Jesus Christ Immanuel *of* Nazareth, Messiah, *and* Saviour *of the* whole world

DARRELL MOWAT

WESTBOW
PRESS®
A DIVISION OF THOMAS NELSON
& ZONDERVAN

WestBow Press books may be ordered through booksellers or by contacting:

WestBow Press
A Division of Thomas Nelson & Zondervan
1663 Liberty Drive
Bloomington, IN 47403
www.westbowpress.com
844-714-3454

Scripture taken from the King James Version of the Bible.

ISBN: 978-1-6642-6621-6 (sc)
ISBN: 978-1-6642-6620-9 (e)

Print information available on the last page.

WestBow Press rev. date: 5/4/2022

CONTENTS

PREFACE

This book came into being after plans to write at least three other books in its place. It was a sort of process in bringing forth the most important ideas that the Holy Bible speaks of, namely that the Old Testament prophecies, laws and history, continue to point to Jesus Christ Immanuel of Nazareth as the Messiah, and Saviour of the whole world (John 5:39). With that idea in mind, early on in my grown-up spiritual walk with God, after my eyes were opened and I was made more perceptive to God's truth, I began to be concerned about the faith of those whom follow the God of the Old Testament, but did not necessarily believe that the Jesus of Nazareth of the New Testament writings was or is the Messiah, the Christ. After doing a lot of research and listening to others about the topic, I decided that I would take as much of the Old Testament prophecies about Jesus, that I knew of, along with other prophetic relationships that the Old Testament speaks of Jesus and the New Testament apostles writings, and attempt to give examples of Jesus of Nazareth's scriptural fulfillment as the Messiah, that other Biblical scholars may not have brought to light yet. Although many of the ideas in this book are not likely new, as the Holy Bible says, "…*there is* no new *thing* under the sun."; I thought it may be a perspective and interpretation of Jesus Christ of Nazareth's life fulfilled in the Scriptures that could be told from a perspective of "…this generation…" (Eccl. 1:9, Matt. 11:16). This book is about Jesus Christ of Nazareth, not only the Jesus Christ mentioned in the New Testament, but about the Jesus Christ Immanuel of all time. It is about His relationship with us today, His desires for us in this lifetime and His plans for us all here on earth and forever more in eternity. Alleluia and praise the LORD. Amen and Amen.

I should say that I have attempted to steer clear of repeating as many references as possible that New Testament writers used to reference Old Testament prophecies being fulfilled in Christ, unless they were absolutely relevant to this book's objectives. Although repeating things can be helpful in remembering important knowledge, I also realize that repetitiveness can seem to become boring and monotonous. With this in mind, God willing, there is some truth, or at least depth of truth, in this book that the reader may not have recognized, fully realized or had knowledge of before reading it. That being said, this does not mean that this book contains all the knowledge on the topic of Jesus Christ of Nazareth, as the Holy Bible says, God's "…understanding *is* infinite." (Ps. 147:5). I would encourage the reader before reading this book to pray about its contents and how you ought to receive them. And I would also encourage the reader to, as the apostle, Paul, says, "Prove all things; hold fast that which is good." (1 Thess. 5:21). Jesus Christ of Nazareth asks us of Himself, to "Take my yoke upon you…my yoke *is* easy, and my burden is light." (Matt. 11:29, 30). The word, easy, in Greek seems to have a root word meaning gentleness, goodness and kindness, Strong's numbers 5543 and 5544, respectively, and can also mean to be useful (Matt. 11:30, Rom. 2:4). Jesus' yoke indeed is useful for us, as He gives us life and life more abundantly (John 10:10). Alleluia and praise the LORD. Amen and Amen.

Last, Jesus admonishes us to build our house on a proper foundation (Matt. 7:24-27, Luke 6:47-49, 14:28-30). In parable, He compares the house built on sand to the house built on a rock, and when a flood and wind comes, the house built on the sand is taken away, whereas the house built on a rock keeps its place (Matt. 7:24-27). This is the choice we have in this lifetime, do we take the time and patience required to seek out and build our house, both spiritually and physically on sand or a rock? This is the choice God gives us, I know for certain that indeed, Jesus Christ of Nazareth is both the spiritual and physical rock that each and every one of us ought to build our house upon. He is that Spiritual Rock of the Old Testament and He is the Creator of all things (Ex. 17:6, Ps. 28:1, 1 Cor. 10:1-4, Rev. 4:11). He is that, Word of God, by the Holy Spirit of God, that became flesh just over two thousand years ago, as of the date of writing this book in 2019 A.D. (John 1:1-3, 14; 14:16-18). I encourage the reader of this book to honestly consider what you believe about this life and this world, and the knowledge of both God and His creation in it, while reading through this book. I encourage you to both read and repent if needed of any understanding that may be against God's will and way, and accept the way of Jesus Christ of Nazareth. As Jesus Christ Immanuel of Nazareth is the way, the truth and the life (John 14:6). Alleluia and praise the LORD. Amen and Amen.

ACKNOWLEDGEMENTS

This book is written for the glory of God and His only begotten Son, Jesus Christ of Nazareth, with His Holy Spirit. To God be the glory forever and ever. Alleluia and praise the LORD. Amen and Amen.

INTRODUCTION

The book of Revelation 1:8 says of God, Jesus Christ of Nazareth and the Holy Spirit, "I am Alpha and Omega, the beginning and the ending, saith the Lord, which is, and which was, and which is to come, the Almighty.". In the light of this idea of God being in the past, present and future, this book will shine the light of God's only begotten Son, Jesus Christ of Nazareth, of the New Testament writings, and spoken of by the Old Testament prophets, on whom God, the Father is, whom Jesus Christ of Nazareth is, and whom the Holy Spirit of God is (Matt. 28:19, 20). And how God relates to us all, through the Old Testament prophets, law and history; through Jesus Christ of Nazareth, prophesied of in the Old Testament and testified of in the New Testament, and through God, the Father's, Holy Spirit given to all whom receive Him, in the name of God's only begotten Son, Jesus Christ Immanuel of Nazareth. Alleluia and praise the LORD. Amen and Amen. The main focus of this book will be about Jesus Christ of Nazareth and how He has fulfilled the Biblical scriptures, both New Testament and Old, but also the prophetic significance of how He will continue to fulfill the Scriptures in this world, and in the "world to come", God willing. Alleluia and praise the LORD. Amen and Amen.

With this all being said, I must acknowledge some things that will be addressed in the chapters to come, namely our sins and blindness of the truth of whom God really is. It says in the book of Revelation that sin has reached to heaven (Rev. 18:5). But Jesus says if a man asks you to walk a mile with him, walk with him two (Matt. 5:41). It can be challenging in this world to place our trust in God, and it can even be a challenge to believe that God is really good and loving based on our own life experience and the witnessing of the corruption of the world around us, at least of the date of writing this book in 2019 A.D.. That all being said, there is a place that God dwells in called the "Most Holy Place", this place physically was the "Most Holy Place", the inner chamber, in the tabernacle in the wilderness and in the first and second temple built in Jerusalem (Ex. 26:34, 1 Kings 6:16, Ezek. 41:4). But it also always has been, is and always will be God, through His Holy Spirit dwelling in our own body, mind and soul (John 2:21, 1 Cor. 3:16, 17; Jude 1:20, 21). My point is that, if we believe, there is a place that sin has never been, but God dwells there. Alleluia and praise the LORD. Amen and Amen. So when reading through this book, consider what I have written, and what the Biblical scriptures say, but most importantly, go to that place that is "Most Holy", in your own mind, or wherever you believe it is, and ask God for yourself, what is the truth of the matter?

As Jesus Christ of Nazareth said, "…the truth shall make you free." (John 8:32). Alleluia and praise the LORD. Amen and Amen.

Last, Jesus admonishes us to "Ask, and it shall be given you; seek, and ye shall find …" (Matt. 7:7). This book has Old Testament scripture quotes, interpretations, and New Testament scripture comparisons, with some reference proofs. I have attempted to develop some sort of a flow and purpose to all of the comparisons, and generally, it is an attempt to bring to light some of the possible character traits and life experience of Jesus Christ of Nazareth, using Old Testament scriptures that have not been addressed before, at least to my knowledge. As Jesus said of Himself in the scriptures, "Search the scriptures; for in them ye think ye have eternal life: and they are they which testify of me." (John 5:39). I am not sure if this is a command or not, but I do not suppose it could hurt to try and learn about Jesus from all of the Scriptures, both New and Old Testament. I have also attempted to "harmonize" some of the New and Old Testament scriptures, regarding Jesus' life experience. As I have learned from studying that each person has a deferring point of view on any given situation, and we need to take these different perspectives into consideration when understanding the "full" picture of whom Jesus, was, is and is to be (Rev. 4:8). That being said, as with my other writing, I have used this same method to address other historical and secular references outside of the Holy Bible to enhance the readers experience and understanding of whom Jesus Christ of Nazareth, God, the Father, and the Holy Spirit are and Their relevance to us all here on earth today. To God be the glory. Alleluia and praise the LORD. Amen and Amen.

CHAPTER 1

That prophet...

*"Greater love hath no man than this, that a man
lay down his life for his friends."*
- JOHN 15:13

Introduction

Anyone reading this knows that you have a life and it came from somewhere. Believers in Jesus Christ understand that our lives come from God Almighty and that we have been given this life for a "greater" purpose here on earth and into eternity. This is the first key in understanding life. That is that life is given, but can also be taken, not that it will be taken and it will perish, but that it can be taken and given again. This is the hope and promise we all have in the life, death, burial and resurrection of Jesus Christ of Nazareth. Arguably the most important point Jesus was trying to make during His ministry, was that He is life, He came to show us that He has authority over it and that no evil, including death can overcome life! The apostle, Paul, spoke candidly about the importance of believing in the resurrection promise. Also saying that if there is no resurrection then our life and our faith are in vain (1 Cor. 15:12-19). The good news is that Christ indeed did rise from the dead and He lives (Matt. 28, 1 Cor. 15:20)! He says if we are faithful in the least of things, then we are faithful also in much (Luke 16:10). What a great promise from God Almighty. This first chapter is about introducing the scriptures of the Old Testament and how they have influenced life here on earth, especially in the preparation for the Messiah, Jesus Christ of Nazareth, whom came into this world, conceived by the Holy Spirit in the virgin, Mary, espoused to Joseph, and born into this world through God, the Father's, mercifully guiding hands (Ps. 22:9, 10; Matt. 1:18-25). Alleluia and praise the LORD. Amen and Amen. Read on to learn more about the scriptures and how they have been fulfilled in Christ Jesus of Nazareth's Holy name. Alleluia and praise the LORD. Amen and Amen.

Jesus and the Old Testament

Jesus and Abraham; The apostle, Paul, in Galatians 3:16 and 17 says, "Now to Abraham and his seed were the promises made. He saith not, And to seeds, as of many; but as of one, And to thy seed, which is Christ. And this I say, that the covenant, that was confirmed before of God in Christ, the law, which was four hundred and thirty years after, cannot disannul, that it should make the promise of none effect.". The law four hundred and thirty years later; from Abraham and new born Isaac to Exodus (Gen. 21:1-10, Ex. 12). The Israelites may not have been in Egypt proper for four hundred years, as some of the passages in the Bible may suggest (Gen. 15:30, Ex. 12:40, 41; Acts 7:6). But from about the day that Hagar, and Ishmael, despised Sarah, and Isaac, it has been said this is when the four hundred year spiritual captivity began (Gen. 16:4, 5; 21:9).[1] Jesus said of Himself, "…Before Abraham was, I am." (John 8:58). He said, "I and *my* Father are one." (John 10:30). Jesus spoke of marrying, and comparing Himself to the bridegroom (Matt. 9:15, 25:1-13). The "Old Testament" God, spoke of being a husband marrying us, His Church (Isa. 54:5). Psalm 69:8 says, "I am become a stranger unto my brethren, and an alien unto my mother's children.". Jesus did do strange things, miracles (Luke 5:17-26). That being said, the book of Job mentions a stranger has not come to earth (Job 15:19). As the apostle, John, says of Jesus, "He was in the world, and the world was made by him, and the world knew him not. He came unto his own, and his own received him not." (John 1:10, 11). Isaiah 53:3 says, "He is despised and rejected of men; a man of sorrows, and acquainted with grief: and we hid as it were our faces from him; he was despised, and we esteemed him not.". This just explains the depths with which God, in Christ Jesus of Nazareth's Holy name, was willing to go to save us from our own corrupt, deprived and sinful nature. Alleluia and praise the LORD. Amen and Amen. Daniel 12:2 says, "And many of them that sleep in the dust of the earth shall awake, some to everlasting life, *and* some to everlasting contempt.". Many of the saints were seen in the streets of Jerusalem at Jesus' resurrection (Matt. 27:52, 53). Daniel 12:3 says, "And they that be wise shall shine as the brightness of the firmament; and they that turn many to righteousness as the stars for ever and ever.". Jesus' face shone like the sun at His transfiguration (Matt. 13:43, 17:2). He was also taken into heaven and received in a cloud, after His resurrection and forty day visitation with His disciples in 31 A.D., about ten days before Pentecost (Acts 1:1-9). He is also referred to as the Light, and the Morning Star (John 8:12, Rev. 22:16). Psalm 22 describes the crucifixion through King David's inspired words, as will be referenced in chapters three and four of this book. Alleluia and praise the LORD. Amen and Amen.

Jesus, Moses, and the Rock; 1 Corinthians 10:1-4 says, "Moreover, brethren, I would not that ye should be ignorant, how that all our fathers were under the cloud, and all passed through the sea; And were all baptized unto Moses in the cloud and in the sea; And did all eat the same spiritual meat; And did all drink the same spiritual drink: for they drank of that spiritual Rock that followed them: and that Rock was Christ.". Psalm 18:2, 31 and 46

---

[1] https://answersingenesis.org/bible-questions/how-long-were-the-israelites-in-egypt/, retrieved 16/03/2022

say, "The LORD *is* my rock, and my fortress, and my deliverer; my God, my strength, in whom I will trust; my buckler, and the horn of my salvation, *and* my high tower. … For who *is* God save the LORD? Or who *is* a rock save our God? … The LORD liveth; and blessed *be* my rock; and let the God of my salvation be exalted. …". Psalm 31:1-3 says, "IN thee, O LORD, do I put my trust; let me never be ashamed: deliver me in thy righteousness. Bow down thine ear to me; deliver me speedily: be thou my strong rock, for an house of defence to save me. For thou art my rock and my fortress; therefore for thy name's sake lead me, and guide me.". Psalm 42:9 says, "I will say unto God my rock, Why hast thou forgotten me? Why go I mourning because of the oppression of the enemy?". Psalm 61:1-3 says, "HEAR my cry, O God; attend unto my prayer. From the end of the earth will I cry unto thee, when my heart is overwhelmed: lead me to the rock *that* is higher than I. For thou hast been a shelter for me, *and* a strong tower from the enemy.". Psalm 62:1, 2, 6 and 7 say, "TRULY my soul waiteth upon God: from him *cometh* my salvation. He only *is* my rock and my salvation; *he is* my defence; I shall not be greatly moved. … He only *is* my rock and my salvation: *he is* my defence; I shall not be moved. In God *is* my salvation and my glory: the rock of my strength, *and* my refuge, *is* in God.". Jesus is also referred to as the chief corner stone in the foundation of our relationship with God, the Father, Almighty, through His Holy Spirit (Eph. 2:19-22). Jesus said, "…Did ye never read in the scriptures, The stone which the builders rejected, the same is become the head of the corner: this is the Lord's doing, and it is marvellous in our eyes?" (Matt. 21:42). Psalm 118:22 says, "The stone *which* the builders refused is become the head *stone* of the corner.". Alleluia and praise the LORD. Amen and Amen.

Of Aaron's priestly robe, Exodus 28:33-35 says, "And *beneath* upon the hem of it thou shalt make pomegranates, upon the hem of the robe round about. A golden bell and a pomegranate, a golden bell and a pomegranate, upon the hem of the robe round about. And it shall be upon Aaron to minister: and his sound shall be heard when he goeth in unto the holy place before the LORD, and when he cometh out, that he die not.". This may represent, Jesus' warning of entering and leaving the tabernacle, like the example of His overturning of the moneychangers tables. If He overturned the moneychangers tables on two separate occasions, the second time He did it, it was just before His crucifixion, burial and resurrection, where after forty days, He ascended up to heaven to sit at the right hand of the Father, until His enemies are made His footstool (Matt. 21:12, 12; John 2:13-16, Acts 1:1-9, 2:32-36). If He did this twice, Jesus entered the tabernacle at the beginning of His ministry and "rang the bells", the "moneychangers tables", and even though He left the physical temple building throughout His ministry, He was still dwelling in the spiritual temple of God Almighty throughout His ministry (Matt. 21:12, 12; John 2:13-16, 19-21). After the second "ringing of the bells", that is overturning of the moneychangers tables, He may have been saying it was His time to finish the work God sent Him to earth to do (Matt. 20:18, 19). This could also be representative of the great sacrifice made in marriage as well, needing a clean temple for a marriage to work properly (Heb. 13:4). Not focusing on money or other idolatrous things, but on the true and pure relationship between husband and wife (1 Tim. 6:10, 1 Cor. 7:28). Alleluia and praise the

LORD. Amen and Amen. Isaiah 16:5 says, "And in mercy shall the throne be established: and he shall sit upon it in truth in the tabernacle of David, judging, and seeking judgment, and hasting righteousness.". Jesus said of Himself, "…I am the way, the truth and the life…" (John 14:6). Isaiah 53:2 says, "For he shall grow up before him as a tender plant, and as a root out of a dry ground: he hath no form nor comeliness; and when we shall see him, there is no beauty that we should desire him.". Jesus was not necessarily a "supermodel" so to speak. Isaiah 53 in general does a good job of describing Jesus' character and prophesied trials. Isaiah 48:12 says, "Hearken unto me, O Jacob and Israel, my called; I am he; I am the first, I also am the last.". He is referred to as the First and the Last, much like He is described of in the book of Revelation (Rev. 1:11, 17; 2:8; 22:13). Comparing Jesus and Joshua, of which the names are the same in the Hebrew language, meaning God saves (Ex. 17:9, Matt. 1:21). Joshua met the Captain of the LORD's Host (Joshua 5:13-15). And the apostle, Paul, refers to Jesus as the Captain of our salvation (Heb. 2:10). 2 Chronicles 13:12 says, "…God himself *is* with us for *our* captain…". Alleluia and praise the LORD. Amen and Amen.

Ancestry

There are two schools of thought on the genealogy of Jesus. Of course, He was born of a virgin, Mary, espoused to Joseph, so the only "physical" ancestry would come from His mother (Matt. 1:18-25). Although Genesis 2:24 says, "Therefore shall a man leave his father and his mother, and shall cleave unto his wife: and they shall be one flesh.", so this is likely why Jesus can also claim His physical ancestry from His earthly father, Joseph. Nevertheless, there are two genealogies, one in Matthew 1, and the second in Luke 3 of Jesus' ancestry, both name Jesus' father, Joseph, and then go on to name different ancestors for each list after King David with the exception of a few, namely Salathiel and Zorobabel (Matt. 1:12, 13, Luke 3:27). The argument of these genealogies is that one is of Mary, Luke 3, and the other is of Joseph, Matthew 1; or that they are both of Joseph and the names are just other given names of the same people in the genealogies.[2] The point is that Jesus indeed descended from David, likely from His mother, as it was custom in Jewish tradition to marry into the same tribal family (Num. 36:6). Although Mary was a cousin of Elizabeth, whose husband and father were Levites, we know this because her husband was a priest at the temple, and it is mentioned that Elisabeth comes from the lineage of Aaron (Luke 1:5). That does not mean that for certain Mary was a Levite. The fact of the matter is, regardless of God's commands and "tradition", people married outside of their tribal family, but some also stayed within. If indeed Mary was a Jew, of the tribe of Judah, than this would be physical evidence of Jesus ancestry to King David. Without that Jesus could still claim the position from His father, Joseph, as I had mentioned earlier, the Bible says two become one flesh, so regardless, Mary

[2] https://www.cgg.org/index.cfm/library/bqa/id/184/why-does-jesus-have-two-different-genealogies-matthew-11-16-luke-323-38.htm, retrieved 16/03/2022

would have taken on Joseph's family ancestry (Luke 1:27). But I do strongly believe that Mary was also a descendant of the tribe of Judah and the house of David, even if the Bible does not expressly say so outwardly. Any and all confusion of Jesus' genealogical heritage, would probably be fulfilled in the prophesy of Daniel and other prophets, "O LORD, righteousness belongeth unto thee, but unto us confusion of faces…", as neither the Old or New Testament prophets and scribes were perfect, only Jesus Christ of Nazareth was and is perfect, and we are perfected through Him (Dan. 9:7, Matt. 5:48). Alleluia and praise the LORD. Amen and Amen.

At least one reference suggests that Heli is the father of Mary, and father in law to Joseph in the New Testament (Luke 2:23). See this reference for more detail on the subject, http://bibleq.net/answer/2926/, retrieved 13/09/2018. That would mean Jacob is the father of Joseph (Matt. 1:16). Now according to Luke's gospel record, Neri is the father of Salathiel (Luke 3:27). The only mention of a Neri, Neriah, in the Old Testament is associated with Jeremiah, when Jeremiah is buying land, Neriah's son received the evidence in the purchase of the land, and a Neriah was with Jeremiah when He is prophesying (Jer. 32:12, 45:1, 51:59). The prophet, Jeremiah, is a Levite (Jer. 1:1). According to Matthew's gospel record, Jechonias is the father of Salathiel (Matt. 1:12). In the Old Testament, Jechonias is the father of Salathiel (1 Chr. 3:17-20). In 1 Chronicles 3:19, Zerubbabel is the son of Pedaiah, a brother of Salathiel. In Ezra and other places in the Old Testament Zerubbabel is mentioned to be the son of Shealtiel (Ezra 3:2, 8; 5:2; Neh. 12:1, Hag. 1:1, 12, 14; 2:2). The Hebrew spelling is the same for both Salathiel and Shealtiel (1 Chr. 3:17, Ezra 3:2). Prophesy or no prophecy, Jesus likely was a physical descendent of David, through His mother, Mary, as per the genealogy mentioned in Luke 3. According to Luke's gospel record, Rhesa is said to be the son of Zorobabel (Luke 3:27). The most similar name to this in the Old Testament, as a son of Zerubbabel is Berechiah (1 Chr. 3:20). Matthew's gospel record says Abiud is the son of Zorobabel (Matt. 1:13). The most similar name to this in the Old Testament, as a son of Zerubbabel is Jushabhesed (1 Chr. 3:20). Abihud is the Hebrew form of the name, Abiud, and is mentioned at least once in the Old Testament, a grandson of Benjamin in 1 Chronicles 8:3. Based on these two Old Testament names, Rhesa seems to be the more reasonable of the two to choose to associate Jesus' physical ancestral relationship with the house of David. Alleluia and praise the LORD. Amen and Amen.

Jeconiah's family descendants were prophesied not to prosper sitting on the throne of David. Jeremiah 22:24-30 says, "…for no man of his seed shall prosper, sitting upon the throne of David, and ruling any more in Judah.". Matthew 1:11 and 12 say, "And Josias begat Jechonias and his brethren, about the time they were carried away to Babylon. And after they were brought to Babylon, Jechonias begat Salathiel; and Salathiel begat Zorobabel…". See the following reference for more information on the subject, https://jewsforjesus.org/publications/issues/issues-v05-n06/the-genealogy-of-the-messiah/, retrieved 27/08/2018. This is an issue then regarding Zerubbabel and all that is prophesied about him in the book of Haggai, if they are the same Zerubbabel. He came back from Babylon with others to build the second temple. How could he have been a king of Judah, with Jeremiah's prophesy being fulfilled in Zerubbabel's grandfather, Jeconiah (1 Ch. 3:17-20)? This would also be at least one reason why the second temple was destroyed in 70 A.D., aside from any other prophecies about it (Matt. 24:1, 2). Also, as scripture indicates, sometimes when a person is referenced, it can be referring to all of their descendants after them. Like when the house of Israel, and it's descendants are referred to as "Jacob", in prophecy and other examples like it (Isa. 2:5, 9:8, 14:1). The only way Jesus could have been King of Israel and Zerubbabel could have been a king of Judah, before Him, is if the prophecy of Jeremiah was finally fulfilled in Jesus. He did not have any physically conceived children during His earthly life according to all of the gospel accounts. Also, Jesus gave authority to His twelve disciples to judge the tribes of Israel (Matt. 19:28). And Zerubbabel was considered a governor, not a king (Hag. 1:1). Prophecy in Zechariah 4:7 says, "Who *art* thou O great mountain? Before Zerubabbel *thou shalt become* a plain: and he shall bring forth the headstone *thereof with* shoutings, *crying,* Grace, grace unto it.". Jesus spoke plainly (John 16:25-29). He is said to be the head corner stone, mentioned earlier (Matt. 21:42, Eph. 2:19-22). He also came in grace and truth (John 1:14). This all brings us to the point that the throne of David is in us all, as we accept Christ Jesus of Nazareth, through His Holy Spirit (John 14:16-18). As the one prophesy says, "…he that is feeble among them at that day shall be as David…" (Zech. 12:8). That all being said, it is easiest to conclude that this prophecy of Jeremiah ended with Jesus Christ of Nazareth, not conceiving physical children with a wife during His earthly ministry. Even Jesus said that the scriptures speak of Himself (John 5:39). Alleluia and praise the LORD. Amen and Amen.

Adam and Jesus; the First and with the Last, the First and the Last (Isa. 41:4, 43:27, 44:6; Luke 3:38, Rev. 1:17, 18). "…Before Abraham was, I am" (John 8:58). "In the beginning was the Word, and the Word was with God, and the Word was God." (John 1:1). "I and *my* Father are one." (John 10:30). Clearly Jesus was both God, and the Son of God. God as a member of the God family, and Son, born into this world through the Holy Spirit, using the vessel of the virgin, Mary, espoused to Joseph (Matt. 1:18-25). He was raised as a child by His parents, Joseph and Mary (Luke 2). His ministering started at the age of about thirty, similarly the Levites start working in the tabernacle of God at that age, according to the Old Testament (Num. 4:3, Luke 3:21-23). He preached the kingdom of God and salvation in His Holy name, that is in the name of Jesus Christ of Nazareth (Matt. 6:33, John 3:14-17). He died on the cross for the forgiveness of our sins at Passover in 31 A.D., He was buried, and He arose the third day to give us the hope and promise of eternal life in His Holy name. On the first day of the week after His resurrection He revealed Himself, first to Mary Magdalene at least, and then to two others, and finally to the apostles and brethren, and after forty days He ascended to sit at the right hand of the Father, until His enemies are made His footstool (Mark 16, Acts 1:1-9, 2:32-36). Jesus has inherited all things by His suffering on the cross (Luke 10:22, John 3:35). God Almighty gave Him this reward, as the Father gives the birthright to His firstborn (Gen. 43:33, Luke 10:22, John 3:35). He has overcome the corruptions of this world, and He has redeemed us from the corruption of this world, by taking on our sins, as a sinless man on the cross, forgiving us of all of our sins (Luke 1:68, John 16:33, 1 Pet. 1:17-21). He died on the cross for the forgiveness of our sins, He was buried and He arose the third day, so that we can also share in God Almighty's inheritance and birthright blessing in the name of Jesus Christ of Nazareth (Rev. 21:7)! Thanks and glory be to God! Alleluia, Amen and Amen. The apostle, Paul, wrote, "For as by one man's disobedience many were made sinners, so by the obedience of one shall many be made righteous." (Rom. 5:19). Adam and Eve were made after the likeness of God (Gen. 1:26). Jesus was made in the likeness of man (Rom. 8:3). I had mentioned in my fifth book, "Heaven, Hell and the Resurrection", that I believe that Jesus is indeed Adam, born again of the Holy Spirit. Jesus said we must be born of the Holy Spirit to see the kingdom of God, and indeed He was born of the Holy Spirit, also as referenced in the previous section and the beginning of this paragraph, Jesus is the "first and the last", so I have no doubt that Jesus is Adam born again (Matt. 1:18-25, John 3:3-7, Rev. 22:13). As Adam is also referenced to be a son of God, in the genealogy of Jesus according to Luke's gospel account (Luke 3:38). 1 Corinthians 15:45 says, "And so it is written, The first man Adam was made a living soul; the last Adam was made a quickening spirit.". Also, one woman whom was healed by Jesus through faith, Jesus called "…Daughter…" (Matt. 9:22). Alleluia and praise the LORD. Amen and Amen.

Jesus, Ruth and Moab; Jesus ancestral line has non-Israelite blood in it from Ruth, a Moabitess woman, whom married Obed, mentioned in the book of Ruth (Ruth 4:9, 10). This is of quite amazing consequence when it comes to prophecy, as we can read regarding the prophecies of Moab (Isa. 11:14; 16, 17, 25:10; Jer. 9:26; 48; Ezek. 25:8-11, Dan. 11:41, Amos 2:1-3, Zeph. 2:8-11). Both Isaiah and Jeremiah prophecy of Moab in the "time of the end", and sure enough, some of Jesus' life can be gleaned from those prophecies as well (Isa. 11:14; 16, 17, 25:10; Jer. 9:26; 48). According to Deutcronomy 23:3, a Moabite cannot enter into the congregation of the LORD until the tenth generation. In Nehemiah 13:1, it says, "…the Moabite should not come into the congregation of God for ever…". King David and his son Solomon, were kings of Israel (2 Sam. 6:20, Neh. 13:26). They were both partially descended from Ruth, a Moabitess (Ruth 4:9, 10; 2 Sam. 5:13, 14; 1 Chr. 2:12-15, Matt. 1:5). If the Nehemiah account were the hard fast truth, Jesus would never be accepted by Israel and therefore would not be able to be King of Israel, never mind David and his descendants otherwise. I think Nehemiah may have interpreted the law incorrectly. Certainly there is some room for discussion, as Ezra and Nehemiah give conflicting records of 666 and 667 for the family population of Adonikam (Ezra 2:13, Neh. 7:18). So there must be some missing piece to the puzzle here. As the apostle, Paul, said, "…let God be true, but every man a liar…" (Rom. 3:4). This just proves that man, whom God has inspired to write the Holy Bible, is not perfect. But God is! Alleluia and praise the LORD, God, the Father, Almighty and His only begotten Son, Jesus Christ of Nazareth. Amen and Amen. Jeremiah 48 also speaks of prophecies of Moab. Some have claimed that Jesus had been in various Asiatic countries and others during His time here on earth. This could be true according to Jeremiah 48:12, it says, "Therefore, behold, the days come, saith the LORD, that I will send unto him wanderers, that shall cause him to wander, and shall empty his vessels, and break their bottles.". He may have been visited in Nazareth by foreign Israelites of the diaspora, that either encouraged or influenced His desire to search out the diaspora in Asia and possibly Europe. This may be where the other accounts of His life came from outside of canonized scripture. That being said the Biblical accounts of Jesus' life here on earth, ought to be the only authority we need. Nevertheless, as Jesus said Himself, "…with God all things are possible." (Matt. 19:26). Alleluia and praise the LORD. Amen and Amen.

Most of Jesus' parables and life lessons were of agrarian society and other practical examples of life (Matt. 6:24-26, 13, 16:6-12, 17:20). This would seem to indicate that His influences were that of an established Israelite, not a worldly person. Even Jesus, Himself, said the gate is strait and the way is narrow (Matt. 7:14). Chapter six has a more thorough overview of Jesus life according to New Testament references. At age twenty, children of Israel begin financial responsibility and are counted among the number for war (Ex. 30:14, 38:26; Num. 1:3, 18). At age twenty five, Levites would be required to start service in the tabernacle of the Lord (Num. 8:24). And at age thirty, Levites are called to begin work in the tabernacle of the Lord; because God is no respecter of persons, this is relevant to all of us in some form or fashion today (Num. 4:3, 23, 30, 35, 39, 43, 47; Acts 10:34, 35). This only leaves eight years from age twelve to twenty for Jesus to travel, but these are formative years, as the scripture would indicate, for Jesus to grow up with His family. I would say that it is highly unlikely that He did travel in His 20's to far reaching places. But just like some college students and twenty somethings do today travel to other countries to experience "the world" and other cultures, it is possible Jesus did also. Also, Jesus was preparing His disciples to spread the gospel message, why would He have revealed Himself to the world previously, before His official ministry started? Would this not cause disruption to God's ministry through Jesus Christ of Nazareth, and His disciples after Him, having separate accounts of His existence from what the Bible says? God is not a God of confusion, and Jesus is the Son of God (1 Cor. 14:33, 1 John 4:15). Also, those whom testified of Him, said "Is not this the carpenter's son?..." (Matt. 13:55). The Old Testament also prophecies of Him being not esteemed (Isa. 53:3, Phil. 2:7). How then could other reports of His possible experiences in the world, outside of the Bible, be true? God knows for certain. Alleluia and praise the LORD. Amen and Amen.

Isaiah 15:9 says, "…waters of Dimon shall be full of blood…lions upon him that escapeth of Moab…". Dimon is likely a place, if we attribute this to the name of "demons", devils and sin in general, this could be associating Jesus' Holy blood shed on the cross for the forgiveness of the sins of mankind. Jesus says, "…If therefore the light that is in thee be darkness, how great *is* that darkness!" (Matt. 6:23). Just like humans have an upright spirit in Christ Jesus of Nazareth (Col. 1:28). Our spirit can also be fallen in sin (Eph. 2:4-7). This is why we need to apply the offering of Jesus Christ's Holy blood shed on the cross to our life, by accepting the Holy Spirit of God in the name of His only begotten Son, Jesus Christ of Nazareth, for the forgiveness of our sins (Rev. 1:5). That is, repent and believe the gospel of Jesus Christ of Nazareth and God, the Father, Almighty and His kingdom! The

Saviour of the world, and Redeemer of all mankind! Praise the LORD, God, the Father, Almighty and His only begotten Son, Jesus Christ of Nazareth! Alleluia and praise the LORD! Isaiah 16:14 says, "...Within three years, as the years of an hireling, and the glory of Moab shall be contemned...". Christ died on the cross for the forgiveness of our sins, three and a half years into His ministry, and was condemned to death because He was the only begotten Son of God, as a sinless man whom died on the cross for the forgiveness of our sins (John 11:49-52). In many respects I think these prophecies for Moab could be on mankind collectively as well. Jeremiah 9:25 and 26 says, "Behold, the days come, saith the LORD, that I will punish all *them which are* circumcised with the uncircumcised; Egypt, and Judah, and Edom, and the children of Ammon, and Moab, and all *that are* in the utmost corners, that dwell in the wilderness: for all *these* nations *are* uncircumcised, and all the house of Israel *are* uncircumcised in the heart.". And the apostle, Paul, says, "For all have sinned, and come short of the glory of God..." (Rom. 3:23). Certainly these prophecies are a call to repentance for us all. This may also describe the "kings" of the world as well, as many monarchies seem to have descended from the throne of David, at least in the west, if not the entire world. But the point is that David, had Moabite ancestors from Ruth. Albeit not much, but the question then may be begged to ask, how much is enough? And how would these prophecies be fulfilled in David's descendants' outside of Jesus? I do not know for certain, only time will tell for sure. Let the truth in all of this be to the glory of God Almighty and Jesus Christ of Nazareth, whom cleanses us of all of our sins, and the sins of our forefathers, regardless of what tribe we come from. We owe our whole life to Him, to Jesus Christ of Nazareth! He deserves all the glory and praise! He is our Saviour and King, the Almighty! Praise Him and worship God in the name of Jesus Christ of Nazareth. Thanks be to God, the Father, Almighty and His only begotten Son, Jesus Christ of Nazareth! Alleluia, and praise the LORD. Amen and Amen.

Jeremiah 48:15-17 may begin the description of Jesus' crucifixion, but of course are related to the descendants of Moab in general as well. Jeremiah 48:28 says, "...leave the cities, and dwell in the rock, and be like the dove that maketh her nest in the sides of the hole's mouth.". This is an admonishment for all of us to start a relationship with Jesus Christ of Nazareth, the Creator of us all, through the Holy Spirit of God! Jeremiah 48:34 says, "...*as* an heifer of three years old...". This likely is speaking of Jesus Christ ministry again, as His ministry physically was likely three and a half years in length, but could also be speaking of His coming out of Egypt with His parents at about that age (Matt. 2:16-21). Jeremiah 48:38 says, "...I have broken Moab like a vessel...". This is likely speaking of Jesus Christ's crucifixion again, like in Isaiah's prophecies of Moab. Jeremiah 48:39 says, "...how hath Moab turned the back with shame!...". Jesus after bearing the cross would have had to turn His back to most, as He passed by during His walk to His crucifixion site (Luke 23:26, 27). Jeremiah 48:42 says, "...destroyed from a people...". Although Jesus was not destroyed spiritually, He was crucified and did die on the cross for the forgiveness of our sins, He was buried and He arose the third day to give us the hope and promise of life everlasting in His Holy name (Matt. 2:13, 12:14)! From a physical perspective He fulfilled this because He did not likely father any "physical" children, during His earthly ministry in the early first century A.D., because He was the Son of God and Saviour of us all! He came first and foremost to bare spiritual children, through our acceptance of His forgiveness, by His life giving blood on the cross. It is with His stripes that we are healed (Isa. 53:5). Praise the LORD. Next Jeremiah 48:44 says, "…I will bring upon it, *even* upon Moab, the year of their visitation, saith the LORD.". This is likely speaking of the "…day of the LORD…", the "…year of recompences…", the final year of the "Great Tribulation" (Isa. 2:12, 34:8, Matt. 24:21). This is an event that has not likely taken place fully yet, as of the date of writing this book in 2019 A.D., as Jesus even spoke of it in His prophecies, namely in Matthew 24. The "Great Tribulation" is the time, just prior to the "Messianic Age"; the "Messianic Age" is said to be a period of one thousand years where Christ rules with His saints, in Spirit, likely (Rev. 20:4). The latter portion of the book of Ezekiel speaks of both of these events in some detail, so does other prophecies in the Old and New Testaments (Ezek. 38-48). Last, Jeremiah 48:46 and 47 say, "Woe be unto thee, O Moab! The people of Chemosh perisheth: for thy sons are taken captives, and thy daughters captives. Yet will I bring again the captivity of Moab in the latter days, saith the LORD. Thus far is the judgement of Moab.". This would seem rather conclusive, but there are other prophecies of Moab in the Bible, just not at the same length as Isaiah and Jeremiah. The point here is that we need Jesus Christ to be saved. His works were finished on the cross as even He said that (John 19:30). He knew His physical time here on earth was for a purpose and that it would be finished and it was. Just like each of us have a certain amount of time here on earth regardless of what tribe we come from. The point in this all, in particular, is that no matter what tribe you come from you can have eternal life in the name of Jesus Christ of Nazareth. He was and is the Son of David, of the tribe of Judah, but still had some relation, like most of us do, to tribes that are "outside" of the tribes of Israel. Alleluia and praise the LORD. Amen and Amen.

"That prophet"

Before the idea of a lying prophet was even introduced into the Bible, as "that prophet"; God said of Himself, "…I AM THAT I AM…" (Ex. 3:14). God through the scriptures actually admits to sending "evil angels", and "creating evil", etc. (Ps. 78:49, Isa. 45:7). Is God a liar, God forbid, in fact He is open and honest in taking the "blame" for the existence of all sorts of evil, including lying, but also He will punish the evil (Job 26:13, Isa. 27:1). God's admittance to the existence of evil under His watch is a foreshadowing of Jesus Christ of Nazareth taking responsibility for, and overcoming sin and death on the cross (John 16:33). Nevertheless, there are a few places in the Bible that mention "that prophet" (Deut. 13:3, 5; 18:20). Deuteronomy 13:1-5 says, "If there arise among you a prophet, or a dreamer of dreams, and giveth thee a sign or a wonder, And the sign or the wonder come to pass, whereof he spake unto thee, saying, Let us go after other gods, which thou hast not known, and let us serve them; Thou shalt not hearken unto the words of that prophet, or that dreamer of dreams: for the LORD your God proveth you, to know whether ye love the LORD your God with all your heart and with all your soul. Ye shall walk after the LORD your God, and fear him, and keep his commandments, and obey his voice, and ye shall serve him, and cleave unto him. And that prophet, or that dreamer of dreams, shall be put to death; because he hath spoken to turn you away from the LORD your God, which brought you out of the land of Egypt, and redeemed you out of the house of bondage, to thrust thee out of the way which the LORD thy God commanded thee to walk in. So shalt thou put the evil away from the midst of thee.". In Ezekiel 14:9 it says, "And if the prophet be deceived when he hath spoken a thing, I the LORD have deceived that prophet, and I will stretch out my hand upon him, and will destroy him from the midst of my people Israel.". John 1:21, 25; 6:14 and Acts 3:23, also speak of "that prophet", when the people are questioning John and speculating about Jesus' role in fulfillment of scripture. So what does God mean by "that prophet", what does He mean by speaking about "other gods", what does He mean "...the LORD have deceived that prophet..."? God is not a God of confusion, so there must be an answer to all of this (1 Cor. 14:33). Ahab, King of Israel, had an experience where a lying spirit was sent to deceive prophets, a true prophet, Micaiah, revealed this to him (1 Kings 22:1-23). Jeremiah lamented that he was deceived by the Lord (Jer. 20:7, 8; Lam. 3:14). Jeremiah's lamentations very much suggest that he could be considered "that prophet" in the perspective that he was confirming the scriptures for the penalties of a prophet that would prophecy lies (Deut. 13:1-5, 18:20, Lam.). Am I saying Jeremiah was a liar, God forbid. But what I am saying is that he struggled with the same struggles that we all struggle with, which is the fight we have not only in the fleshly realm, but the spiritual. As the apostle, Paul, spoke, "For we wrestle not against flesh and blood, but against principalities, against powers, against the rulers of the darkness of this world, against spiritual wickedness in high *places*." (Eph. 6:12). Understanding the account of Jeremiah's trial, is understanding a little better whom "that prophet" is. Alleluia and praise the LORD. Amen and Amen.

On the cross, Jesus said, "...My God, my God, why hast thou forsaken me?" (Matt. 27:46, Mark 15:34). The truth of the matter is that Jesus was and is perfect. He did not have a lying spirit in Him; neither did He die because He was a liar. He died for the forgiveness of our sins. That would include the sins of the "Holy" men and women of God, whom in their lifetime, no doubt, have sinned in some way or another. This would include Jeremiah and any other prophet, including David and Moses, whom had committed sin in their life time. This would explain why much like Jesus, David said in psalm, "My God, my God, why hast thou forsaken me?..." (Ps. 22:1). Even Sarah and Jacob used deception against Jacob's father, Isaac, so that Jacob would receive the birthright blessing over Esau (Gen. 27:6-29). The point is that deception is the oldest sin mentioned in the Holy Bible it would seem, starting with the serpent beguiling Eve in the Garden of Eden (Gen. 2:17, 3:1-5). So what is my point to all of this? It is that Jesus died for the forgiveness of all of our sins. We are to be considered the "body of Christ", and if we are part of His body, of course He would have had to take responsibility as the Son of God and Saviour of the world, for fleshly sin as well as all of the lies we have spoken. That is why Jesus was considered "that prophet", because He was the "Prophet" that would take responsibility for every wrong that has taken place in this world, including the lies that have been spoken by prophets, in the name of God (Deut. 18:15, John 6:14, 7:40). Jesus took responsibility for everything wrong in the world. This may help us understand a little better why he felt so separated from God on the cross, when He said, "…My God, my God, why hast thou forsaken me?" (Matt. 27:46, Mark 15:34). He was literally taking the blame for things that He had not done, nor even conceived of (John 15:25). This also speaks of the blindness that sin causes. He could have said this because He was blinded by our sins, being separated from God momentarily, for the forgiveness of our sins. This is what our sin does; it separates us from fellowship with our Creator, God, because no unrighteousness dwells in Him (John 7:18). In order for God to be Holy, righteous and true, He cannot be tempted with sin, nor does sin dwell in Him, nor can He sin (Jam. 1:13, 14; 1 John 3:5, 9). Jesus even said this about Himself (John 7:16-18). He did not commit Himself to man, because He knew what was in man (John 2:24, 25). He also said, the prince of this world has nothing in Him (John 14:30). Jesus committed His life to God, the Father, whom gave His only begotten Son, to come into the world, to teach us, heal us, forgive us, and ultimately, to save us by dying on the cross, a sinless man, taking all of our sins upon Himself, spilling His Holy and righteous blood for the forgiveness of our sins (John 3:16). He was buried and the third day He arose to give us the hope and promise of eternal life in His Holy name. Alleluia and praise the LORD. Amen and Amen.

Conclusions

Regarding Jesus' ancestry, He is of God, and of the tribe of Judah, to keep it simple (Matt. 1:18-25, Rev. 5:5). The added fact that one of His ancestors at least forty five generations before descended from children of Lot, that is Moab, just goes to show that nobody here on earth has "pure" blood so to speak. Jesus did because His blood came from the Holy Spirit of God, but in His mother's line, it was the same as the rest of us, fleshly man from the line of Adam and Eve originally, whom ate from the tree of knowledge of good and evil in the beginning. I have some understanding in all of this through attempting to know my own genealogical family tree, as I am sure most if not all of us can also. There is some value in learning about the lives of the people whom have passed before us, as the apostle, Paul, says, "Ye are our epistle written in our hearts, known and read of all men: *Forasmuch as ye are* manifestly declared to be the epistle of Christ ministered by us, written not with ink, but with the Spirit of the living God; not in tables of stone, but in fleshy tables of the heart." (2

Cor. 3:2, 3). This is why God gave us His only begotten Son, Jesus Christ of Nazareth, so that no matter which tribe, nation or tongue we come from, we can have eternal life in the name of Jesus Christ of Nazareth! Praise the LORD God, the Father, Almighty and His only begotten Son, Jesus Christ of Nazareth! As the Bible says, "…there is none other name under heaven given among men, whereby we must be saved." (Acts 4:12). That all being said, an aside could be mentioned that the tribes of Simeon, Reuben and Gad, of "ancient" Israel dwelt in these lands mentioned of regarding Moab. And some of these prophecies may be related to their descendants somehow as well. I have written another book on the subject of the tribes of this world in greater detail, descending from the eight people whom came off of the ark of God, Noah built, about 2348 B.C. and I have written books on the "Great Tribulation" and "Messianic Age" as well for the interested reader. Their information can be found in appendix A. That being said, as I have said in the past, we need to refer to the Holy Bible of God, and the Holy Spirit of God, through revelation by Jesus Christ of Nazareth first and foremost for any interpretations or understanding of this life, and any prophecy that is spoken of regarding the possibilities in this world or the world to come! All for the glory of God, the Father, Almighty and His only begotten Son, Jesus Christ of Nazareth! Who reigns and lives forever and ever! All glory and majesty be to His name! Alleluia and praise the LORD! Amen and Amen. The following chapters will speak more about the Old Testament prophecies of Jesus and His prophetic fulfillment in the New Testament scriptures. And in the sixth chapter I will go into more detail about the New Testament Jesus and what He has done for us, summarizing the book in chapter seven. Alleluia and praise the LORD. Amen and Amen. Read on to learn more.

Discussion: Messiah

"But his bow abode in strength, and the arms of his hands were made strong by the hands of the mighty *God* of Jacob; (from thence *is* the shepherd, the stone of Israel:)"
- Genesis 49:24

Some have suggested that there will be a "Messiah" ben Joseph, a messiah coming from the tribe of Joseph, aside from the "Messiah" ben David, Jesus Christ of Nazareth, son of David (Gen. 49:22, 24; Ps. 89:20, 21; Matt. 1:1, Rev. 5:5).[3] Messiah meaning anointed one, as many have been anointed, like King David, of the tribe of Judah (1 Sam. 16:13). However, the reality is that Jesus Christ of Nazareth was the son of Joseph, of the tribe of Judah, "Messiah" ben Joseph, and "Messiah" ben David, Messiah, Son of David (Matt. 1:1, 16; John 1:45). His earthly father's name was Joseph, and His mother's ancestors were of the tribe of Judah, through King David (Luke 3:23-38). Nevertheless, this "idea", may have its roots in the "Messianic Age", and the "prince" of the Israelites during the "Messianic Age" (Ezek.

---

[3] https://www.britam.org/messiah.html, retrieved 16/03/2022

40-48, Rev. 20:2, 6). The reality is; Ephraim, son of Joseph, received the birthright from his grandfather Jacob, also known as Israel (Gen. 48, Jer. 31:9). Joshua, a descendant of Ephraim did "rule" for a time when the "ancient" Israelites were brought into the promised land by God through Joshua's leadership, but Ephraim's position did not last, as a "leader" so to speak (Gen. 49:22-26, Num. 27:17-19, Deut. 33:13-17). The reality is that, in the "Messianic Age", a descendant of Ephraim, may very well hold the position of "prince" for the purposes of worship at the temple during the "Messianic Age", but this would be like other positions of this world, where God is still the ruler above us all (Num. 27:17-19, Ps. 80:2, 89:18; Ezek. 44:3). The quote above if read alone, could even suggest that the "Shepherd" would come from Joseph's descendants, as that is whom the verse is speaking of at first, but verse 25 says, "*Even by the God of thy father, who shall help thee; and by the Almighty, who shall bless thee with blessings of heaven above, blessings of the deep that lieth under, blessings of the breasts, and of the womb:*". Even if it was literal, it was fulfilled through Joshua, son of Non, of the tribe of Ephraim, the son of Joseph, at least once, but even he bowed down to the "…captain of the host of the LORD…", on the way to the "promised land", which was likely Jesus Christ of Nazareth, the great I am (Num. 27:17-19, Jos. 5:13-15, John 8:58, Heb. 2:10). It is clear from this verse that the prophecy is speaking of the Shepherd coming from God, the Father, Almighty, not the descendants of Joseph, son of Israel, first and foremost (Ps. 23:1, 80:1; Eccl. 12:11). And this is why we have Jesus Christ of Nazareth whom is born seemingly with little expectation from the "ruling" Jews at His time, from the tribe of Judah, to save the world from our sins (Ps. 80:1, Eccl. 12:11, Isa. 31:4). Alleluia and praise the LORD. It is He whom is the "Good Shepherd" over us all forever more (Ps. 23:1, John 10:11, 14; Heb. 13:20, 1 Pet. 2:25, 5:4). Regardless of a "Messianic Age" earthly "prince" or not (Ezek. 44:3, Rev. 20:4, 6). That being said, this "prince" of the "Messianic Age", if literal, will fulfill his role, along with his descendants, as God wills it, regardless of my or any other person's interpretation of the matter (Num. 27:17-19, Ps. 80:2). Thanks be to God, the Father, Almighty, and His only begotten Son, Jesus Christ of Nazareth. Praise God and worship Him, in the name of Jesus Christ of Nazareth, through His Holy Spirit. Alleluia and bless Him and let Him receive all of the glory. Amen and Amen.

Discussion Questions

1. What about Jesus as Messiah?

   _____

   _____

   _____

   _____

   _____

2. How can we worship God, believe in Jesus Christ of Nazareth as our Saviour and not be idolatrous according to the commands of the Old Testament?

_____

_____

_____

_____

_____

3. What about those whom worshipped Jesus?

_____

_____

_____

_____

_____

CHAPTER 2

Prophecy and Similitudes in the tribe of Judah and the annual Holyday Feasts

"Search the scriptures; for in them ye think ye have eternal life: and they are they which testify of me."
- JOHN 5:39

Introduction

Jesus is the descendant of David, a king of Israel and a member of the tribe of Judah. In two gospel accounts Jesus' lineage claim descent from the line of King David, from both His earthly parents, although only His mother's is by physical blood as Jesus was conceived in, the virgin, Mary, espoused to Joseph, by the Holy Spirit (Matt. 1:18-25). That being said, God does say, "Therefore shall a man leave his father and his mother, and shall cleave unto his wife: and they shall be one flesh." (Gen. 2:24). So in that light, Joseph was just as much Jesus' physical father as Mary was His mother. This all being said, there are prophecies of Jesus Messiah in the prophecies of blessings for the tribe of Judah, as well as through similitudes in the feasts that were instituted for Israel during the wilderness journey (Gen. 49:9-12, Lev. 23). In this chapter I will speak of these prophecies and some of these similitudes.

Judah – "the lawgiver"

Although prophecies about Judah are for the tribe as a whole, these prophecies no doubt had particular significance for the Messiah, whom came from the tribe of Judah. In this section I will talk about the relationship Jesus has with the prophecies given for the tribe of Judah in general. In Genesis 49:8 it says, "Judah, thou *art he* whom thy brethren shall praise: thy hand *shall be* in the neck of thine enemies: thy father's children shall bow down before thee.". This prophecy was fulfilled completely in Jesus Christ of Nazareth, as it is in His name that we have salvation (Acts 4:12). Genesis 49:9 says, "Judah *is* a lion's whelp: from the prey, my son, thou art gone up: he stooped down, he couched as a lion, and as an old lion; who shall rouse him up?". Jesus is considered the lion of the tribe of Judah (Rev. 5:5). Genesis 49:10 says, "The sceptre shall not depart from Judah, nor a lawgiver from between his feet, until Shiloh come; and unto him *shall* the gathering of the people be.". Although Shiloh came as a place for the tabernacle to rest after the wilderness journey, which may have partially fulfilled this prophecy (Jos. 18:1). Jesus was also no doubt Shiloh, as Shiloh means tranquility and rest, and Jesus is our rest, as mentioned in appendix B. Genesis 49:11 says, "Binding his foal unto the vine, and his ass's colt unto the choice vine; he washed his garments in wine and his clothes in the blood of grapes…". Jesus rode into Jerusalem on an donkey's colt just prior to His crucifixion (Matt. 21:1-7, John 12:14, 15). Jesus considered the wine to represent His blood, at the Passover supper the night of His betrayal (Matt. 26:27, 28). It was Jesus' blood that soaked into His garments after His first smiting, His scourging, then His crown of thorns placed on His head, and after His smiting again, before He was crucified that likely fulfilled "…washed his garments in wine and his clothes in the blood of grapes…" (Gen. 49:11, Matt. 26:67, 27:29, 30; Mark 14:65, 15:15, 17-19; Luke 22:63, 64; John 18:22, 19:1-3). Last, Genesis 49:12 says, "His eyes *shall be* red with wine, and his teeth white with milk.". Although this part of the prophecy could be more ambiguous; Jesus drank wine, it was also prophesied in Isaiah, that He was likely raised on butter and honey, butter being a milk product (Isa. 7:15, Matt. 11:19). As well as the general prophecy that the Israelites and their descendants would live in a land flowing with milk and honey (Ex. 3:8, Jer. 11:5). The purity of His teeth likely also represents the purity of the words that came out of His mouth (John 1:14). Deuteronomy 33:7 says, "And this *is the blessing* of Judah: and he said, Hear, LORD, the voice of Judah, and bring him unto his people: let his hands be sufficient for him; and be thou an help *to him* from his enemies.". Jesus did miracles with His own hands (Matt. 8:3, Luke 11:20). He also was a carpenter, and the son of a carpenter (Matt. 13:55, Mark 6:3). His hands were sufficient for Him. Jesus is also mentioned as the Son of David, of the tribe of Judah (Matt. 1:1, Rev. 5:5). And He sits on the Throne of David, see appendix B for more on this subject of the throne of David (Luke 1:32, 33). Alleluia and praise the LORD. Amen and Amen.

The prophet Daniel was of the tribe of Judah, and He prophesied of Jesus Christ of Nazareth, in the book of Daniel, chapter nine, of the Old Testament (Dan. 1:6, Dan. 9:20-27). The part of his prophecy that I will address here is that the Messiah, would be "…cut off…" and "…in the midst of the week he shall cause the sacrifice and oblation to cease…" (Dan. 9:26, 27). It seems to be common belief, that Jesus was crucified on a Friday, at least as of the date of writing this book in 2019 A.D., but Scripture, and at least a few references I have found and have used in my writing would suggest otherwise. If we take Daniel's prophecy as literal, He was crucified in the middle of the week, on a Wednesday (Dan. 9:27). At least a few Biblical scholars have suggested it was the Passover, Wednesday, of 31 A.D., of which I am agreeable with.[4] I had also read that there was a lunar eclipse around that time, so I did some research on it and found some evidence for a lunar eclipse, the evening after Passover, as Passover would have started the evening before. If this evidence is true, then this is more confirmation of Jesus fulfilment of prophecy regarding the "tribulation" He mentioned. Because He said, "Immediately after the tribulation of those days shall the sun be darkened, and the moon shall not give her light, and the stars shall fall from heaven, and the powers of the heavens shall be shaken: And then shall appear the sign of the Son of man in heaven: and then shall all the tribes of the earth mourn, and they shall see the Son of man coming in the clouds of heaven with power and great glory." (Matt. 24:29, 30; Mark 13:24, Luke 21:25). The earth was dark from the sixth to the ninth hour of Jesus' crucifixion, likely namely from clouds, as seems to be prophesied by Ezekiel (Ezek. 32:6-8, Luke 23:44, 45). Ezekiel 32:6-8 says, "I will also water with thy blood the land wherein thou swimmest, *even* to the mountains; and the rivers shall be full of thee. And when I shall put thee out, I will cover the heaven, and make the stars thereof dark; I will cover the sun with a cloud, and the moon shall not give her light. All the bright lights of heaven will I make dark over thee, and set darkness upon thy land, saith the Lord GOD.". This would seem to describe Jesus' crucifixion, as Jesus said, the scriptures speak of Him (John 5:39). But if indeed there was a lunar eclipse that night around eleven o'clock, this would indeed fulfill the scripture of the moon not giving her light. See appendices C, D and E for references to these ideas, details on Jesus' life timeline and Daniel's seventy week prophecy. Alleluia and praise the LORD. Amen and Amen.

Jesus also said that He would be in the heart of the earth for three days and three nights, using the sign of Jonah in the belly of the whale for three days and three nights (Jonah 1:17, Matt. 12:39, 40). If this is the case, and we take His resurrection as Sunday morning, that would bring His crucifixion, death and burial to the early morning of Thursday. But we know He was crucified during the day according to scripture, and buried before the evening of a High Holyday, the first day of unleavened bread, an annual Sabbath (Matt. 27:1, Mark 15:25, John 19:31). So truthfully, using this evidence alone, we would have to conclude that He was indeed crucified on a Wednesday, and there was a Passover on Wednesday, April 25th, 31 A.D., according to at least one online Hebrew to Roman calendar converting website, and He arose Saturday afternoon, revealing Himself to His disciples, the first day of the week, Sunday; see appendix A for more details on this subject.[5] The idea of Jesus being crucified on a Friday could be argued, also, and some Biblical evidence would suggest it is possible, but that would deny other prophecies being fulfilled in Jesus Christ of Nazareth, namely that in the book of Daniel, chapter nine. So then we are left with a choice of what to believe in all of this. Jesus said that He spoke in parables, He also said that people would see and not perceive and hear and not understand (Matt. 13:14, 15, 34, 35). So it is very possible that a large portion of Christ followers, at least of the date of writing this book in 2019 A.D., are deceived as to the date of Jesus crucifixion, burial and resurrection. The apostle, Paul, said,

---

[4] http://www.wrcog.net/biblelight_crucifixion2.html, retrieved 16/03/2022
[5] http://www.cgsf.org/dbeattie/calendar/?roman=31, retrieved 20/03/2022

"For I would not, brethren, that ye should be ignorant of this mystery, lest ye should be wise in your own conceits; that blindness in part is happened to Israel, until the fulness of the Gentiles be come in." (Rom. 11:25). So whatever the truth of the date and time of Jesus crucifixion, burial and resurrection, there is some purpose to our blindness, whomever has it, but Jesus does desire us to know the truth, and He is the truth, and the truth will make us free (John 8:32, 14:6). Alleluia and praise the LORD. Most importantly we must remember that Jesus came to save us, heal us and forgive us. He was conceived by the Holy Spirit in the virgin, Mary, espoused to Joseph, both of the tribe of Judah (Matt. 1, Luke 3:23-38). He was born and raised a child of Israel, of the tribe of Judah, He had brothers and sisters (Matt. 13:55, 56; Luke 2:41-52, Rev. 5:5). He began His ministry at about the age of thirty, preaching the gospel of the Kingdom of God, healing, forgiving and doing other miracles (Luke 3:21-23, 4:43, 5:15, 20). And ultimately He gave up His life, dying on the cross for the forgiveness of our sins at Passover in 31 A.D., He was buried and the third day He arose to give us the hope and promise of eternal life in His Holy name. Alleluia and praise the LORD. Amen and Amen.

Passover lamb

At Exodus, the Passover lamb was eaten in hast (Ex. 12:11). Jesus told Judas, Jesus' betrayer, to do whatever he was going to do quickly (John 13:27). Jesus was ultimately betrayed, tried and crucified in approximately twelve hours, from Passover dinner, to the crucifixion morning. Moses had contentions with Israel over food, or rather the lack thereof in the wilderness, so God gave them manna to eat (Ex. 16:1-15). Jesus also did miracles of multiplying fishes and loaves of bread (Matt. 14:15-21, 15:32-38). Jesus referred to Himself as the true bread from heaven (John 6:32-35). Jesus, His body and the bread; Psalm 14:4 says, "Have all the workers of iniquity no knowledge? who eat up my people *as* they eat bread, and call not upon the LORD.". Psalm 53:4 repeats the same verse similarly as Psalm 14:4, it says, "Have the workers of iniquity no knowledge? who eat up my people *as* they eat bread: they have not called upon God.". That being said, He instituted the eating of the unleavened bread at the Passover supper, which was already done according to Old Testament laws, the evening before His crucifixion to represent His body given on the cross for the forgiveness of our sins (Ex. 12:8, Matt. 26:26). Bread is made through a process of planting the grain, rain, the heat and sun helping sprout and grow the grain, then the harvesting and winnowing of the grain and grinding of the grain into flour. Then the making of the bread, if leavened, then leaven is added, known as yeast commonly today and is set aside to rise if leaven is in it (Matt. 13:33). Then the bread is baked, with or without leaven, and only then is it ready to be eaten. God has used bread as a sign for His people in the Old Testament and through Jesus it represents His body given for us. We can use this example as the process with which we are planted with the seed of God, grown in Christ, are called, and chosen, sifted and refined, and then are set in the fiery furnace to prepare us to be used for God's greater purposes, whether that be in this life or in preparation for the world to come (Matt. 13:31, 32; 22:14; Luke 22:31, 31; 1 Pet. 4:12). Nevertheless, we have the miracle of Jesus Christ multiplying the fishes and loaves seemingly instantly, giving thanks to God and blessing the increase (John 6:11). Alleluia and praise the LORD. Amen and Amen.

Jesus, His blood and the wine; The blood, according to the Old Testament is sacred, and not to be eaten, because it is the life of a creature (Lev. 17:11). This seems to be in contrast to Jesus asking us to drink His blood, but of course He, Himself, said the words He was speaking were spiritual in nature, that is in similitude (John 6:53-63). This is because He was ultimately saying that His life had to be given for us to receive eternal life, and that He had to spill His blood on the cross so that we could be forgiven of our sins and saved. This is why at the night of Passover supper before His betrayal, He instituted the drinking of the blood of the vine, the wine, to drink in remembrance of Him and His sacrifice on the cross given for us (Matt. 26:27, 28). Psalm 16:5 says, "The LORD is the portion of mine inheritance and of my cup: thou maintainest my lot.". Alleluia and praise the LORD. The similar idea of the process of creating bread can be seen in the creating of the wine representing the blood of Jesus Christ of Nazareth. The seed grows into a vine, the vine develops to be ready to grow fruit, the fruit blossoms and grows, and then the fruit is harvested in its season of ripeness. After this the fruit is pressed, broken, like the seed was grinded, and the juice of that fruit of the vine is collected. After this the process of fermentation takes place with the sugars and the yeast that cause the fruit juices to ferment into alcohol, with natural heat or applied heat, similar to the baking of the bread in the oven, then it is ready to be consumed. In both of these processes the increase can be stored for a time, like grain can be stored, or the grain flour, and even baked bread has a certain albeit small shelf life. Wine is a better example of this, because wine is aged in many cases to bring out more developed flavours in the fermented fruit, also using the storage container to add flavour to the wine. The point here is that we can seem to be set aside or God can be working something in us, but it can seem like a time of sitting, waiting, or boredom, but that does not mean that God does not have a good purpose for it. This is where what Jesus says, "In your patience possess ye your souls.", becomes relevant (Luke 21:19). And just like Jesus multiplied the fishes and loaves, He also seemingly instantly turned water into wine, and the better, likely aged, wine at that (John 2:1-10). So no matter how we look at the bread and the wine, which represent the body and blood of Jesus Christ of Nazareth, and the remembrance of Him giving His life for us on the cross, dying on the cross for the forgiveness of our sins, He was buried and the third day He arose to give us the hope and promise of eternal life in His Holy name. Remember that He is a God of miracles, and that He can and will do His work in us and this world quickly when required. As the Scripture says of Jesus, "Behold, I come quickly…" (Rev. 22:7). Alleluia and praise the LORD. Amen and Amen.

Jesus spoke a teaching in the New Testament in John 6 that was according to some "… an hard saying…" (John 6:60). Simply put He was speaking of His flesh and blood being the offering made for the forgiveness of sins, for Israel and the whole world, on the cross. He said of Himself, "I am the bread of life. Your fathers did eat manna in the wilderness, and are dead. This is the bread which cometh down from heaven, that a man may eat thereof, and not die. I am the living bread which came down from heaven: if any man eat of this bread, he shall live for ever: and the bread that I will give is my flesh, which I will give for the life of the world. The Jews therefore strove among themselves, saying, How can this man give us *his* flesh to eat? Then Jesus said unto them, Verily, verily, I say unto you, Except ye eat the flesh of the Son of man, and drink his blood, ye have no life in you. Whoso eateth my flesh, and drinketh my blood, hath eternal life; and I will raise him up at the last day. For my flesh is meat indeed, and my blood is drink indeed. He that eateth my flesh, and drinketh my blood, dwelleth in me, and I in him. As the living Father hath sent me, and I live by the Father: so he that eateth me, even he shall live by me. This is that bread which came down from heaven: not as your father did eat manna, and are dead: he that eateth of this bread shall live forever." (John 6:48-58). As said, simply put Jesus was prophesying of the offering up of His body, flesh and blood, on the cross for the forgiveness of our sins. The fact of the matter is, in order to eat the flesh of anything; it needs to be slain first. Jesus was without going into detail, saying that He needed to give up His life for the forgiveness of our sins. The other reason why this would have been a hard saying for the Jews is that in Leviticus, there is a command not to eat the blood of the animals which are given up as offerings and sacrifices, mentioned earlier (Lev. 17:12). This is because according to the scriptures, "...the life of the flesh is in the blood..." (Lev. 17:11). As is also mentioned, this blood is an atonement for the sins of the people (Lev. 17:11). But Jesus' blood is different than that of animals; His blood was spilt once for all, forever, for the forgiveness of our sins (Heb. 10:10-14). This is the New Covenant in Jesus Christ of Nazareth, that I will go into greater detail about in chapter four (Jer. 31:31-34, Heb. 8, 12:24). Alleluia and praise the LORD. Amen and Amen.

This all being said, we also need to understand that Jesus, like the prophets before and after Him, also spoke in parables from time to time (Hos. 12:10, Matt. 13:34, 35). So as will be mentioned in other chapters His flesh and blood, were literally going to be given up as an offering for our sins, but Jesus at the Passover supper, the evening before His crucifixion, instituted the memorial of His offering in the breaking of bread and drinking of wine in remembrance of His sacrifice (1 Cor. 11:23-26). Last, He was no doubt suggesting that we need to consume Him, as the Holy Spirit; we need the Holy Spirit to dwell in, through and with us in order to live, so Jesus was giving a fleshly example of this idea of receiving the Holy Spirit into our life, most importantly (John 7:39). As Jesus confirms in John 6:63, He says, "It is the spirit that quickeneth; the flesh profiteth nothing: the words that I speak unto you, *they* are spirit, and *they* are life.". Flesh seems to be equivalent to muscle in the Bible (Ezek. 37:8). Generally, man is made up of according to the Bible; skin, flesh, sinew and bone (Ezek. 37:7, 8). The Bible also mentions the blood, marrow, and heart, as well (Gen. 9:4-6, Job 21:24, Ps. 4:4). The point is that Christ asked us to eat His flesh, which goes below the surface of the skin. He desires us to look deeper into Him and His life than just the surface. And it is the works of Christ that we need to believe in, not just the words He spoke, but the acts that He did!!! He is a miracle worker after all. And He came full of grace and truth (John 1:14). Another word spoken of about His John 6 sermon; I should say that this also likely had something to do with the prophecy of "… The zeal of thine house hath eaten me up." (Ps. 69:9, John 2:17). This prophecy was first referenced in the New Testament, regarding Jesus casting out the money changers from the temple at Passover, accusing them of turning God's temple into a den of thieves (John 2:13-17). But no doubt, God's true temple, that is Christ Jesus of Nazareth, has everything to do with this prophecy (John 2:19-21). Alleluia and praise the LORD. Last, in the book of Revelation, it is the Lamb of God that is worthy to open the seals, the Lamb of God overcomes evil, and the Lamb of God marries His wife (John 1:29, 36; Rev. 5, Rev. 17-19, Rev. 19-22). It is by Christ Jesus of Nazareth that we live, are saved and things are accomplished in this world, and in the "world to come", so place your trust in Him, Jesus Christ of Nazareth, with God, the Father, and His Holy Spirit, first and foremost. Alleluia and praise the LORD. Amen and Amen.

Wilderness journey

Leviticus 16 speaks of the priest laying his hands on and confessing the sins of the people over the head of the scapegoat, that was then sent into the wilderness, bearing the iniquities of the people (Lev. 16:8-10, 20-22). Israel was in the wilderness for forty years, while the generation that knew the ways of Egypt slowly passed away (Num. 14:20-35, 32:13; Deut. 8:2, Jos. 5:6). Jesus was in the wilderness for forty days and forty nights at the beginning of His ministry, fasting, and then was tempted by the devil (Matt. 4:1-11). In Leviticus 25, bondservants were redeemed for a price; they could even redeem themselves if they were able (Lev. 25:48, 49). Jesus paid the price for our redemption (1 Cor. 6:20, 7:23; 2 Pet. 2:1). Jesus also had the ability to redeem Himself (John 10:18). As the scriptures would allow, Leviticus 25:48 and 49 say, "After that he is sold he may be redeemed again; one of his brethren may redeem him: Either his uncle, or his uncle's son, may redeem him, or *any* that is nigh of kin unto him of his family may redeem him; or if he be able, he may redeem himself.". The people around Him at the cross said, "…save thyself. If thou be the Son of God, come down from the cross." (Matt. 27:40). Of course they were ignorant of the fact that He was up there for them, the very people that were yelling at Him, with the other onlookers around them. Regarding manna in the wilderness, as spoken of in the previous section, Jesus says in John 6:32, 48-51, 58, about Himself, "…Verily, verily, I say unto you, Moses gave you not that bread from heaven; but my Father giveth you the true bread from heaven. … I am that bread of life. Your fathers did eat manna in the wilderness, and are dead. This is the bread which cometh down from heaven, that a man may eat thereof, and not die. I am the living bread which came down from heaven: if any man eat of this bread, he shall live for ever: and the bread that I will give is my flesh, which I will give for the life of the whole world. … This is that bread which came down from heaven: not as your fathers did eat manna, and are dead: he that eateth of this bread shall live forever.". We are called to eat His words (Jer. 15:16, John 6:63, 1 Cor. 10:3, 4). Referring to the drink mentioned in the previous section; Jesus is the living waters, He mentioned this to a woman at a well in Samaria (John 4:5-26, 7:38, 39). He said, "But whosoever drinketh of the water that I shall give him shall never thirst; but the water that I shall give him shall be in him a well of water springing up into everlasting life." (John 4:14). In the Old Testament wilderness journey, there is the rock of Horeb, that waters miraculously poured out of after Moses smote the rock at God's command (Ex. 17:5, 6). We are called to drink of the living waters of the Word of God (Jer. 2:13, John 7:37). Jesus calls us to be born of water and spirit; Jesus is the living waters, God is the Holy Spirit (John 3:5-7, 4:24, 7:37). Alleluia and praise the LORD. Amen and Amen.

Conclusion

The tribe of Judah and Jesus Christ of Nazareth; the next two chapters will speak a little more about Jesus and His relationship with the descendants of Judah, namely, king David, along with other topics. Also, regarding the feasts of the LORD, they are written about in Leviticus 23, and they are discussed in greater detail in my seventh book, regarding their "ancient" and present-day purposes, as well as their prophetic meaning, a "…shadow of things to come…" (Col. 2:17). The feasts were for practical purposes according to times and seasons coinciding with plowing, sowing and harvesting. Passover and the Days of Unleavened bread, the Feast of Pentecost, also known as the Feast of Weeks or Feast of First fruits, and then the fall feasts of Trumpets, the Day of Atonement and namely, the Feast of Tabernacles, culminating with the "last day", on the 8th day of the Feast of Tabernacles (Lev. 23). Alleluia and praise the LORD. Amen and Amen. These "Holydays" are also a sign of God's greater plan for mankind, throughout the ages, as well as pointing to Jesus Christ of Nazareth and His salvation plan for all of mankind, culminating with the "last day", the "great day" (Lev. 23:39, John 6:39, 7:37; Rev. 20:11-15). This will conclude God's plan for all of mankind through the resurrection of the dead, and the judgement of both the quick and the dead, by the name of Jesus Christ of Nazareth, some to everlasting life, and possibly some to everlasting death. Nevertheless, this book will continue with the prophetic words spoken of in the Old Testament being compared with Jesus Christ of Nazareth's fulfillment of them. Read on to learn more. Alleluia and praise the LORD. Amen and Amen.

Discussion: Prophecy

"But I will have mercy upon the house of Judah, and will save them by the LORD their God, and will not save them by bow, nor by sword, nor by battle, by horses, nor by horsemen."
- Hosea 1:7

Jesus Christ of Nazareth and His cross, are the best explanation of mercy and salvation for the "…house of Judah…", and all of Israel, and the whole world for that matter. He died on the cross at Passover, in 31 A.D., spilling His Holy and righteous blood on the cross, He was buried and the third day He arose to give us the hope and promise of eternal life in His Holy name. Alleluia and praise the LORD. Amen and Amen. Aside from this, it is possible that during the "Great Tribulation", this world may experience miracles similar to what the Israelites experienced during the plagues of Egypt, there exodus from Egypt, the crossing at the Red Sea, and their sojourn in the wilderness for forty years (Ex., Num., Matt. 24). The "Messianic Age" will likely be ushered in by a miraculous change in our spiritual and physical nature, as the New Testament would suggest, "…we shall be changed." (1 Cor. 15:52, 1 John 6, 8). Alleluia and praise the LORD. Amen and Amen.

Discussion Questions

1. Why do some "Jews" not believe in Jesus Christ of Nazareth, as their Saviour fully yet?

    _____

    _____

    _____

    _____

    _____

CHAPTER 3

Two or three witnesses of Jesus Messiah of Nazareth

"One witness shall not rise up against a man for any iniquity, or for any sin, in any sin that he sinneth: at the mouth of two witnesses, or at the mouth of three witnesses, shall the matter be established."
- DEUTERONOMY 19:15

Introduction

In this chapter I will speak about the "…cloud of witnesses…"; that is the prophets, scribes and common folk, whom testified of Jesus Christ of Nazareth, in vision and prophecy, before He was born into this world in the flesh and then when He was confirmed by the eye witnesses of His presence, as the eternal king of Israel, and Saviour of the whole world (Heb. 12:1). As mentioned above, a matter is established by two or three witnesses, not just because of sin, but also for any truth in general. Jesus said, "…in the mouth of two or three witnesses every word may be established." (Matt. 18:16). He also said, "For where two or three are gathered together in my name, there am I in the midst of them." (Matt. 18:20). The apostle, Paul, said, "Let the prophets speak two or three, and let the other judge." (1 Cor. 14:29). The apostle, Paul, also said, "This *is* the third *time* I am coming to you. In the mouth of two or three witnesses shall every word be established." (2 Cor. 13:1). The point is, we ought to prove what is the truth in any matter, and according to the Holy Bible, this requires at least two witnesses (1 Thess. 5:21). That being said, Jesus did say the gate is strait and the way is narrow to eternal life (Matt. 7:14). Nevertheless, I will speak about some witnesses in this chapter, using the Old Testament law, written by God, through Moses, with the help of his brother Aaron. I will also speak of the testimony of Jesus, through King David, and other Psalmists. And in the last section, Jesus will be spoken about through the writings of the prophet Isaiah. Alleluia and praise the LORD. Amen and Amen. Read on to learn more.

Moses and Aaron

In Deuteronomy Moses prophesied of Jesus Christ of Nazareth saying, "The LORD thy God will raise up unto thee a Prophet from the midst of thee, of thy brethren, like unto me; unto him ye shall hearken; According to all that thou desiredst of the LORD thy God in Horeb in the day of the assembly, saying, Let me not hear again the voice of the LORD my God, neither let me see this great fire any more, that I die not. And the LORD said unto me, They have well *spoken that* which they have spoken. I will raise them up a Prophet from among their brethren, like unto thee, and will put my words in his mouth; and he shall speak unto them all that I shall command him. And it shall come to pass, *that* whosoever will not hearken unto my words which he shall speak in my name, I will require *it* of him." (Deut. 18:15-19). This prophecy was fulfilled in Jesus Christ of Nazareth, and even those whom did not "hearken", testified of the fulfillment of this prophecy, by saying, "…His blood be on us…", when Jesus was being condemned by the people (Matt. 27:25). Jesus said of Himself, "Do not think that I will accuse you to the Father: there is *one* that accuseth you, *even* Moses, in whom ye trust. For had ye believed Moses, ye would have believed me; for he wrote of me. But if ye believe not his writings, how shall ye believe my words?" (John 5:45-47). In a parable Jesus spoke of Lazarus and the rich man, Abraham saying to the rich man, "…They have Moses and the prophets…If they hear not Moses and the prophets, neither will they be persuaded, though one rose from the dead." (Luke 16:29, 31). The Bible says of Jesus after His resurrection, "And beginning at Moses and all the prophets, he expounded unto them in all the scriptures the things concerning himself." (Luke 24:27). Peter, James and John witnessed Jesus' majesty, at the transfiguration during His earthly ministry (Matt. 17:1, 2; 2 Pet. 1:16-18). There may still be a judgement to come, but God's glory and kingdom power was shown in Jesus at His transfiguration before His crucifixion, and then again at His resurrection, before He was taken up into a cloud in heaven (Matt. 17:1-9, John 20). Jesus said we will see Him coming in the clouds (Matt. 24:30). God spoke from the clouds at Jesus' transfiguration about Jesus, "…This is my beloved Son, in whom I am well pleased; hear ye Him." (Matt. 17:5). God's kingdom is coming, and is near, and is in us as we accept His Holy Spirit in the name of Jesus Christ of Nazareth. Alleluia and praise the LORD. Amen and Amen.

Jesus summed up the Ten Commandments in two commandments, and even summed them up in one (Ex. 20:1-17, Matt. 7:12, 22:37-40). He said, "Thou shalt love the Lord thy God with all thy heart, and with all thy soul, and with all thy mind. This is the first and great commandment. And the second *is* like unto it, Thou shalt love thy neighbour as thyself. On these two commandments hang all the law and the prophets." (Matt. 22:37-40). Jesus also said, "Therefore all things whatsoever ye would that men should do to you, do ye even so to them: for this is the law and the prophets." (Matt. 7:12). Leviticus 14 and 15 speak of the cleansing laws for leprosy and other skin diseases, as well as other bodily fluid issues. One of the offerings to be made for the cleansing of these various ailments was a dove (Lev. 14:22). This would compare with the dove like Holy Spirit that descended upon Jesus after His baptism by John in the Jordan, and other comparisons of Jesus' dove likeness, discussed further in the next section of this chapter (Matt. 3:16). The other offering was of a lamb, and the blood from the offering was used partially to mark the "patients" body; the priest would dip his finger in the blood and mark the tip of the right ear, the tip of the right thumb and the tip of the right great toe with blood (Lev. 14:14). When thinking about Jesus on the cross, it is highly likely that His own blood would have fallen on His right ear from the crown of thorns, on His right thumb from His blood issuing from His wounds on His hands, and on His right big toe from the blood issuing from the wounds on His feet (Matt. 27:29, 35; John 20:25). A similar ceremony was spoken of in the book of Exodus, when Aaron was being anointed to become the "High Priest". He was anointed with oil, and fitted with a crown as well, which Jesus also received before His crucifixion (Ex. 29:6, 7; Matt. 27:29). Jesus was anointed with oil by a woman before His crucifixion, and He said, wherever the gospel is preached this act will be spoken of (Mark 14:3-9). Alleluia and praise the LORD. Amen and Amen.

The point of all this, is to show the depths that Jesus Christ of Nazareth went, to cleanse us of our sins, and how He has become "High Priest" of God for us all forever (Isa. 59:17, Heb. 3:1, 2). Not only this, but He did heal both a leper, and a woman whom had an issue of blood twelve years (Matt. 8:2-3, 9:20-22; Mark 1:40-42). He even asked the man to give the offering commanded by Moses for a witness to the temple authorities of the healing (Matt. 8:4, Mark 1:43, 44). Albeit, the cleansed leper did not listen and instead told people about the miracle that Jesus did for him (Mark 1:45). The point in all of this is that Jesus simplified all of the ritualistic behaviour required by Biblical law to be cleansed of diseases and to serve God in His "temple". In healing, He simply said, "… go, and sin no more." (John 8:11). It was not only Jesus that did these miracles, but His disciples and has continued throughout history unto today (Mark 6:12, 13; 16:15-18). Many continue to be healed today by the miraculous healing power in the name of Jesus Christ of Nazareth, by faith, through the Holy Spirit (Eph. 2:8, 9). And now with Jesus Christ of Nazareth as High Priest forever, we can go boldly to the throne of grace in His name, with our prayers and petitions for ourselves and on behalf of others as intercessors. But Jesus is that great Ambassador, and Intercessor between us and God, now and forever more, by His shed blood on the cross for the forgiveness of our sins! And He is our hope of eternal life in His Holy name, through His burial and His resurrection three days later! Praise the Lord God Almighty, and His only begotten Son Jesus Christ of Nazareth! Also, Aaron having received a similar ceremony for cleansing, would be representative of us all being sinners and needing forgiveness and cleansing for our sins (Lev. 29:20, 21). As, "… God is no respecter of persons…" (Acts 10:34). As the Bible says, "For all have sinned, and come short of the glory of God…" (Rom. 3:23). It is by the blood of the eternal lamb, Jesus Christ of Nazareth, that we have forgiveness of our sins and eternal life! Repent and believe the gospel! Alleluia and praise the LORD. Amen and Amen.

David and other Psalmists

Although the Psalms are used throughout this book to point to Jesus, as the prophesied Messiah, in this section I will go into greater detail using the Psalms to describe the New Testament account of Jesus' life here on earth. At the beginning of His earthly life, Jesus was conceived, by the Holy Spirit, in and born to the virgin, Mary, espoused to Joseph (Matt. 1:18-25). And within two years of His childhood, He was visited by "kings", often known as the "three wise men", but called "wise men", without a specific number of them given and He was given gifts of gold, frankincense and myrrh (Matt. 2:1-11, 16). In Psalm 68:18 it says, "Thou hast ascended on high, thou hast led captivity captive: thou hast received gifts for men; yea, *for* the rebellious also, that the LORD God might dwell *among them*.". And Psalm 68:29 says, "Because of thy temple at Jerusalem shall kings bring presents unto thee.". After this time Jesus was sent to Egypt with His parents to flee from king Herod's desire to destroy the Messiah (Matt. 2:13-15). There are a couple psalms that point to this prophesied event. Psalm 68:31 says, "Princes shall come out of Egypt; Ethiopia shall soon stretch out her hands unto God". This was also likely fulfilled when a disciple of Jesus, Philip, met an Ethiopian eunuch, during the Ethiopian's travel to worship at Jerusalem after Jesus' resurrection (Acts 8:26-40). Nevertheless, in Psalm 80:8 it also says, "Thou hast brought a vine out of Egypt: thou hast cast out the heathen, and planted it.". I will speak more of Jesus as the vine in chapter five. And last Psalm 71:5 speaks of Jesus' relationship with God's house in His youth, it says, "For thou *art* my hope, O Lord GOD: *thou* art my trust from my youth.". This is likely in regards to the time Jesus spent at the temple during the feast of Passover, when His parents had already started to travel home unwittingly without Jesus, when He was twelve (Luke 2:41-52). The point of all of this is that Jesus' early life alone is spoken of in the Psalms. Alleluia and praise the LORD. Amen and Amen.

Next is the beginning of Jesus' three and a half year ministry, preaching of the Kingdom of God. It starts with His baptism with the Holy Spirit descending on Him like a dove (Matt. 3:16). In Psalms 55:6 it says, "And I said, Oh that I had wings like a dove! *For then* would I fly away, and be at rest.". And in Psalm 57:1-3 it says, "Be merciful unto me, O God, be merciful unto me: for my soul trusteth in thee: yea, in the shadow of thy wings will I make my refuge, until *these* calamities be over past. I will cry unto God most high; unto God that performeth *all things* for me. He shall send from heaven, and save me *from* the reproach of him that would swallow me up. Selah. God shall send forth his mercy and his truth.". The mercy and truth being that of the Holy Spirit that descended upon Jesus like a dove (John 14:16, 17; Gal. 5:22, 23; Eph. 5:9). Also Psalm 63:7 says, "Because thou hast been my help, therefore in the shadow of thy wings will I rejoice.". In Psalm 68:13, it seems to describe the significance of the dove as a sign, "Though ye have lien among the pots, *yet shall ye be as* the wings of a dove covered with silver, and her feathers with yellow gold.". After this a voice from heaven says, "…This is my beloved Son, in whom I am well pleased." (Matt. 3:17). In Psalm 2:7 it says, "I will declare the decree: the LORD hath said unto me, Thou *art* my Son; this day have I begotten thee.". Next, Jesus was led up of the spirit into the wilderness, fasting for forty days, and then tempted by the devil (Matt. 4:1-11). In Psalm 55:7 it says, "Lo, *then* would I wander far off, *and* remain in the wilderness. Selah". Another great event of Jesus' life is His transfiguration (Matt. 17:1-9, Mark 9:2-9, Luke 9:28-36). Jesus' face was said to have shined as bright as the sun and He was seen speaking with Elijah and Moses, then a bright cloud overshadowed them and God spoke from the cloud (Matt. 17:2, 3, 5). This experience likely fulfils a few Psalms, the Psalms talk of God's cloud, and the shadow of the Almighty (Ps. 17:8, 18:11, 36:7, 57:1, 63:7, 91:1, 97:2, 99:7, 104:3, 105:39). The Psalms also speak of asking for God's face to shine upon the people of God (Ps. 31:16, 50:2, 67:1, 80:1, 3, 7, 19; 119:135). Psalm 67:1 says, "God be merciful unto us, and bless us; *and* cause his face to shine upon us; Selah.". Nevertheless there are many more Psalms that speak of Jesus' life, and in reality the whole Bible speaks of Jesus, as He is the living Word of God, and the Bible is the written Word of God, the two are inseparable. If you have a Bible, I would recommend searching these Psalms out, and if you do not have a Bible, may the Almighty provide one for you. God bless. Alleluia and praise the LORD. Amen and Amen.

Now I will speak about Jesus' betrayal and judgement, using the Psalms. His betrayal began with Judas conspiring with the religious authorities of Jesus' day. Judas accepted a bribe for the betrayal of Jesus (Matt. 26:15). In Psalm 26:10 it says, "In whose hands *is* mischief, and their right hand is full of bribes.". After the declaration of Judas' betrayal, by the sign of dipping his bread into the same cup as Jesus at the Passover supper, and then the institution of the bread and wine in remembrance of Jesus, Jesus and the disciples went to the garden of Gethsemane to pray (Matt. 26:21-36). Psalm 63:6 says, "When I remember thee upon my bed, *and* meditate on thee in the *night* watches.". During this time, Judas had already gone out to bring the authorities to capture Jesus (John 13:27-30). Psalm 41:9 and 10 says, "Yea, mine own familiar friend, in whom I trusted, which did eat of my bread, hath lifted up *his* heel against me. But thou, O LORD, be merciful unto me, and raise me up, that I may requite them.". This verse may very well be testimony that Judas and the "religious authorities" will receive forgiveness in the final resurrection of the dead, God only knows for certain (Ps. 68:30, 69:22-28). Later, in the account in Matthew it seems as if Judas verbally repented of his act of betrayal to the chief priests and elders before he killed himself (Matt. 27:3-5). Nevertheless, Jesus in the garden of Gethsemane facing His accusers is next (Matt. 26:36, Mark 14:32, John 18:1). When they approached, Jesus went forth and asked, "Whom seek ye?", and they said Jesus of Nazareth, when Jesus said, "I am *he*.", His accusers went backward and fell to the ground (John 18:4-6). In Psalm 40:14 it says, "Let them be ashamed and confounded together that seek after my soul to destroy it; let them be driven backward and put to shame that wish me evil.". And, at Judas' defence, he betrayed Jesus conveniently, and he told the authorities to take and lead Jesus away safely (Mark 14:11, 44). Next is Jesus with Pontius Pilate, Pilate declared that he found no fault in Jesus and washed his own hands clean of the crucifixion process (Matt. 27:24). In Psalm 26:6 and 7 it says, "I will wash mine hands in innocency: so will I compass thine alter, O LORD: That I may publish with the voice of thanksgiving, and tell of all thy wondrous works.". This would also indicate Christ as the altar of God, which indeed He is eternally. Alleluia and praise the LORD. Amen and Amen.

Last, let us talk of His crucifixion, burial and resurrection. In Psalm 89:38-52 it goes into detail of how he bore our reproach and sin, as well as in Psalm 69:7-20. Jesus was offered gall to drink when He was first being crucified, but He did not receive it (Matt. 27:34). Psalm 69:21 says, "They gave me also gall for my meat; and in my thirst they gave me vinegar to drink.". Jesus endured accusations, demands and insults while He was being crucified on His cross (Matt. 27:39-44). Psalm 57:4 says, "My soul *is* among lions: *and* I lie *even among* them that are set on fire, *even* the sons of men, whose teeth *are* spears and arrows, and their tongue a sharp sword.". At the end of Jesus' crucifixion He echoed the words of King David spoken in psalm saying, "My God, my God, why hast thou forsaken me? …" (Ps. 22:1). After speaking His feeling of separation from God, His Father, just prior to Jesus giving up His ghost after hours on His cross, Jesus spoke that He was thirsty, and He did indeed receive the vinegar He was given Him that time, completely fulfilling what was spoken in Psalm 69:21 earlier (John 19:29, 30). After this He said, "…It is finished…" (John 19:30). Psalm 31:5 seems to speak of Jesus giving up the ghost, it says, "Into thine hand I commit my spirit: thou hast redeemed me, O LORD God of truth.". He spoke similar words on the cross before giving up His Holy Spirit to God, the Father (Luke 23:46). And Psalm 60:1-3 speaks of the tearing of the veil of the temple from top to bottom, and the earthquake (Matt. 27:51-54). Psalm 60:1-3 says, "O GOD, thou hast cast us off, thou hast scattered us, thou hast been displeased; O turn thyself to us again. Thou hast made the earth to tremble; thou hast broken it: heal the breaches thereof; for it shaketh. Thou hast shewed thy people hard things: thou hast made us to drink the wine of astonishment.". Psalm 64 seems to go into detail about the process of Jesus' trial and crucifixion. Psalm 64:9 says, "And all men shall fear, and shall declare the work of God; for they shall wisely consider of his doing.". A centurion and others said, "…Truly this was the Son of God.", according to Matthew's gospel account (Matt. 27:54). The Psalms also speak of Jesus' resurrection, Psalm 16:10 says, "For thou wilt not leave my soul in hell; neither wilt thou suffer thine Holy One to see corruption.", as well as others (Ps. 57:5-11, 66:7-20). Before Jesus' ascension He called for His disciples to make disciples of all nations (Matt. 28:19, 20). Psalm 67:5 says, "Let the people praise thee, O God; let all the people praise thee.". In chapter six I will continue with the topic of the timeline of the life of Jesus Christ of Nazareth, using some more Psalms as well as other Old Testament and New Testament scripture, to draw this book to its general conclusions. Alleluia and praise the LORD. Amen and Amen.

Isaiah and the "bigger picture"

Isaiah 7:14 speaks of Jesus, it says, "Therefore the Lord himself shall give you a sign; Behold, a virgin shall conceive, and bear a son, and shall call his name Immanuel.". This is speaking of Jesus Christ of Nazareth, He was conceived of the Holy Spirit, in Mary, a virgin. An angel visited both Joseph, whom Mary was espoused to and Mary, and warned them of the conception by the Holy Spirit (Matt. 1:20, Luke 1:26-35). Isaiah 8 continues this account but branches out to the bigger picture of God's relationship with Israel, His chosen people. Both Samaria and Jerusalem are mentioned, which are examples of the Northern tribes whom went into captivity in approximately 700 B.C., as Samaria, and Judah with those tribal remnants that stayed with them, as Jerusalem, whom went into captivity in approximately 600 B.C., Jesus being a member of the tribe of Judah (Rev. 5:5). Judah, went into captivity to Babylon, and has a relationship with Assyria (Isa. 7:17). And Samaria, that is idolatrous Israel, went into captivity by Assyria, and could be compared with Babylon (Isa. 7:8, 9). This is an aside to the direct life of Jesus Christ of Nazareth, in Biblical prophecy, but understanding where the tribes of Israel likely were during Jesus' ministry paints the bigger picture of life in first century A.D.. They were a part of the larger empires at the time, namely the Roman Empire, during Jesus' three and a half year "earthly" ministry (John 11:48, Acts 16:37). See appendix F for more details on tribal and church history, and this subject of tribal history is spoken of in greater detail in my book, "Origin of Mankind". Isaiah 8:13-18 says, "Sanctify the LORD of hosts himself; and *let* him *be* your fear, and *let* him *be* your dread. And he shall be for a sanctuary; but for a stone of stumbling and for a rock of offence to both the houses of Israel, for a gin and for a snare to the inhabitants of Jerusalem. And many among them shall stumble, and fall, and be broken, and be snared, and be taken. Bind up the testimony, seal the law among my disciples. And I will wait upon the LORD, that hideth his face from the house of Jacob, and I will look for him. Behold, I and the children whom the LORD hath given me *are* for signs and for wonders in Israel from the LORD of hosts, which dwelleth in mount Zion.". The entirety of this verse is spoken of in the New Testament in various places, Jesus is considered a "stumblingblock" to some (1 Cor. 1:23, 10:4). Of course, His ministry along with that of His disciples caused many to fall, namely because of established religious hypocrisy of His time, and challenges to "status quo". Jesus said, If our righteousness does not exceed that of the religious authorities we cannot enter into the kingdom of God (Matt. 5:20). And Jesus and His disciples have been called to do and be signs, wonders and miracles, which is what Isaiah prophesied (John 4:48, Acts 5:12). Alleluia and praise the LORD, Amen and Amen.

Isaiah 9 is probably the most detailed of the chapters of Isaiah's book that speaks of Jesus Christ as the Messiah, and God. Isaiah 9:1 and 2 says, "Nevertheless the dimness *shall* not *be* such as *was* in her vexation, when at the first he lightly afflicted the land of Zebulun and the land of Naphtali, and afterward did more grievously afflict *her by* the way of the sea, beyond Jordan, in Galilee of the nations. The people that walked in darkness have seen a great light: they that dwell in the land of the shadow of death, upon them hath the light shined.". This speaks of Jesus in Galilee, as "...the light...", which is referenced in New Testament Scripture (John 8:12, 9:5, 12:36). Isaiah 9:4 says, "For thou hast broken the yoke of his burden, and the staff of his shoulder, the rod of his oppressor, as in the day of Midian.". This speaks of Jesus' courageous act of taking all of our sins upon Himself on the cross. This all being said, Isaiah 9:5, likely speaks of the prophesied "Great Tribulation" to come upon this world, which Jesus spoke about during His ministry (Matt. 24). Isaiah 9:6 and 7 say, "For unto us a child is born, unto us a son is given: and the government shall be upon his shoulder: and his name shall be called Wonderful, Counsellor, The mighty God, The everlasting Father, The Prince of Peace. Of the increase of *his* government and peace *there shall be* no end, upon the throne of David, and upon his kingdom, to order it, and to establish it with judgement and with justice from henceforth even for ever. The zeal of the LORD of hosts will perform this.". These are the verses that are often used to describe Jesus as the Messiah, using the Old Testament prophecies relating to the New Testament accounts. This also speaks of God's church, "the Body of Christ", as Jesus is the head and we, the church, are the members of the Body of Christ (1 Cor. 12:27, Eph. 5:23). Isaiah 9:8 says, "The Lord sent a word into Jacob, and it hath lighted upon Israel.". This speaks of the Holy Spirit conception of Jesus, as mentioned earlier (John 1:1-3). Isaiah 9:9-21 speaks of the terrors of God that have come upon fallen and rebellious Israel, His discipline using surrounding nations and the infighting caused by rebellion from God, which is mentioned in the time of the Judges and Kings of Israel, and has continued to take place throughout history. This is also likely prophetic in nature, of the world we live in today in general, as well as the prophesied coming "Great Tribulation" and the "1000 years of Christ's rule with His saints", which have not likely taken place yet, as of the date of writing this book in 2019 A.D. (Matt 24, Rev. 20:4). This is the reality of Bible prophecy, because Jesus Christ of Nazareth is the Spirit of prophecy, and as life still carries on after His resurrection and ascension, there are still Biblical prophesies that have yet to take place, that even Jesus Christ of Nazareth, Himself spoke of (Matt. 24, Rev. 19:10). He preached about the kingdom of God, and its coming to earth. He taught us to pray about Him, "Thy kingdom come, Thy will be done in earth, as *it is* in heaven." (Matt. 6:10). This is the "bigger picture" of Jesus' ministry, He preached about the Kingdom of God, He taught about repentance for the forgiveness of our sins, and He taught about the resurrection, judgement, and life everlasting in His Holy name. Alleluia and praise the LORD. Amen and Amen.

Isaiah 10 and 11 go into greater detail about history and prophecies to come, about our day, the "Great Tribulation" and the "1000 years of Christ's rule with His saints", also known as the "Messianic Age" (Matt. 24, Rev. 20:4). John the Baptist said Jesus would baptize with the Holy Spirit and fire, namely fiery trials, trials that test us during our life here on earth, and Jesus spoke of the meek inheriting the earth (Isa. 10:16-19, Matt. 3:11, 12; 5:5). Isaiah mentions a "remnant" and a "consumption", which is likely related to the "Great Tribulation" and the "Messianic Age", as well as the "final judgement" of mankind (Isa. 10:20-23, Rom. 9:27, 28; Rev. 11:13). Isaiah 10:24-34 speaks of God's promised protection during these times of trials. We have hope in God's protection, because of Jesus Christ of Nazareth, the Saviour of the whole world. Isaiah 10:27 says, "And it shall come to pass in that day, *that* his burden shall be taken away from off thy shoulder, and his yoke from off thy neck, and the yoke shall be destroyed because of the anointing.". Jesus is the Anointed One, the Messiah, and we have His anointing in receiving His gift of eternal life in His Holy name, through fellowship with and the indwelling of His Holy Spirit. Isaiah 11 will be spoken of in chapter five, referring to

Jesus as the prophesied "Branch". Philip, a disciple of Jesus Christ of Nazareth, said of Jesus in the New Testament, "...We have found him, of whom Moses in the law, and the prophets, did write, Jesus of Nazareth, the son of Joseph." (John 1:45). The knowledge of Jesus Christ of Nazareth as God is a challenging one to accept for some, at the least it needs prayerful consideration. A rather simple way of looking at it would be to consider a man whom is both a father and a son in this life. We are born into a family which makes us a "son" or daughter of somebody, but we also have the opportunity to bear children, so if we have children we are also considered parents, a "father" or a mother. This is the easiest way to explain the dual nature of Jesus Christ of Nazareth or anyone else for that matter. Even He called at least one He healed, Daughter, and this speaks of His relationship with the "first" Adam, as was spoken of in chapter one (Matt. 9:22). That being said, from the perspective of Jesus Christ of Nazareth, there is still one higher than He, and He is known as, the Father, Our Father, the Father of lights, Abba, JAH, God, the LORD, etc. (Gen. 2:4, Ps. 68:4, Matt. 11:27, 19:17; Mark 14:36, Jam. 1:17). Jesus did say of Himself, "I and *my* Father are one." and "...I *am* in the Father, and the Father in me..." (John 10:30, 14:11). Nevertheless, for practical purposes, our life here on earth and forever more is in Christ Jesus of Nazareth, whom died on the cross for the forgiveness of our sins, He was buried and the third day He arose to give us hope for an eternal life in His Holy name. Aside from this both the Psalms and Jesus, Himself, describe the friendly and loving nature of our Creator. Just like a friend here on earth, often the more we learn of someone the more comfortable we become with them. This is the same with God, as we learn more about Him, the more intimate, loving and kind our relationship becomes with Him and the rest of His creation. This being the first and great commandment; "Thou shalt love the Lord thy God with all thy heart, and with all thy soul, and with all thy mind." (Matt. 22:37, 38). Alleluia and praise the LORD. Amen and Amen.

Conclusion

Jesus said in Luke 24:44 of Himself, "...These *are* the words which I spake unto you, while I was yet with you, that all things must be fulfilled, which were written in the law of Moses, and *in* the prophets, and *in* the psalms, concerning me.". A key to understanding Jesus Christ of Nazareth is that He is eternal. Jesus said of Himself, "...Before Abraham was, I am." (John 8:58). A New Testament writer, the apostle, Paul, spoke of Christ being with the Israelites in the wilderness, as mentioned in chapter one and two (1 Cor. 10:1-4). Psalm 61:6 and 7 say, "Thou wilt prolong the king's life: *and* his years as many generations. He shall abide before God for ever: O prepare mercy and truth, *which* may preserve him.". This is the same "mercy and truth" spoken of in Psalm 57:3, and I compared with the Holy Spirit. The reality is that God's Holy Spirit is the Spirit of life, mercy and truth, it gives us life and we live through Him, in Him and by Him. And it is in the name of Jesus Christ of Nazareth that God's Holy Spirit has been sent to us to give us mercy, truth and life everlasting! I will speak of the Holy Spirit of God in greater detail in chapter six, but for now it is important to understand that we need the Holy Spirit dwelling in us to maintain a healthy relationship with our Creator and others (Ps. 42:11, 43:5, 67:2). Alleluia and praise the LORD. Amen and Amen.

There are many other prophecies and witnesses of Jesus Christ of Nazareth, as the Messiah, mentioned in the Old Testament. Jesus and David's relationship in Psalm 55:16 says, "As for me, I will call upon God; and the LORD shall save me.". This is the relationship Jesus Christ of Nazareth desires to have with each and every one of us. And you can have that relationship with Him if you ask His Holy Spirit to dwell in you and you in Him forever more. Many of the Psalms speak of God as being, terrible, horrible and even a persecutor (Ps. 66:3, 5; 68:35; Jer. 29:18). All of this can be put into proper perspective with the light of the life of Jesus Christ of Nazareth. He is the Saviour of the whole world, He bore our shame, our reproach, He took on our sins on the cross, He was buried and He arose three days later to give us a hope and a future. Jesus Christ of Nazareth endured the "wrath" of God on the cross for the forgiveness of our sins. This is the ultimate sacrifice; Christ died on the cross for the forgiveness of our sins, He was buried and He arose three days later to give us hope for eternal life in His Holy name. Psalm 55:22 says, "Cast thy burden upon the LORD, and he shall sustain thee: he shall never suffer the righteous to be moved.". Jesus said much the same thing in the New Testament, "Come unto me, all *ye* that labour and are heavy laden, and I will give you rest." (Matt. 11:28). This is the key to having a relationship with your Creator, God Almighty, in Jesus Christ of Nazareth, through His Holy Spirit. He came not to condemn us, but to save us (John 3:17). He came to give us eternal life in His Holy name. He desires that we repent and turn to Him, casting all of our burdens upon Him. Jesus said of Himself, "Take my yoke upon you, and learn of me; for I am meek and lowly in heart: and ye shall find rest unto your souls." (Matt. 11:29). If you are carrying a burden too heavy to bear, give it to Jesus Christ of Nazareth in prayer. You will not regret the decision, I promise you this. Alleluia and praise the LORD. Amen and Amen.

Just like I do throughout this book, the New Testament authors also reference Old Testament Scripture to prove Jesus Christ's authenticity as the Messiah, King of Israel, and Saviour of the whole world. This book may be a great start for understanding Jesus Christ as the Messiah, and our Saviour. But if you truly desire the wisdom, understanding and faith that come along with having a personal relationship with your Creator, ask God to give you His Holy Spirit, the Spirit of truth, asking the Spirit of Jesus Christ of Nazareth to dwell in you, with you and through you forever. It is through God's Holy Spirit, that we live, by the name of Jesus Christ of Nazareth, the hope of the resurrection and eternal life in His Holy name (Deut. 30:20). Aside from this reading, your own Bible will provide you with the spiritual nourishment to guide you in your daily journey with Christ and others, and fellowshipping with other believers will provide you with the "communal" or "social" aspect of having a relationship with God. As Jesus said, "A new commandment I give to you, That ye love one another; as I have loved you, that ye also love one another." (John 13:34). Jesus said, "...the hour cometh, and now is, when the true worshippers shall worship the Father in spirit and in truth..." (John 4:23). Jesus said, "God is a Spirit..." (John 4:24). Last, the Holy Bible says, that without faith we cannot please God (Heb. 11:6). And Jesus said, "... If ye have faith as a grain of mustard seed ye shall say unto this mountain, Remove hence to yonder place; and it shall remove; and nothing shall be impossible unto you." (Matt. 17:20). So, if you are questioning your relationship with God, the Father, Almighty or your place in His plans for you in this world or the "world to come", do not worry or be anxious, just have faith, which is a free gift from God, by grace, and believe on, God's only begotten Son, Jesus Christ of Nazareth, through His Holy Spirit, given to us, for your hopes, plans and dreams (Eph. 2:8, 9). Amen and Amen. Later, I will speak more about the Holy Spirit in chapter six, along with our faith in Jesus Christ of Nazareth in general. Alleluia and praise the LORD. Amen and Amen.

Discussion: Witnesses

"Either his uncle, or his uncle's son, may redeem him, or *any* that is nigh of kin unto him of his family may redeem him; or if he be able, he may redeem himself."
- Leviticus 25:49

Understanding that God gave Jesus Christ of Nazareth the ability to resurrect Himself is very important, because it is by Jesus Christ of Nazareth's payment for our sins on the cross that we to can be resurrected unto eternal life someday. Jesus even said of faith in Himself, "And whosoever liveth and believeth in me shall never die. ..." (John 11:26). These again are powerful words, but the reality is in Jesus Christ of Nazareth. He died on the cross for the forgiveness of our sins, shedding His Holy and righteous blood, He was buried and He arose the third day, conquering death and giving us the hope of redemption of our own body, soul and spirit, someday unto eternal life in His Holy name. Glory be to God. Even King David, knew Jesus Christ of Nazareth as his Saviour. He said, "The LORD said unto my Lord, Sit thou at my right hand, until I make thine enemies thy footstool." (Ps. 110:1). How much more evidence do we need? Jesus said of Himself, "...Before Abraham was, I am." (John 8:58). He is the Rock of the Old Testament and the Lamb of God, the Son of God, whom gave His life up on the cross for the forgiveness of our sins. He spilt His Holy and righteous blood on the cross, He died on the cross, He was buried and the third day He arose to give us the hope and promise of eternal life in His Holy name. Praise the LORD God, the Father, Almighty and His only begotten Son, Jesus Christ of Nazareth, with His Holy Spirit. Alleluia and praise the LORD. Amen and Amen.

Discussion Questions

1. How did Jesus Christ of Nazareth have the ability to resurrect Himself?

_____

_____

_____

_____

_____

2. Why does Jesus Christ of Nazareth have the ability to resurrect Himself?

_____

_____

_____

_____

_____

3. What does this mean for us?

_____

_____

_____

_____

_____

CHAPTER 4

Key of David

"...preaching of Jesus Christ, according to the revelation of the
mystery, which was kept secret since the world began..."
- ROMANS 16:25

Introduction

The Bible speaks about the "key of David" at least twice (Isa. 22:22, Rev. 3:7). Understanding the purpose of a key is to open a lock that is holding closed a door for some purpose, is part of the "key" to understanding and opening the door to reveal what the "key of David" is used for. Although I will describe this key in greater detail and the purpose of it, the simple truth is that the key of David, lays in having faith in, believing on and following the life of Jesus Christ of Nazareth, whom died on the cross for the forgiveness of our sins, shedding His Holy and righteous blood, He was buried and He arose the third day to give us the hope and promise of eternal life in His Holy name. Alleluia and praise the LORD. The key to understanding the entirety of the Holy Bible, all of its lessons, parables, commandments and prophecies, is to place our trust in Jesus Christ of Nazareth and "believe on" Him (John 1:12, 13). He is the revealer of all truth, as He is the light, the way, the truth, and the life (John 12:46, 14:6). With all that being said, I will continue in this chapter to talk about the "key of David", as well as some other prophecies about Jesus Christ of Nazareth and things to come here on earth, that Jesus prophesied of during His own earthly ministry, as well as did the other Old and New Testament prophets by the Holy Spirit. Last, I will talk about the New Covenant, Jesus has made with us, according to Old Testament prophecies, compared with the acts of His life giving covenant He made with us through His own Holy and righteous blood sacrifice as an eternal sin offering He made for us on the cross for the forgiveness of our sins. Alleluia and praise the LORD. Amen and Amen. Read on to learn more.

Key of David

Isaiah 22:20-25 says, "And it shall come to pass in that day, that I will call my servant Eliakim the son of Hilkiah: And I will clothe him with thy robe, and strengthen him with thy girdle, and I will commit thy government into his hand: and he shall be a father to the inhabitants of Jerusalem, and to the house of Judah. And the key of the house of David will I lay upon his shoulder; so he shall open, and none shall shut; and he shall shut, and none shall open. And I will fasten him *as* a nail in a sure place; and he shall be for a glorious throne to his father's house. And they shall hang upon him all the glory of his father's house, the offspring and the issue, all vessels of small quantity, from the vessels of cups, even to all the vessels of flagons. In that day, saith the LORD of hosts, shall the nail that is fastened in the sure place be removed, and be cut down, and fall; and the burden that *was* upon it shall be cut off: for the LORD hath spoken *it*.". These verses have everything to do with Jesus Christ of Nazareth, of course they were no doubt fulfilled literally by Eliakim, but the similitudes regarding Jesus' life are difficult to ignore. Jesus was clothed with a robe, of scarlet or purple, at His crucifixion (Matt. 27:28, Mark 15:17). As mentioned in the previous chapters, He has the government of God, on His shoulders, through the Holy Spirit of God (Isa. 9:6). He is also a Father, and He has the key of David, according to Revelation 3:7, mentioned below (John 10:30). Jesus was fastened with nails to the cross for the forgiveness of our sins, a sure place of salvation for all (John 20:25, Col. 2:14). He has inherited the throne of David, and of God (Matt. 1:32, Rev. 3:21). And Jesus has inherited all things (Matt. 11:27). Through His burial and resurrection three days later, the burden has been cut off, and now we live through His Holy Spirit given to all freely (John 16:7). Alleluia and praise the LORD. Amen and Amen. Eliakim seems to be a Levite, a son of Hilkiah, possibly a descendant of Zadok, of the priests mentioned in Ezekiel's prophecies (2 Kings 18:18, 1 Chr. 6:12, 13; Ezek. 44:15). That being said, there is also an Eliakim, renamed Jehoiakim by Pharaoh of Egypt, He was a son of King Josiah, of the tribe of Judah (2 Kings 23:34). It may even be possible that, through Jesus' mother, Mary, Jesus may have lineage from Eliakim, son of Hilkiah, but this is only speculation (Luke 1:5, 36). Nevertheless, Jesus is High Priest of the Eternal, but from the tribe of Judah in the flesh for certain (Heb. 3:1, Rev. 5:5). Revelation 3:7 says, "And to the angel of the church in Philadelphia write; These things saith he that is holy, he that is true, he that hath the key of David, he that openeth, and no man shutteth; and shutteth, and no man openeth…". Jesus took all of our sins upon Himself, and gave us the opportunity to be a kingdom of priests, a royal priesthood, kings and priests of God (Ex. 19:6, 1 Pet. 2:9, Rev. 1:7). Jesus said, "Henceforth I call you not servants…but I have called you friends…" (John 15:15). Regarding King David, 2 Samuel 12:10 says, "Now therefore the sword shall never depart from thine house; because thou hast despised me, and hast taken the wife of Uriah the Hittite to be thy wife.". David's house was cursed, because of His adultery with Bathsheba whom He took to wife, and murdered Uriah the Hittite, Bathsheba's husband at the time (2 Sam. 11, 12:1-9). But Jesus is "…I am." and Jesus was and is also the root of David, so Jesus

Christ of Nazareth has overcome this "curse" (John 8:58, Rev. 5:5). See appendix B for more details on the throne of David. Alleluia and praise the LORD. Amen and Amen.

Jesus said on the cross, almost just before giving up His Holy Spirit, "…My God, my God, why hast thou forsaken me?" (Matt. 27:46, Mark 15:34). These same words, as mentioned in chapter one and three, were spoken of by King David in Psalm (Ps. 22:1). 1 Corinthians 1:25 says, "Because the foolishness of God is wiser than men; and the weakness of God is stronger than men.". God is not flesh, first and foremost, in the fleshly realm this could be considered a weakness, but it is not, His Holy Spirit is stronger than our flesh (John 4:24). Alleluia and praise the LORD. Amen and Amen. This was shown when Jesus gave up the ghost, the Holy Spirit, and died on the cross for the forgiveness of our sins (Luke 23:46, John 19:30). And the power of the Holy Spirit was shown at His resurrection (Matt. 28:18). Alleluia and praise the LORD. Amen and Amen. The wisdom of man was to crucify Jesus Christ of Nazareth without a cause (Ps. 35:7, 19; 69:4; Isa. 44:24-28, Jer. 4:22, John 11:47-52, 15:25; 1 Cor. 3:19). Jesus said to God, the Father, "… Father, forgive them; for they know not what they do. …" (Luke 23:34). Interestingly enough, the common word "without a cause" or "without cause" in the Old Testament, which can mean vain, nothing, free, innocent, Strong's number 2600; has a root word meaning amongst other things, graciousness, Strong's number 2580 (Ex. 21:2, 11; Num. 11:5, 1 Kings 2:31, Prov. 1:9). This would explain Judas Iscariot saying, "…lead *him* away safely.", when betraying Jesus in the garden of Gethsemane (Mark 14:44). That being said, in Proverbs 31 it says, "Favour *is* deceitful…", the same Hebrew word used for grace (Prov. 31:30, Zech. 4:7). And the apostle, Paul, said, "…let God be true, but every man a liar…" (Rom. 3:4). So nevertheless, the foolishness of God was that Jesus, the Son of God, a perfect man, took all of our sins upon Himself on the cross (Prov. 24:9, John 3:16, 1 Cor. 3:19). Spilling His Holy and righteous blood on the cross for the forgiveness of all of our sin, He died and He was buried, and the third day He arose to give us the hope and promise of eternal life in His Holy name. Alleluia and praise the LORD. Amen and Amen. Also, Jesus warned against being angry "…without a cause…", hating our brother and accusing others of foolishness. He said, "But I say unto you, That whosoever is angry with his brother without a cause shall be in danger of the judgment: and whosoever shall say to his brother, Raca, shall be in danger of the council: but whosoever shall say, Thou fool, shall be in danger of hell fire." (Matt. 5:22). And the apostle, Paul, does speak of the love of Christ that passes knowledge (Eph. 3:19). So no matter, our reality ought to be in Jesus Christ of Nazareth, through His Holy Spirit, and in fellowship with God, the Father, in Jesus Christ of Nazareth's Holy name. Jesus died on the cross for the forgiveness of our sins at Passover in 31 A.D., spilling His Holy and righteous blood on the cross, He was buried and He arose the third day to give us the hope and promise of eternal life in His Holy name. Alleluia and praise the LORD. Amen and Amen.

Jesus, David and the throne; Regarding Jeremiah 30:9-11, the name David may possibly be used for a greater prophetic fulfillment in Jesus, especially. Like the name Jacob is used in Jeremiah to describe the descendants of Jacob, not Jacob himself necessarily. Jesus sits on the throne of David, as mentioned in chapter two and three, see appendix B for more about Jesus and David's throne. Psalm 22:6 says, "But I *am* a worm, and **no man**; a reproach of men, and despised of the people.". There are other places in the Holy Bible that speak about "no man", in various ways. And I think it is interesting, if we are to consider that, Jesus Christ of Nazareth has fulfilled this idea of being "no man", because He is the Son of God also, and God. Alleluia and praise the LORD. Amen and Amen. Hosea 11:9 says, "I will not execute the fierceness of mine anger, I will not return to destroy Ephraim: for **I *am* God, and not man**; the Holy One in the midst of thee: and I will not enter into the city.". The point here is that God is God, not man, first and foremost. And Jesus is God; He was with God from the beginning, the Word made flesh (John 1:1-14). That being said, the devil possessed men, mentioned in the gospel according to Matthew, allowed "no man" into the city (Matt. 8:28). Even after Jesus cast the devils out of the men, He was encouraged to leave the place by the people of the city, and He did leave (Matt. 8:34). So this is literal, and would suggest that Jesus is also not, "no man", He is also Man, Ishi, in Hebrew, and the Son of man, through Mary, a virgin at the time of Jesus' earthly birth, His earthly mother, whom Jesus was conceived in by the Holy Ghost (Gen. 2:23, Hos. 2:16, Matt. 1:18-25, 8:20, 9:6). Of course, these are just interpretations of things, but the point is we are nothing without Christ Jesus of Nazareth, and God, the Father, Almighty, through His Holy Spirit, which made us, and keeps us. Alleluia and praise the LORD. Amen and Amen. Zechariah 12:8 says, "In that day shall the LORD defend the inhabitants of Jerusalem; and he that is feeble among them at that day shall be as David; and the house of David *shall be* as God, as the angel of the LORD before them.". So the reality is that we all have hope in the name of Jesus Christ of Nazareth, and can receive the same blessings as King David, as the book of Revelation speaks of making us "…kings and priests unto God and his Father…" (Rev. 1:6). Alleluia and praise the LORD. Amen and Amen. Having a relationship with Jesus Christ of Nazareth, and understanding His relationship with, knowledge of, and understanding in, the Old Testament scriptures is essentially the "Key of David". This is the "key" that Jesus Christ of Nazareth has given to all of His faithful believers, no matter what tribe, tongue or nation we descend from. In Jesus Christ of Nazareth, we are baptized into the kingdom of God, and born of God through the Holy Spirit of our Lord and Saviour, Jesus Christ of Nazareth (Mark 1:8, John 1:33, Acts 1:5, 11:16; 1 John 2:29, 3:9, 4:7, 5:1, 4, 18). If you doubt this, confess with your mouth that Jesus Christ has come in the flesh, because only by the Holy Spirit can someone confess Jesus Christ has come in the flesh (Rom. 10:9, Phil. 2:11, 1 John 4:2). Alleluia and praise the LORD. Amen and Amen.

Jesus and Jerusalem

In Daniel 9:24-27, seventy weeks are determined upon Israel and Jerusalem. Daniel 9:24 says, "Seventy weeks are determined upon thy people and upon thy holy city, to finish the transgression, and to make an end of sins, and to make reconciliation for iniquity, and to bring in everlasting righteousness, and to seal up the vision and prophecy, and to anoint the most Holy.". Jesus' crucifixion at Passover for the forgiveness of the sins of the whole world, in 31 A.D., His burial and His resurrection three days later, fulfilled a great portion of this prophecy physically, and spiritually He fulfilled all of this prophecy (John 19:30, Rev. 19:10). Daniel 9:25 says, "Know therefore and understand, *that* from the going forth of the commandment to restore and to build Jerusalem unto the Messiah the Prince *shall be* seven weeks, and threescore and two weeks: the street shall be built again, and the wall, even in troublous times.". Artaxerxes reconfirmed the decree for the building of the second temple after Cyrus had made it some decades earlier (Ezra 7:11). Artaxerxes likely made the decree in approximately 457 B.C. and Ezra the priest went back to Jerusalem at that command with some Israelites, see appendix A – Messiah for more detail (Ezra 7:12-28). And indeed according to the accounts in Nehemiah and Ezra, the street and the wall were built in "… troublous times." (Ezra 4:7-16, Neh. 4). Daniel 9:26 says, "And after threescore and two weeks shall Messiah be cut off, but not for himself: and the people of the prince that shall come shall destroy the city and the sanctuary; and the end thereof *shall be* with a flood, and unto the end of the war desolations are determined.". Jesus Christ of Nazareth, Messiah, was "… cut off, but not for himself…". Jesus died for us, at Passover in 31A.D., on the cross for the forgiveness of our sins, He was buried and He arose three days later for our hope and promise of eternal life in His Holy name. Daniel 9:27 says, "And he shall confirm the covenant with many for one week: and in the midst of the week he shall cause the sacrifice and the oblation to cease, and for the overspreading of abominations he shall make *it* desolate, even until the consummation, and that determined shall be poured upon the desolate.". Jesus confirmed the covenant with us for three and a half years and was "…cut off…", dying on the cross for the forgiveness of our sins, causing the need for animal sacrifice and oblations to cease (Dan. 9:26, Heb. 9:12). As well, in 70 A.D., Rome destroyed the second temple, making it "…desolate…" (Dan. 9:27). Using the time in Daniel 9:25, we come to approximately 27 A.D. for the "…Messiah the Prince…", which is highly likely when Jesus started His three and a half year ministry, each day for a year (Num. 14:34, Ezek. 4:6). Sixty nine weeks is equivalent to 483 years using the "day for a year" principle mentioned in Numbers 14:34 and Ezekiel 4:6. The last week of this 70 week prophecy, was partially Jesus' three and a half year ministry, with the last three and a half days, or years likely being the "Great Tribulation", whom Jesus and the prophets have spoken about throughout the Bible (Matt. 24, Mark 13, Luke 21). The culmination of all of this leading to the 1000 years of Christ's rule with His saints, sometimes known as the "Messianic Age" (Rev. 20:4, 6). I have mentioned these two topics in other places in this book briefly and have written books on both of the subjects for the interested reader. Nevertheless for practical purposes, Jesus did indeed forgive us and He died on the cross for the forgiveness of our sins, at Passover in 31 A.D., spilling His Holy and righteous blood, He was buried and He arose three days later to give us a hope and promise of eternal life in His Holy name. See appendix E for a visual timeline of this prophecy. Praise the LORD God, the Father, Almighty and His only begotten Son, Jesus Christ of Nazareth,

Saviour of the whole world and Redeemer of all of mankind. Alleluia and praise the LORD. Amen and Amen.

Although I will not speak about the subject in detail, as I have addressed it in other writings, namely the book I wrote regarding the "Messianic Age", "The Day Star and Us". Part of the reason that the fulfillment of Daniel 9:24-27, namely Daniel 9:24 is not likely complete is because, according to the book of Revelation; God has set apart, 144 000 people, chosen from the tribes of Israel, likely throughout history to be a part of Christ's rule in the "Messianic age", spiritually first and foremost (Rev. 7, 20:6). Because of the concept of the "body of Christ", mentioned in the New Testament writings of, the apostle, Paul of Tarsus, the fulfillment of "…anoint[ing] the most Holy…", may not be complete until all of the saints or the 144 000, have fulfilled their lives and purposes here on earth prior to the "Messianic Age" (Dan. 9:27). That would be to prepare them for their reward and responsibility as part of the "first fruits" of God with Christ Jesus in God's kingdom, here on earth and in eternity (Rom. 8:23, Jam. 1:18, Rev. 4:4). That being said, we are all a part of God's kingdom with Christ, and participants in the blessings and eternal reward of life with God, through faith in Jesus Christ of Nazareth, as the Bible says, "…God is no respecter of persons…" (Acts 10:34). As I have written in other books and will continue to testify, the reader must keep in mind that these writings are, at least in part, "interpretations" of what Biblical Scripture says. The Bible says, "For we know in part, and we prophesy in part." (1 Cor. 13:9). I am not saying I am wrong or doubtful on most or any of these ideas, but it is only fair to let the reader decide, for yourself, what the truth is according to Biblical Scripture. As the Bible says, "Prove all things; hold fast that which is good." (1 Thess. 5:21). With that being said, keep an open mind in reading through the remainder of this book and let the Holy Spirit of God, the Father, Almighty in Jesus Christ of Nazareth lead you to the truth in all of these matters and all others in this life and forever more. Praise the LORD. That also being said, I have referenced other works in most of the topics written in this book, and although most of this book's interpretation is "original" thought, albeit hopefully God inspired, there are many books and writings on the same subjects outside of this book that can be found. A list of references can be found in appendix C. I have and will continue to maintain that the Holy Bible of God ought to be the first and foremost authority on the subject of truth, outside of any revelation by the Holy Spirit of God, the Father, through Jesus Christ of Nazareth (Rev. 19:10). If you are truly seeking an honest and open relationship with God and others, I would suggest a personal relationship with Jesus Christ of Nazareth, repenting you of your sins and accepting His offering of forgiveness by His Holy and righteous blood shed on the cross for us, He died on the cross and He was buried, and the third day He arose for our hope and promise of eternal life in His Holy name. And I would suggest the Bible as your go to reference book of choice for truth in this life and life in the "world to come". To God be the Glory. Alleluia and praise the LORD. Amen and Amen.

Last, regarding Jerusalem, the "…abomination that maketh desolate…" and prophecy (Dan. 9:27, 11:31, 12:11). Three of the New Testament gospel writers gave account of it, according to Jesus' prophesying; first in Matthew 24:15 it says, "…abomination of desolation, … stand in the holy place…"; in Mark 13:14 it says, "…abomination of desolation…standing where it ought not…"; and in Luke 21:20 it says, "…Jerusalem compassed with armies, then know that the desolation thereof is nigh.". The key to understanding this "…abomination that maketh desolate…", is in Luke's account. He says "…when ye shall see Jerusalem compassed with armies…" (Luke 21:20). This can be taken from a historical, present-day and prophetic perspective, and even a literal and somewhat spiritual one. Let us start with the spiritual and literal historical perspective. Jesus asked His disciples to sell and buy swords, two were purchased and one was used by Peter to cut off the ear of the High Priest's servant, whose ear Jesus also healed, all at Jesus' betrayal in the garden of Gethsemane (Matt. 26:51, 52; Luke 22:36-38, 50, 51; John 18:26). In this same place He was indeed approached by the armed servants of the religious authorities (Matt. 26:47). And then He was given over to the armed guards of the Roman authorities, and He was smote, scourged, platted with a crown of thorns, mocked and smote again (Matt. 27:29-31, Mark 15:15, John 19:1-3). He was tried, being surrounded by the Jews and Roman armed guards, and common folk alike, and then led away to be crucified, with a great company following (Luke 23:27, John 19:4-42). Regarding the word "setup", mentioned in Daniel's prophecy (Dan. 12:11). This would be speaking of them setting Him up on the cross (Luke 23:33). And regarding the word "…where it ought not…", this would be Jesus dying on the cross for the forgiveness of our sins, not His own (Mark 13:14, John 11:49-52). He did not deserve to die, because He was a sinless man, perfect (John 15:35). He died for the forgiveness of our sins, not His own. And this brings us to "…stand[ing] in the Holy place…" (Matt. 24:15). Jesus of course was standing so to speak on the cross, but also the judgement made by sinners to crucify Jesus was no doubt fulfillment of this, albeit it was prophesied to happen, and needed to in order for us to be healed, saved and receive eternal life in Jesus Christ of Nazareth's Holy name. Nevertheless, this prophecy also has other historical significance, as mentioned earlier, when the Romans apparently offered swine's blood on the altar of the temple in Jerusalem in around 70 A.D. and then destroyed the temple and the city. This also can be seen in more recent history with the various empires fighting over Jerusalem; the Muslims, Crusaders of the middle ages, and onto today. In the 20th century, there was the mandate of Palestine, by the British government, and then a transition of power in 1948, and a United Nations vote to make Israel a nation state in 1949. But under some UN mandate Jerusalem seems to be a disputed city, as of the date of writing this book in 2019 A.D., dividing east and west Jerusalem. Zechariah 12:2 says, "Behold, I will make Jerusalem a cup of trembling unto all the people round about, when they shall be in the siege both against Judah *and* against Jerusalem.". Nevertheless, we will have to wait and see what is to come of this prophecy in years to come, but a Psalm admonishes us to pray for the peace of Jerusalem (Ps. 122:6). And Jesus speaking to a woman in Samaria, said, "… the hour cometh, when ye shall neither in this mountain, nor yet at Jerusalem, worship the Father.…But the hour cometh, and now is, when the true worshippers shall worship the Father in spirit and in truth…" (John 4:21, 23). So the reality is in Jesus Christ of Nazareth, whom has been given all power in heaven and in earth (Matt. 28:18). He died on the cross for the forgiveness of our sins, spilling His Holy and righteous blood for us, He was buried and the third day He arose to give us the hope and promise of eternal life in His Holy name. Alleluia and praise the LORD. Amen and Amen.

New Covenant

Jeremiah 31:31 says, "Behold, the days come, saith the LORD, that I will make a new covenant with the house of Israel, and with the house of Judah.". This new covenant has come by the blood of Jesus Christ of Nazareth shed for us on the cross for the forgiveness of our sins. He died on the cross, He was buried and He arose from the dead on the third day, giving us the hope for eternal life in His Holy name. Praise the LORD God, the Father, Almighty, and His only begotten Son, Jesus Christ of Nazareth. Jesus said, "A new commandment I give unto you, That ye love one another; as I have loved you, that ye also love one another." (John 13:34). He said that our righteousness ought to be greater than that of the scribes and the Pharisees, as mentioned in the previous chapter (Matt. 5:20). He even asks us to be perfect like God (Matt. 5:48). He gave us a new covenant, a Holy, Spiritual, "heavenly" covenant, that came from God by His only begotten Son, Jesus Christ of Nazareth, the Saviour of the whole world, and Redeemer of all of mankind. Praise the LORD GOD, the Father, Almighty, and His only begotten Son, Jesus Christ of Nazareth, through His Holy Spirit. This covenant is fulfilled in Jesus Christ of Nazareth dying on the cross for the forgiveness of our sins, He was buried and the third day He arose to give us the hope and promise of eternal life in His Holy name. And His words of the giving of God's Holy Spirit to all, about ten days after Jesus' ascension into heaven, Jesus' ascension happening forty days after His resurrection from the grave (John 16:7, Acts 1:1-9, 2:1-21). The Holy Spirit was poured out on Pentecost in 31 A.D., it was poured out on the twelve apostles and witnessed by the brethren, Peter spoke of this prophetic fulfillment referencing the book of Joel, and three thousand were baptized to receive the Holy Spirit that day (Joel 2:28-32, Acts 2:1-41). Regarding Leviticus 26 curses and eating the flesh of sons and daughters, continuing the thought of eating Jesus' flesh and blood, mentioned in chapter two (Matt. 26:26-28, John 6:53). In Jesus Christ's blood the curses of the Old Testament have been completely removed from us (Gal. 3:13, 14; Rev. 22:3, 4). I do not desire to turn the reader from accepting Jesus Christ of Nazareth as your Saviour, by speaking of all of these terrible prophecies and curses that have been spoken of in the Holy Bible, but I desire you to understand the depths with which Jesus has gone to be your Saviour and Messiah (Ps. 51:6, Eph. 3:18, 19). He loves you and He gave His life for you. This is what I desire you to understand. Not only this, but He has given you eternal life in His Holy name. Is this not a wonderful truth? In Christ Jesus of Nazareth, we have life everlasting. Not only this, but Jesus says of Himself in relation to us, "…I am come that they might have life, and that they might have *it* more abundantly." (John 10:10). This is the Saviour that we serve, a living God, a life giving God, a God of provision, a God of creation, a God of love, a God of peace, a God of truth and a God of light, an Almighty and everlasting God. Alleluia and praise the LORD. Amen and Amen.

Ezekiel 16 describes in some respects the development of Israel, Judah, and the Gentile nations, our sins and God's redemption of us in Jesus Christ of Nazareth's Holy name. I will write about it first and foremost from the perspective of fulfillment in Christ, but the reader, if you care to read the prophecy can look at it from your own perspective, and in light of our own sins being contrasted with the light of Christ. But ultimately we must remember that Jesus came to forgive us and save us from our sins. Alleluia and praise the LORD. Amen and Amen. Ezekiel 16:4 describes Jesus' birth in a very simple manner, albeit He was swaddled with cloth (Luke 2:7). Jesus was born in a manger, in Bethlehem, and this was also prophesied about in the Old Testament (Mic. 5:2, Matt. 2:1, Luke 2:7). Ezekiel 16:5 likely describes in a crewed manner, the birth of Jesus and the announcement of His birth made to the shepherds by the angel of the Lord, and the witnessing of the heavenly host appearing with Him (Luke 2:8-14). Then the shepherds visited Jesus and made the announcement publicly known in the city (Luke 2:15-18). Ezekiel 16:9 speaks of Jesus' baptism physically and by the Holy Spirit spiritually, and the anointing by a woman or women, physically on the feet and head (Matt. 3:13-17, Mark 14:3-9, Luke 2:37, 38; John 11:2, 12:3). Ezekiel 16:14 speaks of Jesus preaching the gospel of the kingdom of God (Matt. 4:23). Ezekiel 16:15-43 speaks of Jesus and sinners, fallen Israel, backsliding believers, and the church apostasy, even denominational and religious divide (Ezek. 16:24-26, 28-31, 33). Ezekiel 16:40 seems to speak about the martyrdom of some true believers, and ultimately, the penalty Jesus Christ of Nazareth paid for our sins on the cross (Matt. 24:9, Acts 7:59, 60; Rev. 2:13). This really can show the depths that Christ went to and suffered for our rebelliousness. If we believe, Psalm 51:6 says, "Behold, thou desirest truth in the inward parts: and in the hidden *part* thou shalt make me to know wisdom.". Ezekiel 16:44-59 speak of Sodom, Samaria and Jerusalem; as mentioned in chapter three, Samaria is likely the Northern tribes of Israel that went into captivity in 700 B.C., and Jerusalem is likely Judah and those of the tribes of Israel whom stayed with Judah throughout history. Sodom in general likely represents the "gentile" nations of the world (Ezek. 16:48, 49). And it is said that Sodom's sins are not even as abundant as Jerusalem's sins (Ezek. 16:47, 48). This describes the brokenness of the covenant God made with Israel in the wilderness, and the need for Jesus to take our shame and brokenness upon Himself on the cross. In Ezekiel 16:60-63 it speaks of the "...everlasting covenant.". God made an everlasting covenant with us through the blood of Jesus Christ of Nazareth on the cross. This is a call to the Jews, the lost sheep of Israel, and all who believe in the God of Israel to accept Jesus Christ of Nazareth as the everlasting covenant (Heb. 13:20, 21). Much of Ezekiel 16 is graphic in detail, but sometimes God needs to use these examples to wake us up to receive our attention of what He has done, is doing, and is going to do for us, through us and around us in this life here on earth, in the lives of our descendants, and in the "world to come". Alleluia and praise the LORD. Amen and Amen.

Regarding Jesus' birth place specifically, there has been some suggestion that He was born in the "…tower of Edar.", the "…tower of the flock…", also known as Migdal Edar (Gen. 35:21, Mic. 4:8-10). This was a tower that is said to have been used by shepherds that watched over the flocks used to provide the sacrificial unblemished lambs for the temple offering at Jerusalem. This same tower was said to have been used as a birthing location for the young lambs, in the base of the tower no doubt. And it is suggested that this tower was located on the road to Jerusalem from Bethlehem, possibly east of the road, between Rachel's tomb and Bethlehem (Gen. 35:19-21). Micah 4:8-10 says, "And thou, O tower of the flock, the strong hold of the daughter of Zion, unto thee shall it come, even the first dominion; the kingdom shall come to the daughter of Jerusalem. Now why dost though cry out aloud? *is there* no king in thee? Is thy counsellor perished? For pangs have taken thee as a woman in travail. Be in pain, and labour to bring forth, O daughter of Zion, like a woman in travail: for now shalt thou go forth out of the city, and thou shalt dwell in the field, and thou shalt go *even* to Babylon; there shalt thou be delivered; there the LORD shall redeem thee from the hand of thine enemies.". The daughter of Jerusalem likely references, the virgin, Mary, and the first dominion likely references both Jesus Christ of Nazareth, as "…I am.", but also the opportunity for Mary and Joseph, as saints to have the same opportunity as Adam and Eve did, someday (Gen. 1:26-28, John 8:58). According to the New Testament scriptures there was no room at the inn, so Mary and Joseph could very well have gone forth out of the city of Bethlehem into the field, and given birth to Jesus in the "…tower of the flock…" (Mic. 4:10, Luke 2:7). The reference to Babylon, which can mean confusion, Strong's number 894, but also likely points to the tower of Babel, may be a sign of the towering structure Jesus may have been born in (Gen. 11:4-9, Mic. 4:10). There is one particular 19th century scholar named, Alfred Edersheim, a European Jewish convert to faith in Jesus Christ of Nazareth, whom seems to have visited the site and wrote about the site's historical significance. There are also at least a few references on the internet that agree similarly with this idea. The New Testament scriptures seem to describe Jesus being born in the "city of David" and the shepherds went to Bethlehem to visit the new born Messiah (Luke 2:11, 15). And there has been a suggestion that Jesus was born in the stable section of a home, where it was common for people to allow their animals to dwell in safely at night. This is also possible, as the same Greek word used for "manger", that the new born baby Jesus was lying in, is also used to describe a stall that houses a person's ox or ass, Strong's number 5336 (Luke 2:7, 13:15). So whatever the truth of this is, the most important thing to remember is that Jesus was first conceived by the Holy Spirit of God in the virgin, Mary, espoused to Joseph, and then born of the virgin, Mary, espoused to Joseph after the about nine month gestation period (Matt. 1:18, 25). He was raised as a child of Israel and had brothers and sisters (Matt. 13:55, 56; Luke 2:41-52). He started His earthly ministry at about the age of thirty, healing, doing miracles and forgiving sin (Luke 3:21-23). And ultimately, after three and a half years of ministry, He died on the cross for the forgiveness of our sins, as a perfect man, He took all of our sins upon Himself, spilling His Holy and righteous blood, He was buried and He arose the third day to give us all the hope and promise of eternal life in His Holy name. Alleluia and praise the LORD. Amen and Amen.

Conclusion

Speaking of Daniel's prophecy a bit further regarding the "…abomination that maketh desolate…" (Dan. 9:27, 11:31, 12:11). Daniel 9:27 says, "And he shall confirm the covenant with many for one week: and in the midst of the week he shall cause the sacrifice and the oblation to cease, and for the overspreading of abominations he shall make *it* desolate, even until the consummation, and that determined shall be poured upon the desolate.". As had been mentioned, this was fulfilled in Jesus Christ of Nazareth being "…cut off…", in the "…midst of the week…", crucified on a Wednesday, at Passover in 31 A.D., saying "…It is finished…" (John 19:30). But in the greater plan of God, no doubt this has everything to do with the fulfillment of all prophecy in the Holy Bible, including the "Great Tribulation", the "Messianic Age" and then the final judgment, which will finally likely consume all of the earth, as the apostle, Peter, spoke of and Jeremiah mentioned seeing the earth "…without form, and void…" (Jer. 4:23, 2 Pet. 3:10-13). And then finally the "…new heavens and a new earth, wherein dwelleth righteousness.", which is mentioned in greater detail in Daniel 12 (2 Pet. 3:13). Daniel 11:31 says, "And arms shall stand on his part, and they shall pollute the sanctuary of strength, and shall take away the daily *sacrifice,* and they shall place the abomination that maketh desolate.". This has everything to do with Jesus' crucifixion, the authorities and common folk, including our own sin, putting Jesus Christ of Nazareth on the cross. His body is the sanctuary of God, and it was polluted by our sins, for the forgiveness of our sins (John 2:21). The daily sacrifice was taken away, in two ways, Jesus' life was taken from Him, or at least given up, and we no longer need to atone for our own sins by the blood of bulls, sheep, goats and birds (Heb. 9:12). Jesus is the eternal Passover Lamb of God. He died on the cross for the forgiveness of our sins, spilling His Holy and righteous blood, He was buried and the third day He arose to give us the hope and promise of eternal life in His Holy name. Alleluia and praise the LORD. Amen and Amen. Daniel 12 :11 says, "And from the time *that* the daily *sacrifice* shall be taken away, and the abomination that maketh desolate set up, *there shall be* a thousand two hundred and ninety days.". Albeit I wrote a book about the "Great Tribulation", called "Time, Times and a Dividing of Time-What did John really see?". We need to remember that Jesus has fulfilled all scripture during His life growing up, His three and a half year earthly ministry, and finally at His death on the cross for the forgiveness of our sins, His burial of three days in the grave, His resurrection on the third day, and then His revealing to His disciples for about forty days after His resurrection, and then ascension into heaven, and ten days after that, at the feast of Pentecost in 31 A.D., the outpouring of His Holy Spirit for all to receive, and we receive Him, as we pray, repent, forgive, receive forgiveness for our sins and obey Him in the Holy Spirit and in truth. Alleluia and praise the LORD. Amen and Amen.

The division of east and west Jerusalem by ethnic and religious lines, in 1948, would in some sense fulfill the scripture spoken of by Zechariah. Zechariah 14:3 and 4 say, "Then shall the LORD go forth, and fight against those nations, as when he fought in the day of battle. And his feet shall stand in that day upon the mount of Olives, which *is* before Jerusalem on the east, and the mount of Olives shall cleave in the midst thereof toward the east and toward the west, *and there shall be* a very great valley; and half of the mountain shall remove toward the north, and half of it toward the south.". This is still prophetic I believe in the coming of the Lord Jesus Christ and the establishment of the "Messianic Age", which will likely include the "Great Tribulation", but no doubt, Jesus Christ of Nazareth, through the Holy Spirit is fully in control of the dividing lines that have been made in Jerusalem in generations past, including in recent history, unto this day. As He even said of Himself, "Think not that I am come to send peace on earth: I came not to send peace, but a sword.", and also, "Suppose ye that I am come to give peace on earth? I tell you, Nay; but rather division…" (Matt. 10:34, Luke 12:51). The point in all of this is to understand that Jesus Christ of Nazareth is fully in control of all of these events that have happened here on earth, and will continue to be in control of them forever. Alleluia and praise the LORD. Amen and Amen. And of course Jesus Christ of Nazareth spent time on the Mount of Olives alone and with His disciples; before being carried into Jerusalem triumphantly as King of Israel on an donkey's colt the Sunday before His crucifixion, and then prophesying on the mount about the "great tribulation" on the Monday, and finally Tuesday evening into Wednesday morning He spent time there with His disciples praying before His betrayal to the religious authorities by Judas Iscariot (Matt. 21:1-7, 24, 26:30-56; Mark 11:1-7, 13, 14:26-50; Luke 19:29-38, 21:37, 22:39-53; John 8:1). As Jesus Christ is, I AM, so Jesus is always there in Jerusalem and everywhere through His Holy Spirit of God (Ex. 3:14, John 8:58). As Jesus revealed to the Samaritan woman in conversation, "The woman saith unto him, Sir, I perceive that thou art a prophet. Our fathers worshipped in this mountain; and ye say, that in Jerusalem is the place where men ought to worship. Jesus saith unto her, Woman, believe me, the hour cometh, when ye shall neither in this mountain, nor yet at Jerusalem, worship the Father. Ye worship ye know not what: we know what we worship: for salvation is of the Jews. But the hour cometh, and now is, when the true worshippers shall worship the Father in spirit and in truth: for the Father seeketh such to worship him. God *is* a Spirit: and they that worship him must worship *him* in spirit and in truth. The woman saith unto him, I know that Messias cometh, which is called Christ: when he is come, he will tell us all things. Jesus saith unto her, I that speak unto thee am *he*." (John 4:19-26). Alleluia and praise the LORD. Amen and Amen.

The other thing that Jesus said about all of this is to not judge by what we see, but in righteousness judge (John 7:24). That is we can only judge by the righteousness of God, and ultimately, all things are in His control and power, through His only begotten Son, Jesus Christ of Nazareth, by His Holy Spirit (Matt. 28:18). Alleluia and praise the LORD. Amen and Amen. Jesus even said He did not come to condemn, but to save (John 3:17). He also said He judges no man (John 8:15). And Jesus is our example, so we ought not to judge others unless we desire to be judged (Matt. 7:1). This all being said, in the book of Revelation it says, "He that is unjust, let him be unjust still: and he which is filthy, let him be filthy still: and he that is righteous, let him be righteous still: and he that is holy, let him be holy still." (Rev. 22:11). This is the freedom we have in Jesus Christ of Nazareth, to allow people freedom to do as they please, and to allow God to work in us all through His Holy Spirit. Alleluia and praise the LORD. Joel 3:16 says, "The LORD also shall roar out of Zion, and utter his voice from Jerusalem; and the heavens and the earth shall shake: but the LORD *will be* the hope of his people, and the strength of the children of Israel.". Of course this was also fulfilled when Jesus cried out on the cross and gave up the ghost, and the rocks were rent and the veil of the temple was torn in two (Matt. 27:46, 50, 51). The good news is that we know now, He arose from His death, after His burial for three days in the grave, for our hope and promise of eternal life in His Holy name. Alleluia and praise the LORD. See appendices A, B and G for more details on the Messiah, David's throne, and Jerusalem, respectively. The next chapter will discuss in greater detail the temple and Jesus' relation with it through His body. Alleluia and praise the LORD. Amen and Amen. Read on to learn more.

Discussion: New Covenant

"…now is made manifest, and by the scriptures of the prophets, according to the commandment of the everlasting God, made known to all nations for the obedience of faith…"
- Romans 16:26

Faith is required to believe in Jesus Christ of Nazareth. And this does not come by works, but is a gift from God, the Father, Almighty. We can search the scriptures all we desire, and listen to all the rabbis, preachers, teachers, and read all of the Bible study books, etc., but the reality is that we do not receive faith from God by doing, but it is a free gift (Eph. 2:8, 9). Jesus Christ of Nazareth calls us to wait for Him (Luke 12:35, 36). We grow our faith by doing all of the earlier mentioned things including worshipping God, and fellowshipping, but that initial "seed" of faith is not of this world. It is of God, this is the miracle of our adoption into the "…kingdom of God…", into the family of God (Matt. 6:33, Mark 10:29, 30; Eph. 3:14-19). God's kingdom is not of this world. Praise the LORD God, the Father, Almighty, and His only begotten Son, Jesus Christ of Nazareth. Alleluia and praise the LORD. Thanks be to God. Amen and Amen. When reading through this chapter's discussion questions, consider your faith, and where it comes from. Consider your "…first love…", where it all started, and turn to the true God that loves you, in Jesus Christ of Nazareth's Holy name (Rev. 2:4). You will not regret it. Jesus said we are to come to Him as little children (Matt. 18:3). Children are generally great in faith, and lack in knowledge, especially worldly knowledge (1 Kings

3:7). This may be the first step, to you realizing, whom your Saviour really is. He is not of this world (John 18:36). He was not known by this world (John 1:10). And He only reveals Himself truly, to those whom He loves, and desires to continue His relationship with. That means you and I. To God be the glory. But do not take my word for it, listen to the "...still small voice." for yourself (1 Kings 19:12). That is the Holy Spirit of God, in Jesus Christ of Nazareth. Alleluia and praise the LORD. Amen and Amen.

Discussion Questions

1. Where ought we to worship God?

   _____

   _____

   _____

   _____

   _____

2. What about fellowship?

   _____

   _____

   _____

   _____

   _____

3. What about the "Messianic Age"?

   _____

   _____

   _____

   _____

   _____

CHAPTER 5

The Temple, The Body, The Vine

"For I am persuaded, that neither death, nor life, nor angels, nor principalities, nor powers, nor things present, nor things to come, Nor height, nor depth, nor any other creature, shall be able to separate us from the love of God, which is in Christ Jesus our Lord."
- ROMANS 8:38, 39

Introduction

In the last chapter I spoke about the relationship between Jesus and King David, in this chapter I will speak about the relationship between Jesus' and the physical temple, as well as His body as the temple of God, and last regarding Jesus relationship with natural creation including with us as individuals and a part of His Body, that is the church of God. Alleluia and praise the LORD. Read on to learn more.

Ezra, Isaiah, Haggai, Zerubbabel, Jesus and the Temple

In this section I will talk about the parallels between the physical temple of the Old Testament in relationship with Jesus Christ of Nazareth, God's temple of Jesus Christ of Nazareth, and the temple of God, the Father, through a living relationship with His Holy Spirit in Christ Jesus of Nazareth's Holy name. In Ezra, Zerubbabel first comes to Jerusalem with supporters, after a royal decree by Cyrus, after seventy years in captivity in Babylon (Ezra 2). This parallels Jesus coming to Jerusalem with His supporters, the days leading up to His crucifixion (Matt. 21:1-9, Mark 11:1-10, Luke 19:28-44, John 12:12-15). Then Zerubbabel and his supporters built the foundations of the temple and shouted and cried for joy, during this time (Ezra 3:8-13). Much like in Jesus' time, when His supporters were laying clothing and branches in Jesus' path and shouting "…Hosanna…" (Matt. 21:8, 9; Mark 11:8-10, Luke 19:36-38, John 12:13). Then Zerubbabel and his supporters saw opposition to the temple building, and had to stop for some time (Ezra 4). Jesus experienced a similar opposition to His claimed kingship, by the established religious authorities of His day (Matt. 21:10-16, Luke 19:39-48). The opposition of the temple building continued with some sort of judicial trial of the opposition to the work of building the second temple of God, in Jerusalem (Ezra 5). As Jesus also endured His trial for the claim of His Messianic position and fulfillment of Old Testament prophecies of the Messiah, King of Israel, and Saviour of the whole world before the governor and the people, that led to His crucifixion, death, burial and resurrection three days later (Matt. 27, 28). Then we have the continuation and completion of work on the second temple in Jerusalem and continuation of its service for the glory of God by the people of God (Ezra 6-8). With the parallel of the triumphant resurrection of Jesus Christ of Nazareth, witnessed by His disciples on the first day of the week, and during the time of visitation before His ascension into heaven, and then confirmed by the outpouring of His Holy Spirit at Pentecost in 31 A.D., on His disciples, and on all whom believed, unto today and forever more (Matt. 28, Mark 16, Luke 24, John 20, 21; Acts 2:1-21). The point here is that God's physical temple that men's hands have built is a "shadow" of God's heavenly temple and more importantly salvation in Jesus Christ of Nazareth, as Jesus affirmed, we as people, are God's temple of His Holy Spirit (John 2:21, 14:20, 15:4). This is that very sacred relationship that our Creator desires to have with us, through the indwelling of His Holy Spirit, through our body, in our mind and with our soul. Much like the priests through the Holy Spirit interacted with and worshipped God at His physical temple in the wilderness and in Jerusalem, throughout the centuries, until Jesus' time, now in homes, churches, synagogues, etc., and likely again, in and at a temple, in the so called "Messianic age", mentioned in Ezekiel's prophecies (Ezek. 40-48). Alleluia and praise the LORD. Amen and Amen.

In the Book of Haggai, during the same time as Ezra, God speaks to Haggai, to speak to Zerubbabel and Joshua (Hag. 1:1). He first admonishes that the people are saying, "…The time is not come, the time that the LORD's house should be built." (Hag. 1:2). God then goes on and questions the people, "*Is it* time for you, O ye, to dwell in your ceiled houses, and this house *lie* waste?" (Hag. 1:4). God was asking is it not time to build the house of God? And He admonishes them to "… Consider your ways." (Hag. 1:5, 2:10-19). Jesus experienced similar opposition during His ministry on this earth, and even Jesus, Himself considered much during His ministry; Jesus and His mother at the wedding supper, Jesus and His brothers about attending the Feast of Tabernacles, Jesus in the garden of Gethsemane praying before His crucifixion, etc. (Matt. 26:36-45, John 2:1-4, 7:1-5). Next, God calls the people to, "Go up to the mountain, and bring wood, and build the house; and I will take pleasure in it, and I will be glorified, saith the LORD." (Hag. 1:8, 2:9). Jesus spoke about the glory He was going to receive as well, when His body, the temple of God, would be resurrected, He was even glorified in His life before the crucifixion, because of His miraculous existence and works (Matt. 1:18-25, John 17). In Haggai, God then gives example after example of the peoples failure to prosper, because of their disobedience, through failed crops, and other labours, so they turned to God and obeyed His command (Hag. 1:9-15). This would be equivalent to Jesus stirring up the spirit of the people during His ministry to follow Him and after His resurrection to continue the work of building the church through, signs, wonders and miracles, and publishing the gospel of the kingdom of God to all the nations (Matt. 4:19, 20; 28:19, 20). The second chapter of Haggai's book continues with encouraging the people saying, "Yet now be strong, O Zerubbabel, saith the LORD; and be strong, O Joshua, son of Josedech, the high priest; and be strong, all ye people of the land, saith the LORD, and work: for I *am* with you, saith the LORD of hosts: *According to* the word that I covenanted with you when ye came out of Egypt, so my spirit remaineth among you: fear ye not." (Hag. 2:4, 5). God then goes into a more prophetic tone, and says, "For thus saith the LORD of hosts; Yet once, it *is* a little while, and I will shake the heavens, and the earth, and the sea, and the dry *land;* and I will shake all nations, and the desire of all nations shall come: and I will fill this house with glory saith the LORD of hosts." (Hag. 2:6, 7, 21-23). This likely pointed to an earthquake that took place at Jesus' crucifixion, but even Jesus prophesied of a time in history, that has not likely yet taken place, as of the date of writing this book in 2019 A.D., where the earth would shake and wars would erupt, and other prophets, namely Ezekiel and John, prophesied of this time of the heavens and the earth shaking, with wars erupting, culminating with a time where the nations of the earth would turn to worship God at His temple in Jerusalem (Ezek. 38-48; Hag. 2:9, Matt. 24, Rev. 5-20). This Zerubbabel, governor of Judah, in approximately 487 B.C, was likely an ancestor of Jesus Christ of Nazareth, through His mother physically, as spoken of in chapter one (Hag. 1:1, Matt. 1:12, 14; Luke 3:27). So it is no doubt that these prophecies are related to Jesus as well, as Jesus is the Word of God, and all scripture is inspired by and created through, and fulfilled in Him (Rev. 4:11). That all being said, Jesus did say, "But the hour cometh, and now is, when the true worshippers shall worship the Father in spirit and in truth...", so we need to put these prophecies into proper perspective, in our daily relationship with our Creator, in Jesus Christ of Nazareth, through His Holy Spirit (John 4:23). Alleluia and praise the LORD. Amen and Amen.

Isaiah prophesied quite a bit about not only Jesus, but about Israel and the tribes of Israel and their descendants in general, throughout the ages, continuing today and into the age to come. Isaiah 56:7 calls God's temple, "...an house of prayer...", as Jesus confirmed (Matt. 21:13, Mark 11:17, Luke 19:46). And the later chapters of Isaiah, namely Isaiah 60-66 speak of Jesus and some of the things He also prophesied of, as well as in a greater way, John, in the Book of Revelation, through the inspiration of the Holy Spirit. Isaiah 60:19 speaks of Jesus being our light. Isaiah 61:1 speaks of Jesus (Luke 4:18-21). Isaiah 61:2 speaks of the great tribulation, which Jesus spoke of (Matt. 24, Mark 13, Luke 21). Isaiah 61:3-11 speaks of the "Messianic age" (Rev. 20:4, 6). Isaiah 62:1-3 speaks of the establishment of Jerusalem as a praise. Jesus spoke of worshipping God in Spirit and in truth (John 4:23). Isaiah 62:4 and 5 speak of peoples' relationship with Zion and God. This is all fulfilled in God's gift to us by His Holy Spirit, through faith in God's only begotten Son, Jesus Christ of Nazareth. Isaiah 62:6 speaks of the New Heavens and a New Earth (2 Pet. 3:13, Rev. 21:1). I have spoken of this subject in greater detail in my book, "Heaven, Hell and the Resurrection", but most important is to understand our relationship with God through His Holy Spirit, in the name of God, the Father's, only begotten Son, Jesus Christ of Nazareth. Isaiah 62:7-11 speaks of redemption and blessings of the people of God in His courts of holiness, salvation from God, and the praise of Jerusalem. Jesus fulfilled this all, as He has stood in our place of condemnation, as we are all sinners under the law of God. Jesus took all of our sins upon Himself, on the cross, and died for the forgiveness of our sins on the cross, shedding His Holy and righteous blood for the forgiveness of our sins, He was buried and the third day He arose to give us the hope and promise of eternal life in His Holy name. However this is also prophetic regarding the general "atmosphere" of the so called "Messianic Age", during the prophesied final one thousand years of this earth's present history (Ezek. 40-48, Rev. 20:4, 6). Alleluia and praise the LORD. Amen and Amen.

Isaiah 63:1-6 speaks more of wrath and the great tribulation, which Jesus spoke of, as mentioned above and in previous chapters (Matt. 24, Mark 13, Luke 21). Isaiah 63:8 and 9 speak of Jesus and the Holy Spirit (Matt. 28:20). Isaiah 63:10-14 speaks of rebellion, remembrance of God's mercy in the past, and Jesus admonishes us to "...go ye and learn what *that* meaneth, I will have mercy..." from the very world around us, that God has authority over through His only begotten Son, Jesus Christ of Nazareth (Matt. 9:13, John 1:1-3, Rev. 4:11). Isaiah 63:15-19 speaks of calling on God for help and the return of the tribes of Israel to the land God has promised them, and I have written books about the topics of God's promises and the history of the tribes in general, called "The Day Star and Us" and the "Origin of Mankind", the latter speaking about amongst other things, the western civilizations generally being descendants of the tribes of Israel. Most importantly this has been fulfilled in Christ for all of mankind, through His life, death on the cross for the forgiveness of our sins, His burial, and His resurrection three days later for the hope and promise of eternal life in His Holy name (John 10:14-16). Isaiah 63:18 also likely speaks of Ezra's time of return from captivity in Babylon to rebuild the temple, as well as of Jesus and His crucifixion. This is why Jesus Christ of Nazareth came, He came for the lost sheep of Israel, and for the gentile sheep He has intended to bring into His fold (John 10:14-16). Isaiah 64 speaks of calling on God for help, much like Jesus did in the garden of Gethsemane (Matt. 26:36-45). Isaiah 65:1-7 speaks of the abomination of Israel, compared to Jesus upbraiding the temple money changers, as a den of thieves (Matt. 21:12, 13). Isaiah 65:8-16 and 19-25 speak of a remnant and forgiveness. Isaiah 65:17 speaks of the New Heaven and a New Earth mentioned amidst prophecy of the "Messianic Age", likely because of the similarity between the two experiences (Rev. 20, 21, 22). But ultimately Jesus admonishes us to recognize that the kingdom of God, through His Holy Spirit is in us, it does not come with observation (Luke 17:20, 21). Isaiah 66:1-4 speaks of the greatness of God. Jesus said no one is good but God, and one of the fruits of the Holy Spirit is goodness (Gal. 5:22, 23). Isaiah 66:5-11 prophecies of Jesus and His virgin birth, as well as likely reestablishment of Israel as a nation state in 1948 A.D. (Matt. 1:18-25). Isaiah 66:12-24 speaks of things to come, the "Great Tribulation", and the "Messianic Age", as of the date of writing this book in 2019 A.D. (Matt. 24, Rev. 20:4, 6). It may seem that much of Isaiah has a lot to do with prophecy and not much to do with Jesus Christ of Nazareth, but the reality is "…the testimony of Jesus is the spirit of prophecy." (Rev. 19:10). Because Jesus Christ of Nazareth is the Word of God, when we speak of the testimony of Jesus Christ of Nazareth, it comes naturally that we would prophecy as well. To sort out any confusion of the order of some of these events I have mentioned regarding the "Great Tribulation" and the "Messianic Age", you can see appendix E for more details. Alleluia and praise the LORD. Amen and Amen.

What Jesus endured in the Body

In Exodus 20:24-26 it says, "An altar of earth thou shalt make unto me, and shalt sacrifice thereon thy burnt offerings, and thy peace offerings, thy sheep, and thine oxen: in all places where I record my name I will come unto thee, and I will bless thee. And if thou wilt make me an altar of stone, thou shalt not build it of hewn stone: for if thou lift up thy tool upon it, thou hast polluted it. Neither shalt thou go up by steps unto mine altar, that thy nakedness be not discovered thereon.". This describes well the nature of Jesus as the altar, made of the earth, born in the flesh; not made by man's hands, conceived by the Holy Spirit; and created in the same physical stature as man, that is, He is the Son of man, born of the virgin, Mary, at the time, likely in late 4 B.C. (Matt. 1:18-25, John 5:26, 27). Alleluia and praise the LORD. In John 8:6 it says, "Jesus stooped down, and with *his* finger wrote on the ground…". He also spit on the ground and made clay anointing the eyes of a blind man, miraculously healed, after he was told to wash in the pool of Siloam (John 9:6, 7). He was very much a man of the natural earth, but at the same time the Son of God, and Creator of all things (John 1:1-14). Alleluia and praise the LORD. Regarding Jesus' judgement and crucifixion, Isaiah 52:14 says, "…his visage was so marred more than any man, and his form more than the sons of men…". Spiritually speaking His stature as the Son of God, and Immanuel, God with us was marred. He accused those amongst Him of being faithless and unbelievers (Matt. 17:17, 20; Mark 9:19, Luke 9:41). Some of His friends accused Him of being crazy and were ready to deliver Him up for that reason (Mark 3:21). Then the religious authorities accused Him of being Beelzebub, the prince of the devils, essentially accusing Him of being Satan, which was of course, not true (Mark 3:22-26). Zechariah 12:2 says, "Behold, I will make Jerusalem a cup of trembling unto all the people round about, when they shall be in the siege both against Judah *and* against Jerusalem.". This was fulfilled in 70 A.D. and has been fulfilled throughout the centuries after that, and may still be fulfilled in the future as of the date of writing this book, in 2019 A.D., but we must also look at this first from the perspective of how it was fulfilled with Jesus Christ of Nazareth. He was on the Mount of Olives the night of His betrayal and went about a stone's throw away to the Garden of Gethsemane; this is where He prayed to God to take the cup from Him (Luke 22:39-42). But then He prayed to God, the Father, "… not my will, but thine, be done." (Luke 22:42). In the Gospel according to Luke, it is said that

He sweat as if it was like "…great drops of blood falling down to the ground." (Luke 22:44). I suppose this describes the heaviness and possibly even, terror and fear Jesus may have felt because of the things that were about to come upon Him, without cause, but ultimately for the sake of God, the Father, and for the forgiveness of all of our sins. Alleluia and praise the LORD. Amen and Amen.

Isaiah 53:5 says, "But he *was* wounded for our transgressions, *he was* bruised for our iniquities: the chastisement of our peace *was* upon him; and with his stripes we are healed.". Proverbs 3:11 and 12 say, "My son, despise not the chastening of the LORD; neither be weary of his correction: For whom the LORD loveth he correcteth; even as a father the son *in whom* he delighteth.". The point here is that Jesus Christ of Nazareth received the chastening for all of our sins. We can have peace in our mind, with God, and with others in this world because Jesus Christ of Nazareth died on the cross for the forgiveness of all of our sins, He was buried, and He arose the third day for our hope and promise of eternal life in His Holy name. As Isaiah 53:6 says, "All we like sheep have gone astray; we have turned every one to his own way; and the LORD hath laid on him the iniquity of us all.". We have gone astray, and Jesus Christ of Nazareth came to make us free, to save us and deliver us from our sins, to Shepherd us and bring us back to green pastures with the rest of the sheepfold (Matt. 18:11-13). All of our sins were taken upon Jesus Christ of Nazareth on the cross at Passover in 31 A.D.. Alleluia and praise the LORD. Amen and Amen. Isaiah 53:7 says, "He was oppressed, and he was afflicted, yet he opened not his mouth: he is brought as a lamb to the slaughter, and as a sheep before her shearers is dumb, so he openeth not his mouth.". At the judgement, before Pontius Pilate, during the scourging and smiting, and on the cross, there were false witnesses, questions, and other accusers and tempters that Jesus did not answer (John 18:38, 19:9). And more than that, He said, "…Father, forgive them; for they know not what they do. …" (Luke 23:34). Isaiah 53:8 says, "He was taken from prison and from judgement: and who shall declare his generation? For he was cut off out of the land of the living: for the transgression of my people was he stricken.". After Jesus' trial by the religious authorities and Pontius Pilate, He was taken to the place called, the place of a skull, Golgotha in Hebrew, to be crucified (John 19:16-18). Isaiah 53:9 says, "And he made his grave with the wicked, and with the rich in his death; because he had done no violence, neither *was any* deceit in his mouth.". He was crucified like the two malefactors on either side of Him, but He had done no wrong (Luke 23:32, 33). He was also, prepared for burial and buried in an honourable man's new tomb, Joseph of Arimathea, a counsellor (Matt. 27:59, 60; Mark 15:42-46, Luke 23:50-53, John 19:38-42). The good news is that after His burial, three days later, Jesus arose to give us all the hope and promise of eternal life in His Holy name, Jesus Christ of Nazareth. Alleluia and praise the LORD. Amen and Amen.

Isaiah 51:17 says, "Awake, awake, stand up, O Jerusalem, which hast drunk at the hand of the LORD the cup of his fury; thou hast drunken the dregs of the cup of trembling, *and* wrung *them* out.". As mentioned this speaks of Jesus receiving God's wrath upon Himself for the forgiveness of our sins. He literally drank vinegar, from a sponge, on a branch of hyssop and gave up the Holy Ghost on the cross for the forgiveness of our sins (John 19:29, 30). He spilt His Holy and righteous blood, died on the cross, He was buried and the third day He arose to give us the hope and promise of eternal life in His Holy name. Alleluia and praise the LORD. Amen and Amen. Isaiah 51:21-23 says, "Therefore hear now this, thou afflicted, and drunken, but not with wine: Thus saith thy Lord the LORD, and thy God *that* pleadeth the cause of his people, Behold, I have taken out of thine hand the cup of trembling, *even* the dregs of the cup of my fury; thou shalt no more drink it again: But I will put it into the hand of them that afflict thee; which have said to thy soul, Bow down, that we may go over: and thou hast laid thy body as the ground, and as the street, to them that went over.". This describes Jesus and the disciples of Christ in general being willing to give up our life for Jesus Christ of Nazareth and God, the Father, through His Holy Spirit (John 15:13). That being said, the fulfillment of the cup being put into the hand of those that afflict us was fulfilled in that the people whom were asking that Jesus be crucified said, "…His blood be on us, and on our children." (Matt. 27:25). Strangely enough this may have actually worked in their favour, because that is exactly what we need to be healed, we need the blood of Jesus Christ of Nazareth to cover us and cleanse us, for the forgiveness of our sins (Matt. 26:28). Isaiah 52:15 says, "So shall he sprinkle many nations; the kings shall shut their mouths at him: for *that* which had not been told them shall they see; and *that* which they had not heard shall they consider.". Certainly, Pontius Pilate fulfilled this role in some respect also (Matt. 27:19). Alleluia and praise the LORD. Amen and Amen. Last, Isaiah 52:13 says, "Behold, my servant shall deal prudently, he shall be exalted and extolled, and be very high.". Jesus was exalted on a number of occasions, being called, Christ, King of Israel, Saviour, The LORD, God, etc. by some, even His crucifixion exalted Jesus and God, the Father's, merciful and loving nature (Matt. 16:16, John 1:49, 4:42, 20:28). But ultimately, after His crucifixion, death and burial, He arose the third day, and He revealed Himself to His disciples for forty days afterward, and then ascended into heaven to sit at the right hand of the Father, our God, and Creator. Alleluia and praise the LORD. Amen and Amen.

The Vine, and the Branch

After Jesus' birth, visitation by the "wise men", and fleeing to Egypt with His parents at the age of two, Jesus came out of Egypt, just like the children of Israel did (Ex. 12:31-51, Matt. 2:14-21). Psalm 80:7-19 says, "…Thou hast brought a vine out of Egypt: thou hast cast out the heathen, and planted it. Thou preparedst *room* before it, and didst cause it to take deep root, and it filled the land. The hills were covered with the shadow of it, and the boughs thereof *were like* the goodly cedars. She sent out her boughs unto the sea, and her branches unto the river. Why hast thou *then* broken down her hedges, so that all they which pass by the way do pluck her? The boar out of the wood doth waste it, and the wild beast of the field doth devour it. Return, we beseech thee, O God of hosts: look down from heaven, and behold, and visit this vine; And the vineyard which thy right hand hath planted, and the branch *that* thou madest strong for thyself. *It is* burned with fire, *it is* cut down: they perish at the rebuke of thy countenance. Let thy hand be upon the man of thy right hand, upon the son of man *whom* thou madest strong for thyself. So will not we go back from thee: quicken us, and we will call upon thy name. Turn us again, O LORD God of hosts, cause thy face to shine; and we shall be saved.". Jesus was also broken, plucked, laid waste, and devoured by His persecutors during His ministry, especially physically during His final day of condemnation, dying on the cross for the forgiveness of our sins, spilling His Holy and righteous blood, He was buried, but He arose the third day for our hope and promise of eternal life in His Holy name. Alleluia and praise the LORD. Amen and Amen. Jesus Christ of Nazareth is in relation to God, the Father, "…the man of thy right hand…" and "…the son of man *whom* thou madest strong for thyself." (Ps. 80:17, Luke 2:40, Rom. 8:34). This is also prophetic in the nature of Israel as a whole going into captivity throughout the nations of this world, with the psalmist, calling on God to save us (Ps. 80:19). Of course his prayers were answered in Jesus Christ of Nazareth, Saviour of the whole world, deliverer of Israel and Redeemer of all of mankind, by His just work on the cross. And the prophetic nature of this psalm, like the Holy Bible in its entirety, will continue to be fulfilled in the calling and salvation of each one of us, as we repent of our sins and accept the blood of Jesus Christ of Nazareth to cleanse us of our sins, in order that we may receive eternal life in His Holy name. Alleluia and praise the LORD. Amen and Amen.

Isaiah 11:1-5 says, "And there shall come forth a rod out of the stem of Jesse, and a Branch shall grow out of his roots: And the spirit of the LORD shall rest upon him, the spirit of wisdom and understanding, the spirit of counsel and might, the spirit of knowledge and of the fear of the LORD; And shall make him of quick understanding in the fear of the LORD: and he shall not judge after the sight of his eyes, neither reprove after the hearing of his ears: But with righteousness shall he judge the poor, and reprove with equity for the meek of the earth: and he shall smite the earth: with the rod of his mouth, and with the breath of his lips shall he slay the wicked. And righteousness shall be the girdle of his loins, and faithfulness the girdle of his reins.". The remainder of Isaiah 11 likely speaks of the "Messianic Age" and the time working toward it, with Jesus Christ of Nazareth and the Holy Spirit of God performing these prophesies through mankind and the rest of God's creation (Isa. 11:6-16). In Jeremiah 23:5 and 6, it says, "Behold, the days come, saith the LORD, that I will raise unto David a righteous Branch, and a King shall reign and prosper, and shall execute judgment and justice in the earth. In his days Judah shall be saved, and Israel shall dwell safely: and this *is* his name whereby he shall be called, The LORD OUR RIGHTEOUSNESS.". This is fulfilled in the name of Jesus Christ of Nazareth, and the prophesies coinciding with it continue to be fulfilled today, in the "ingathering" of the descendants of Israel, from the north country and scattered abroad, to the modern day nation state of Israel physically, and the spiritual awareness of believers in Jesus Christ of Nazareth, as our Lord and Saviour (John 10:16). He also prophesied similarly again saying, "…she…", "…the LORD our righteousness…" (Jer. 33:16). This would indicate the female component of God and Jesus Christ of Nazareth

(Gen. 1:26, 27). Of course, Jesus Christ of Nazareth represents both the male and the female of "mankind"; God is not a respecter of persons, male or female (Acts 10:34). But it also represents the importance of the marriage relationship, as Jesus spoke of as well (Isa. 54:5, 61:10; Matt. 19:4-6). Jesus said, "O Jerusalem, Jerusalem, *thou* that killest the prophets, and stonest them which are sent unto thee, how often would I have gathered thy children together, even as a hen gathereth her chickens under *her* wings, and ye would not!" (Matt. 23:37). This again could be compared to Jesus and Adam's relationship with his wife, Eve, as well, mentioned in chapter one (Gen. 1:26, 27, 1 Cor. 15:45, Rev. 1:11, 17; 2:8, 22:13). Jeremiah 23:7 and 8 says, "Therefore, behold, the days come, saith the LORD, that they shall no more say, The LORD liveth, which brought up the children of Israel out of the land of Egypt; But, The LORD liveth, which brought up and which led the seed of the house of Israel out of the north country, and from all countries whither I had driven them; and they shall dwell in their own land.". Alleluia and praise the LORD. Amen and Amen.

Zechariah chapters three and six, both speak of "the Branch", as reference to Christ. Zechariah 3:8 says, "Hear now, O Joshua the high priest, thou, and thy fellows that sit before thee: for they *are* men wondered at: for, behold, I will bring forth my servant the BRANCH.". Zechariah 6:12 says, "And speak unto him, saying, Thus speaketh the LORD of hosts, saying, Behold the man whose name *is* The BRANCH; and he shall grow up out of his place, and he shall build the temple of the LORD…". There were palm tree branches lain out before Jesus, when riding into Jerusalem on the donkey's colt (Matt. 21:8, Mark 11:8, Luke 12:12, 13; John 12:12, 13). Also, the branch of hyssop was used to give Jesus vinegar from a sponge at the final moments of His life during His crucifixion; albeit the King James Version does not expressly say it was a branch of hyssop, just hyssop (John 19:29). Jesus said of Himself, "I am the true vine, and my Father is the husbandman. Every branch in me that beareth not fruit he taketh away: and every *branch* that beareth fruit, he purgeth it, that it may bring forth more fruit. Now ye are clean through the word which I have spoken unto you. Abide in me, and I in you. As the branch cannot bear fruit of itself, except it abide in the vine; no more can ye, except ye abide in me. I am the vine, ye *are* the branches: He that abideth in me, and I in him, the same bringeth forth much fruit: for without me ye can do nothing. If a man abide not in me, he is cast forth as a branch, and is withered; and men gather them, and cast *them* into the fire, and they are burned. If ye abide in me, and my words abide in you, ye shall ask what ye will, and it shall be done unto you." (John 15:1-7). In this parable Jesus refers to us as "branches" of Himself, the Vine (John 15:2, 4-7). This is because, as He explains and in greater detail the apostles explain in the epistles, especially, the apostle, Paul, we are the "Body of Christ" and members of His body (1 Cor. 12:27). Just like a vine has branches, Jesus Christ of Nazareth is also the head and we are the members of His Body (Eph. 1:22, 23). He is the vine and we are the branches (Isa. 60:21, John 15:5). But ultimately Jesus Christ of Nazareth is the "THE LORD OUR RIGHTEOUSNESS", the "BRANCH", as the body of God, Immanuel, God with us (Jer. 23:5, 6; 33:16; Zech. 3:8, 6:12; Matt. 1:23). Alleluia and praise the LORD. Amen and Amen.

Conclusion

The apostle, Paul, speaks in his letter to the Ephesians to put on the whole armour of God. He says, "Finally, my brethren, be strong in the Lord, and in the power of his might. Put on the whole armour of God, that ye may be able to stand against the wiles of the devil. For we wrestle not against flesh and blood, but against principalities, against powers, against the rulers of the darkness of this world, against spiritual wickedness in high *places.* Wherefore take unto you the whole armour of God, that ye may be able to withstand in the evil day, and having done all, to stand." (Eph. 6:10-13). Jesus says, "Take no thought for the morrow: for the morrow shall take thought for the things of itself. Sufficient unto the day *is* the evil thereof." (Matt. 6:34). Continuing, the apostle, Paul, says, "Stand therefore, having your loins girt about with truth, and having on the breastplate of righteousness…" (Eph. 6:14). Jesus Christ of Nazareth is our righteousness, He is the truth (Matt. 3:15, John 14:5). Next, the apostle, Paul, says, "And your feet shod with the preparation of the gospel of peace…" (Eph. 6:15). Jesus washed the feet of His disciples, and asks us to do the same, that is we are called to be servants of God and Christ, not masters, judges and dictators of men (John 13:3-17). Ephesians 6:16 says, "Above all, taking the shield of faith, wherewith ye shall be able to quench all the fiery darts of the wicked.". Faith comes from Jesus Christ of Nazareth, through the Holy Spirit, which is a gift from God, the Father, by grace not by works, and Jesus Christ of Nazareth is Faithful (Eph. 2:8, 9; Rev. 1:5, 3:14, 19:11,). Alleluia and praise the LORD. Amen and Amen. Ephesians 6:17 continues, "And take the helmet of salvation, and the sword of the Spirit, which is the word of God…". Jesus says our salvation comes by patience, that is longsuffering, and Jesus is our longsuffering, our patience, whom endured on the cross for us, He was buried and He arose the third day to give us hope and the promise of eternal life in His Holy name. Alleluia and praise the LORD. Amen and Amen. Ephesians 6:18 says, "Praying always with all prayer and supplication in the Spirit, and watching thereunto with all perseverance and supplication for all saints…". This is the reality we have in Jesus Christ of Nazareth, whom asks us to watch and pray always (Matt. 26:41, Mark 13:33). Alleluia and praise the LORD. Amen and Amen.

God was shown to have a Body, in Jesus Christ of Nazareth. Psalm 11:5 says God has a soul, and Jesus revealed that living soul of God, in Himself, He became a fleshly soul, like Adam and Eve, Noah, and every other soul God has ever created (Gen. 2:7, 1 Pet. 3:20). And God is a Spirit, He is the Holy Spirit (John 4:24). This is the threefold nature of God, but also, the threefold nature of every living being, God has created. This is why it is important for us to have a full relationship with God, the Father, Almighty, by Jesus Christ of Nazareth, His only begotten Son, through His Holy Spirit. Alleluia and praise the LORD. The Bible speaks of the body, soul and spirit, receiving a new heart of flesh, and a new spirit, the Holy Spirit, and our regeneration (Ezek. 18:31, 36:26; Matt. 19:28, Rev. 21:1-5). This is the redemption we have in the name of Jesus Christ of Nazareth, born of water and spirit, Jesus the living waters, and God, the Holy Spirit, as mentioned in chapter two (Jer. 17:13, John 4:24, 7:37, 38).

Alleluia and praise the LORD. In the bigger picture we are members of the Body of Christ (1 Cor. 12:27). The church of God, the "…general assembly and church of the firstborn…" (Heb. 12:23). And we are all one in Christ Jesus of Nazareth's Holy name (John 17:22, 23). Isaiah 60:21 says of God's people in His land, "Thy people also *shall be* all righteous: they shall inherit the land for ever, the branch of my planting, the work of my hands, that I may be glorified.". This is referring to God's creation as the branch, like Jesus said (John 15:1-7). This is why it is important to follow Jesus Christ of Nazareth, so that we are not cut out of the Vine, that is Jesus Christ of Nazareth, and God, the Father, rooted in the Word of God, the Holy Spirit of God. In the next chapter I will speak about Jesus Christ of Nazareth, His life in general, His miracles, and His relationship with God, through the Holy Spirit, read on to learn more. Alleluia and praise the LORD. Amen and Amen.

Discussion: Holy Spirit

"And if thou wilt make me an altar of stone, thou shalt not build it of hewn stone: for if thou lift up thy tool upon it, thou hast polluted it."
- Exodus 20:25

This verse is actually quite revealing about our relationship with God, through Jesus Christ of Nazareth, God's only begotten Son. He was crucified on the cross, we polluted Jesus, by lifting up a hammer and nail against His body on the cross. But there is more to it than that. We can come up with so many different ideas of how the "future" is going to be and how mankind ought to live, with all of these fancy gadgets and technologies, but forget the Creator, whom gave us the ability to build all of these things. God is not looking for a fancy manmade altar for us to worship at. He just desires us to follow Him. He is a Spirit. That is what Jesus tells us (John 4:24). Jesus said, "…the hour cometh, and now is, when the true worshippers shall worship the Father in spirit and in truth: for the Father seeketh such to worship him." (John 4:23). Also, we must remember that this also points to Jesus Christ of Nazareth being conceived by the Holy Ghost, not by mans hand. (Matt. 1:18-25). Another reason why Jesus was not polluted from the womb, was because He was conceived by the Holy Ghost, by God, the Father (Matt. 1:18-25) This all points to God's ability to prepare "works", materials, etc., ahead of time for us, as the Bible says is the case (Eph. 2:10). We must also remember that we were created in the womb, by God (Isa. 44:2). Our very existence is a miracle. Praise the LORD God, the Father, Almighty and His only begotten Son, Jesus Christ of Nazareth. The idea of "genetically modified organisms", "chemical" and "nuclear" weaponry, "cloning", man's interference in the natural birthing process and the like, maybe signs of our rebellion against the natural way God had intended for mankind to be fruitful and multiply from the beginning (Gen. 1:28). That all being said, He did indeed send His only begotten Son, Jesus Christ of Nazareth to die on the cross for the forgiveness of our sins, whatever they may be, at Passover in 31 A.D.. Thanks be to God. So whatever the truth is in all of this, we have an advocate with the Father in Christ Jesus of Nazareth, through His Holy Spirit, that has, will and does cleanse us of all of our sins, as we accept Jesus Christ of Nazareth and His truth into our life. We have freedom to learn and develop as children of God, in Christ Jesus of Nazareth. Praise the LORD God, the Father, Almighty, and His only begotten Son, Jesus Christ of Nazareth. This all being said, I will say, of course I am not perfect yet either, so I need God's forgiveness through Jesus Christ of Nazareth, as well as anyone else. So follow Him, all for God's glory. Praise Him. Alleluia. Amen and Amen.

Discussion Questions

1. How could Jesus Christ of Nazareth be conceived by the Holy Spirit?

_____

_____

_____

_____

_____

2. What about the "Messianic Age" temple?

_____

_____

_____

_____

_____

CHAPTER 6

─────

Jesus and His cross

"He was taken from prison and from judgement: and who shall declare his generation? For he was cut off out of the land of the living: for the transgression of my people was he stricken."
- ISAIAH 53:8

Introduction

Daniel prophesied about Jesus, when he spoke of the Messiah that was to be "…cut off…" and "…in the midst of the week…cause the sacrifice and oblation to cease…" (Dan. 9:26, 27). If we use the day for a year principle in the Bible, Jesus was "…cut off…" in the middle of a seven day or seven year ministry (Ezek. 4:6). He was crucified three and a half years into His ministry for the forgiveness of our sins, at Passover in 31 A.D., He was buried and the third day He arose to give us the hope and promise of eternal life. The key here is that that prophecy of Messiah, may not have been completely fulfilled, which in part requires the concept of the "second coming" of Christ (Matt. 16:27). The Bible speaks about a time of trouble that is to come on this world like has never been before nor ever will be again (Matt. 24). This time is known as the "great tribulation", the completion of the seven day or seven year ministry of Jesus Christ of Nazareth (Matt. 24:21, Rev. 2:22, 7:14). Unfortunately, the second half of Jesus' ministry is not going to be the same as the first half. As Hebrews 12:25-29 says, "See that ye refuse not him that speaketh. For if they escaped not who refused him that spake on earth, much more *shall not* we *escape,* if we turn away from him that *speaketh* from heaven: Whose voice then shook the earth: but now he hath promised, saying, Yet once more I shake not the earth only, but also heaven. And this *word,* Yet once more, signifieth the removing of those things that are shaken, as of things that are made, that those things which cannot be shaken may remain. Wherefore we receiving a kingdom which cannot be moved, let us have grace, whereby we may serve God acceptably with reverence and godly fear: For our God *is* a consuming fire.". The good news is that the "great tribulation" is not likely the end, the

"Messianic Age" will likely follow it, then the final judgement, and the new heaven and a new earth (Rev. 20, 21, 22). Jesus was treated with distain and hatred by some, and gratitude and joy by others. It is during this prophesied future time, the "great tribulation", that Jesus will continue His ministry but with trials that are to come on this world, unlike any this earth has ever experienced, as of the date of writing this book in 2019 A.D. (Matt. 24). Jesus is the Alpha and Omega, the beginning and the end (Rev. 1:8). He lives and will live forever. That all being said, read on to learn about the life of Jesus as a man here on earth, as the Lord of the Old Testament and as the Word of God that will live forever more! Alleluia and praise the LORD. Amen and Amen.

Jesus Christ of Nazareth; Early Years

Jesus, when asked how to attain eternal life, said plain and simply, "…keep the commandments." (Matt. 19:17). The man He was talking with then admonished that he did such (Matt. 19:20). Jesus then said, "…If thou wilt be perfect, go *and* sell that thou hast, and give to the poor, and thou shalt have treasure in heaven: and come *and* follow me." (Matt. 19:21). The point of all of this is, that Jesus Christ of Nazareth, never came to destroy the law, He came to fulfil it, He came to "perfect" it (Matt. 5:17). The law is spiritual, it is mankind that perverts and changes laws to suit selfish gain. As the saying goes, "absolute power corrupts". Chapter two and three of the book of the prophet Jeremiah describe the corruption that the northern tribes of Israel and Judah fell into in the Old Testament. Jesus of course called the religious authorities out during His ministry for their corruption and hypocrisy and unfortunately, the same problems still remain today, as the apostle, Peter, and other apostles mention in their epistles, as of the date of writing this book in 2019 A.D. (Matt. 6:2, 5, 16; 1 Pet. 2:1-5). So now that we know the basics of where Jesus was coming from and what He stood for, who is Jesus of Nazareth really? Well, without going to much further; 1 Corinthians 10:4 says, "And did all drink the same spiritual drink: for they drank of that spiritual Rock that followed them: and that Rock was Christ.". This basically sums up who Jesus was, is and always will be, that being said, let us go into greater detail of the life and lessons of the man named, Jesus of Nazareth. Alleluia and praise the LORD. Amen and Amen.

For this next portion of describing who Jesus Christ of Nazareth is, I will use prophecies spoken of in the book of Daniel, chapter eleven, to compare with Jesus' life timeline according to the New Testament accounts. That being said, I realize that Daniel's prophecies have been fulfilled in other ways in the past, as I and others have written about, and are still prophetic, as God does not change (Mal. 3:6). Let us start with Daniel 11:20, it says, "Then shall stand up in his estate a raiser of taxes *in* the glory of the kingdom: but within a few days he shall be destroyed, neither in anger, nor in battle.". This very well could mark the coming of the Messiah, Jesus Christ of Nazareth in the flesh, as Joseph and Mary had to travel to Bethlehem of Judah to pay their tax, that Caesar Augustus decreed for the world to pay, as Joseph was a noted descendant of Judah (Luke 2:1-5). This was the time when Mary was well along in her pregnancy with Jesus, whom was conceived by the Holy Spirit in her before Mary and Joseph had consummated their marriage (Matt. 1:18-25). Next, we have Daniel 11:21, it says, "And in his estate shall stand up a vile person, to whom they shall not give the honour of the kingdom: but he shall come in peaceably, and obtain the kingdom by flatteries.". This very well describes king Herod's attempts to keep his governing status in Judaea as a Roman governor, when he heard from the wise men come from the east that the king of the Jews was born, that is, Jesus Christ of Nazareth (Matt. 2:1-7). He spoke to the wise men with flatteries in regards to Jesus, saying, "...Go and search diligently for the young child; and when ye have found *him,* bring me word again, that I may come and worship him also." (Matt. 2:8). Nevertheless, he likely felt threatened, certainly his actions would seem to show that to be the case, as he commanded all of the children under the age of two in the area of Bethlehem to be destroyed, after the wise men did not return to him, and Joseph, Mary and the young child, Jesus, fled into Egypt, because of warnings from God in a dream (Matt. 2:12-18). Daniel 11:22-29 could describe other events in Jesus' life, namely, Joseph, Mary and Jesus' return out of Egypt soon after king Herod's death, and dwelling in Nazareth, to keep distance from king Herod's successor, his son, Archelaus (Matt. 2:19-23). Alleluia and praise the LORD. Amen and Amen.

Aside from this, other events mentioned in the New Testament of Jesus' youth are His circumcision on the eighth day, possibly just before Yom Kippur, the Day of Atonement, in the fall of 4 B.C., this would have likely been about two years before Joseph, Mary and Jesus fled into Egypt, likely around the fall of 2 B.C. (Lev. 23:27-32, Matt. 2:14-16, Luke 2:21). As mentioned above, Joseph, Mary and Jesus returned from Egypt, possibly in the spring of 1 B.C., as there is some evidence in the writings of a Jewish historian, Josephus, and some other scholarly references, that king Herod, may have died around this time (Matt. 1:20). See the reference appendix C for details on these references, and appendix D for a proposed timeline of Jesus' earthly life. One other notable event of Jesus' young childhood, before going into Egypt was His dedication by His parents at the temple according to the law of God, after Mary's time of purification according to the law of God, the first born is to be dedicated to the LORD (Ex. 13:2, Lev. 12:4, 6-8; Luke 2:22-27). While in the temple Jesus was prophesied over and spoken of by a man named Simeon, and a widow named Anna (Luke 2:25-38). Twelve years later, after their sojourn in Egypt and their return to Nazareth of Galilee, the young family went up to Jerusalem for the feast of Passover in Jerusalem (Luke 2:41, 42). Jesus had stayed behind in Jerusalem at this time, while His parents began their travel back to Nazareth, unknowing that Jesus was still in Jerusalem (Luke 2:43-45). They returned to look for Him and found Him in the temple speaking to and asking questions of the doctors (Luke 2:46). This was the first sign of Jesus', to say the least, "peculiar" abilities, as "...all that heard him were astonished at his understanding and answers." (Ex. 19:5, Luke 2:47). Nevertheless, he returned to Nazareth with His mother and earthly father, Mary and Joseph and was subject unto them, as one of the commands of God says to "...honour thy father and thy mother..."

(Ex. 20:12, Matt. 15:4, Luke 2:48-52). Although some have suggested that Jesus travelled during His early life, before His recorded ministry, which is possible and I addressed this in chapter one of this book. It is hard for me to believe that He did much if any traveling outside of the boundaries of physical Biblical Israel on the east side of the Mediterranean Sea. I say this because His parables and lessons given during His ministry are references to agrarian society, and would have been known from His experiences of life in Israel, albeit He could have learned them elsewhere (Matt. 19:26). He was the son of a carpenter, Joseph, and Jesus was a carpenter (Matt. 13:55, Mark 6:3). And He had brothers and sisters; with this all in mind, a good son would know doubt have helped His family with their business as much as possible, especially knowing that, for Himself, He would be physically leaving this earth, early on in His grownup years (Mark 6:3). That is, Jesus Christ of Nazareth died on the cross for the forgiveness of our sins, spilling His Holy and righteous blood, He was buried and He arose the third day, giving us the hope and promise of eternal life in His Holy name, and about forty days later He was taken up to heaven to a cloud (Acts 1:1-9). Alleluia and praise the LORD. Amen and Amen.

Jesus Christ of Nazareth; Ministry, Practicality and Miracles

Although this section does not pickup directly at the beginning of Jesus ministry at the age of about thirty, likely in the fall of 27 A.D., it gives some comparisons of Jesus teachings during His ministry with some Old Testament examples and the practical application of His teachings today. Jesus said of Himself, "…For he that is not against us is on our part." (Mark 9:38-40). The common people heard him gladly (Mark 12:37). Jesus spoke about the value of marriage (Isa. 58, Mark 10:2-12). Regarding bells in Church and "wedding bells", this can be seen in Aaron's priestly garment in the Old Testament, as mentioned in chapter one (Ex. 28:33-35). Isaiah 54:5 says of God, "For thy Maker *is* thine husband…" (Isa. 54:5). We are called to have Jesus Christ of Nazareth dwell in us, through His Holy Spirit given to us, in order to reflect the nature of Jesus Christ of Nazareth and the fruit of the Holy Spirit in our family (Mal. 2:15, Gal. 5:22, 23). This command of marriage is not broken with Jesus. As Jesus said, "…he…made them male and female…For this cause shall a man leave father and mother, and shall cleave to his wife…What God hath joined together, let not man put asunder." (Matt. 19:4-6). Regarding the emotion of hate and enemies, we are to follow Jesus Christ of Nazareth, first and foremost (Matt. 5:54, Luke 14:25-27). The first commandment is to have no other gods before the true God (Ex. 20:3, Matt. 22:37). Those who follow Jesus are His family (Mark 3:35). He says, "…whosoever shall smite thee on thy right cheek, turn to him the other also.", and Jesus says to take up our cross daily, and follow Him (Lam. 3:30, Matt. 5:39, Luke 9:23). Jesus created family for a purpose in the beginning. But what He is saying is that when it comes time to choose between an earthly person and a relationship with Jesus Christ of Nazareth, our relationship with Jesus Christ of Nazareth must come first. Jesus knew what was in man (Ps. 94:11, John 2:24, 25). That is, "For all have sinned, and come short of the glory of God…" (Rom. 3:23). Jesus forgave the adulterous woman. He stood before the counsel, when a woman was brought in to be judged for adultery and said, "…He that is without sin among you, let him first cast a stone at her.", and one by one they left in shame, as they through their actions admitted they were sinners (John 8:1-11). This fulfills the prophecy of Hosea 4:14, it says, "I will not punish your daughters when they commit whoredom, nor your spouses when they commit adultery: for themselves are separated with whores, and they sacrifice with harlots: therefore the people that doth not understand shall fall.". Rahab and her descendants, including Jesus, if He is her descendant, through Salmon, would be included in this Old Testament prophecy. This is just more proof of Jesus' sinless life, even though He was born of an earthly woman, whose maternal ancestors were, at least one foreigner, Ruth, and possibly one foreign "harlot", Rahab (Jos. 2:1, Ruth 4:13, Matt. 1:5, Luke 3:32). This should be great news for all of us, both men and women, as God, the Father, Almighty forgives us of our fornications, adulteries and all sorts of wickedness, spiritually, physically and otherwise. As we have all come short of the glory of God (Rom. 3:23). We have all sinned, "…there is none that doeth good, no, not one." (Ps. 14:3). Psalm 38:12-14 says, "They also that seek after my life lay snares *for me:* and they that seek my hurt speak mischievous things, and imagine deceits all the day long. But I, as a deaf *man,* heard not; and *I was* as a dumb man *that* openeth not his mouth. Thus I was as a man that heareth not, and in whose mouth *are* no reproofs.". Jesus very much fulfilled these verses, even at His own judgement, he did not come to condemn, but to save (John 3:17). He said to, "…go, and sin no more." (John 8:11). Alleluia and praise the LORD. Amen and Amen.

This all being said, Deuteronomy 17:14-20 speaks of true kingship, and the qualities that a husband should have. Not many possessions, wives, horses, gold and silver, but diligent in studying the word of God and obeying His commands (Deut. 17:14-20). David and Solomon failed to keep these commandments "perfectly" and is part of the reason why their kingdoms were challenged, and fell, as prophesied, albeit there is still some evidence for the existence of the Davidic lineage in the British monarchy, through a daughter of King Zedekiah, fleeing to Ireland (Jer. 43:6, 7). See appendix B for more details on the throne of David and Jesus' relationship with it. But Jesus has taken up this sceptre promise forever spiritually, as the only begotten Son of God and a son of David of the tribe of Judah, through His mother, Mary (Matt. 1:18-25, Luke 3:23-38, Rev. 5:5). Jesus Christ of Nazareth died on the cross for the forgiveness of our sins, He was buried and the third day He arose for our hope and promise of eternal life in His Holy name. Even Solomon confirms the vanity of going after all of the earthly things, as he did (Eccl. 1:2). He says, "Let us hear the conclusion of the whole matter: Fear God, and keep his commandments: for this *is* the whole *duty* of man." (Eccl. 12:13). And again, the reality is in Jesus Christ of Nazareth, as He is that perfect husbandman (Matt. 5:48, Luke 13:32, John 10:30, 17:23). He has come for His bride in the flesh and continues to sojourn with us through His Holy Spirit until the end. And on that final day we will stand before Him without condemnation and will be with Him forever more in the New

Heavens and a New Earth (Isa. 65:17, 2 Pet. 3:13, Rev. 21:1-5). Alleluia and praise the LORD. Regarding children, Jesus said of Himself, "…Suffer the little children to come unto me, and forbid them not: for of such is the kingdom of God. Verily I say unto you, Whosoever shall not receive the kingdom of God as a little child, he shall not enter therein." (Mark 10:14, 15). Jesus refers to His disciples, us, as children (Mark 10:24). Also, even though Jesus tells us to leave all and follow Him (Luke 14:33). He confirms that He asked us to, but clearly gives it all back and one hundred fold in this life (Mark 10:29, 30). He says, "Verily I say unto you, There is no man that hath left house, or brethren, or sisters, or father, or mother, or wife, or children, or land, for my sake, and the gospel's, But he shall receive an hundredfold now in this time, houses, and brethren, and sisters, and mothers and children, and lands, with persecutions; and in the world to come eternal life. But many *that are* first shall be last; and the last first." (Mark 29-31). This confirms that when we "sacrifice" family life, friends and belongings, to follow Jesus, He gives them back again and one hundred fold, with eternal life. Praise the LORD God, the Father, Almighty and His only begotten Son, Jesus Christ of Nazareth. He truly is the redeemer, whom gives life and life more abundantly (John 10:10). Alleluia and praise the LORD. Thanks be to God, the Father, and His only begotten Son, Jesus Christ of Nazareth. Amen and Amen. Alleluia and Amen.

The reason why some of the "authorities" and others may not have believed that Jesus is the Messiah, maybe because of all of the miracles that other prophets had performed in the Old Testament era, and any other miracles false "messiahs" may have done. Some examples of Old Testament miracles are an axe head floating to the surface of the water, comparing to Jesus walking on water (2 Kings 6:1-7, Matt. 14:22-33). Manna from heaven in the wilderness journey, as well as Elijah and the miracle of oil and flour not diminishing, which could be compared to Jesus multiplying the fishes and the loaves, albeit twice, and then again upon His resurrection, He called His disciples to cast a net on the other side of the boat and they caught one hundred and fifty three fish (Ex. 16, 1 Kings 17:9-16, Matt. 14:15-21, 14:32-38; John 21:1-11). The raising of the dead, which both Elijah and Jesus did (1 Kings17:17-24, Matt. 9:18, 19, 23-25; John 11:1-45). Nevertheless, this does not excuse a person from believing in Jesus Christ of Nazareth, as the Messiah, the Christ and the only begotten Son of God. But it is possible that some of these men and women for that matter; may have been converted upon His resurrection, like Saul had his calling after persecuting the church, being renamed Paul (Acts 7:58-60, 9:1-30, 13:9). It is hard to know for sure, regardless, we all need to focus on our own salvation first and foremost (Phil. 2:12). And then help others with their own salvation (Matt. 28:19, 20). The miracle Jesus did that arguably no other prophet had done was open the eyes of the blind (Isa. 42:7, John 9:32). Albeit, the prophet, Elisha prayed to God to blind an army with blindness and then he prayed to have them healed after leading them for his purposes (2 Kings 6:18-20). This is two-fold in its message. Jesus not only healed the physical sight of the blind, but He also opens our eyes spiritually to the truth of our life in Him. He also healed a woman who had an issue of blood twelve years and had been treated by many doctors, but none could heal her (Luke 8:43). She believed in Jesus and her faith in

Him healed her (Luke 8:44-48). Sometimes we cannot explain why things happen in life, and this is ok. The Holy Bible says, "…lean not unto thine own understanding." (Prov. 3:5). Mark 5:36 says, "…Be not afraid, only believe.". Jesus Christ of Nazareth is that miraculous healer, and His spirit, the Holy Spirit is working these miracles and greater than these today. Jesus said that it would happen and it has been and will happen (Mark 16:15-18). Not only this, but He said of us, His followers, that we would do greater miracles than He had done during His earthly ministry, but still through Him (John 13:16, 14:12). This truth alone would explain the miraculous world of technology and innovation we live in today. That all being said, the greatest miracle Jesus truly did that no other prophet or man of God has done was forgive us all of our sins, not just one person's sin, but everyone's sins (John 3:16). He did this, a sinless man taking our sins upon Himself on the cross, He died on the cross for the forgiveness of our sins, spilling His Holy and righteous blood, He was buried and the third day He arose to give us the hope and promise of eternal life in His Holy name. Alleluia and praise the LORD. Amen and Amen.

Jesus and the Holy Spirit

Jesus said, "…This is the work of God, that ye believe on him whom he hath sent." (John 6:29). Psalm 66:3-5 says, "Say unto God, How terrible *art thou in* thy works! Through the greatness of thy power shall thine enemies submit themselves unto thee. All the earth shall worship thee, and shall sing unto thee; they shall sing *to* thy name. Selah. Come and see the works of God: *he is* terrible *in his* doing toward the children of men.". As mentioned in the chapter three conclusion, this verse can be put into proper perspective in the light of Jesus Christ of Nazareth, whom has taken all of our sins upon Himself on the cross, and has forgiven us all of our sins. He has suffered the wrath of God for us, He died on the cross, spilling His Holy and righteous blood for us on the cross, He was buried and the third day He arose to give us hope for a future in this world and of eternal life in His Holy name in the world to come. Alleluia and praise the LORD. Amen and Amen. Jesus, the living waters and the woman at the well, "…the hour cometh, and now is, when the true worshippers shall worship the Father in spirit and in truth…" (Isaiah 12:3, John 4:23). The Holy Bible also says that we cannot please God without faith (Heb. 11:6). But this comes from God freely, as Jesus Christ of Nazareth, is the author and finisher of our faith (Eph. 2:8, 9; Heb. 12:2). Alleluia and praise the LORD. Amen and Amen.

The Holy Spirit was poured out on Pentecost in 31 A.D. (Acts 2:1-21). Deuteronomy 30:20 says of God and us, "…he *is* thy life, and the length of thy days…" (Deut. 30:20). Jesus spoke about God, the Father, being in Him, and He, Jesus, being in God, the Father (John 14:11). This describes the nature of God's Holy Spirit, that is, it seems to penetrate, and be a part of all of God's creation, as many religions in this world tend to believe. If we consider that everything is made of some amount of energy, whether it be the dust of the earth, a grain of sand or the sun. And as mentioned above, God's power is great, as well Jesus said of Himself, after His resurrection, "…All power is given unto me in heaven and in earth." (Matt. 28:18). This would explain why He was able to turn water into wine, walk on water, and the like miracles; He had, has, and always will have, all authority over all creation (Rev. 4:11). Alleluia and praise the LORD. The point is that God's Holy Spirit is omnipresent, everywhere. And Jesus desires us to follow Him, and to experience God, the Father, like Jesus did and does (John 15:4). The Old Testament says of God, "But the word *is* very nigh unto thee, in thy mouth, and in thy heart, that thou mayest do it." (Deut. 30:14). Of course Jesus Christ of Nazareth is the "Word of God", it is through Jesus Christ of Nazareth and God, the Father's, Holy Spirit that we live and breathe, as God, the Father, and Jesus Christ of Nazareth are one, through His Holy Spirit (John 1:1-3, 10:30). And He desires us to be one with Him (John 17:11-23). Alleluia and praise the LORD. Amen and Amen.

The Comforter, the Holy Spirit, is Jesus Christ of Nazareth and God, the Father, and is in us as we receive Him by faith in Jesus Christ of Nazareth, God, the Father's, only begotten Son (John 14:16-18). Alleluia and praise the LORD. The apostle, James, said that "…faith without works is dead…" (Jam 2:20). Jesus said, "…This is the work of God, that ye believe on him whom he hath sent." (John 6:29). That is, believe on Jesus Christ of Nazareth. Alleluia and praise the LORD. Amen and Amen. The apostle, Paul, says of God, "For we are his workmanship, created in Christ Jesus unto good works, which God hath before ordained that we should walk in them." (Eph. 2:10). Psalm 68:19 says, "Blessed *be* the Lord, *who* daily loadeth us *with benefits, even* the God of our salvation. Selah.". The point in all of this is that God put us on earth for a purpose, and He shares His authority and responsibilities with us, as He decides. As the Holy Bible says, "…God *is* faithful, who will not suffer you to be tempted above that ye are able; but will with temptation also make a way to escape, that ye may be able to bear *it*." (1 Cor. 10:13). A faithful walk and personal relationship with Jesus Christ of Nazareth, our Saviour, daily, hourly, and all of the time makes it much easier than trying to sort out life ourselves. Prayer, praise, and thanksgiving to God for everything and in all circumstances, is very helpful in this faith journey we all have here on earth. See appendix F for more on this topic of faith. Glory be to God, the Father, Almighty and His only begotten Son, Jesus Christ of Nazareth. Alleluia and praise the LORD. Amen and Amen.

Conclusion

Jesus was and is, and always will be, the only begotten Son of God, conceived of the Holy Spirit, but fully man through His virgin birth in His earthly mother, Mary, espoused to Joseph, her husband (Matt. 1:18). He is the Saviour of this world and all who ever have and ever will live in it. Jesus Christ Immanuel of Nazareth is the only name under heaven whereby we can be saved (Acts 4:12). He lived on this earth 2000 years ago as of the date of writing this book in 2019 A.D.. He died on the cross at Passover in 31 A.D., for the forgiveness of our sins, spilling His Holy and righteous blood on the cross, He was buried and the third day He arose to give us the hope and promise of eternal life in His Holy name. And forty days after first revealing Himself resurrected, He was taken into heaven, being received in a cloud and He currently sits at the right hand of the Father, God, in heaven until all His enemies are made His footstool (Acts 1:1-9). And He poured out His Holy Spirit on Pentecost in 31 A.D., to dwell with us and in us forever (Acts 2:1-21). Jesus will be with us in Spirit unto the end, for all those who believe, and will resurrect those whom put their faith and trust in Him at the last day, to everlasting life with Him and Almighty God, the Father, forever (Matt. 28:20). Alleluia and praise the LORD. Amen and Amen. Jesus came to make us free (John 8:32, 14:6). Jesus explained the law in simple terms so that anyone could understand and follow it. He simply said, "Therefore all things whatsoever ye would that men should do to you, do ye even so to them: for this is the law and the prophets." (Matt. 7:12). See appendix F for more information on the "Golden Rule". Jesus came for the lost sheep of Israel, He is the "Great Shepherd" of Israel, and has other sheep not of this fold (Matt. 15:24, John 10:1-16, Heb. 13:20, 21). Jesus suffered and died on the cross for all of mankind, for the forgiveness of our sins, He spilt His Holy and righteous blood for us on the cross, He was buried and He arose the third day to give us all the hope and promise of eternal life in God, the Father's, eternal kingdom. Alleluia and praise the LORD. Amen and Amen.

Regarding the "great tribulation" mentioned at the beginning of this chapter's introduction, in other places in my writing, and in the Holy Bible of God. We must remember that Jesus Christ of Nazareth took the sins of all of mankind upon Himself on the cross; this is that hope and promise of Salvation, preservation and protection we have in the name of Jesus Christ of Nazareth, by His Holy and righteous blood spilt on the cross for the forgiveness of our sins. He died and He was buried and the third day He arose giving us the hope and promise of eternal life in His Holy name. Alleluia and praise the LORD. Amen and Amen. One of the signs of the "great tribulation" is that the sun will be darkened (Matt. 24:29). Well this happened at Jesus' crucifixion, as mentioned in chapter two (Luke 23:45). The point in mentioning this and other prophecies regarding the "great tribulation" and associating them with Jesus Christ of Nazareth's ministry in the first century A.D., is to know that Jesus Christ of Nazareth took the "wrath" of God upon Himself on that cross for all of us at Passover in 31 A.D. (Rom. 5:8-11). The entire purpose of Jesus' life and ministry is to save us from the wrath of God, which we deserve because of our sinful rebellion against Him and His commandments, starting with our fore parents, Adam and Eve in the Garden of Eden (Gen. 3, Rom. 5:8-11). In return, He freely gives us the hope and promise of eternal life in God's everlasting kingdom, and life more abundantly here on earth now (Matt. 10:8, John 10:10). Alleluia and praise the LORD. Amen and Amen. All we need to do is believe, and this is a gift from God, not by our own works, it is by God's grace that we are saved, so that no man can boast (Eph. 2:8, 9). So, regardless of trials in this world, a "great tribulation" or our own personal life trials; God knows them all, and He is with us in them all (Matt. 28:20, John 14:16-18). He loves us and desires us to turn to Him and trust in Him, in repentance, asking

Him for forgiveness of our sins and receiving His forgiveness by faith freely given to those whom will receive it. Do you believe that Jesus Christ of Nazareth died for you on that cross at Passover in 31 A.D., and spilt His Holy and righteous blood for you, forgiving you of your sins, He being buried and He arising the third day to give us the hope and promise of eternal life in His Holy name? If so, praise God, the Father, and give Him thanks, in the name of His only begotten Son, Jesus Christ of Nazareth. Alleluia and praise the LORD. Amen and Amen. And He has given each of us, of His Spirit, that is His Holy Spirit, to dwell in us and with us forever (1 John 4:13). Alleluia and praise the LORD. Amen and Amen.

Discussion: Miracles

"And it shall come to pass afterward, that I will pour out my spirit upon all flesh; and your sons and your daughters shall prophesy, your old men shall dream dreams, your young men shall see visions: And also upon the servants and upon the handmaids in those days will I pour out my spirit."
- Joel 2:28, 29

This was confirmed to have taken place at Pentecost in 31 A.D., but may very well have a greater fulfillment in the "Messianic Age". That being said, we can experience this "outpouring" of the Holy Spirit today, as we accept Jesus Christ of Nazareth as our Saviour and Redeemer. It is by His blood that we are healed. Jesus did wonderful miracles before God's miracle through Him on the cross. He multiplied fishes and loaves, He walked on water, He prophesied, and He healed the sick (Matt. 14:15-21, 22-33; 15:32-38; Mark 13, Luke 4:40). One of the notable miracles was that He healed the sight of the blind, which was a true sign of whom He is (John 9). This was a sign of what He has, is and will continue to do physically and spiritually to this world. He admonishes us to, "…anoint thine eyes with eye salve…" (Rev. 3:18). Jesus came to heal us from our blindness, which came through ours and our forefathers' sins, first in Adam and Eve (Rom. 5:14). He has come to show us that we were created to be like Him, sons and daughters of God, children of God, the Father, Almighty. We did not come from some evolutionary chain, or another planet, etc. (John 1:12, 13). We came from God, the Father, Almighty, through His Holy Spirit, in Christ Jesus of Nazareth's Holy name. Alleluia and praise the LORD. Amen and Amen.

Discussion Questions

1. Is Jesus really the only begotten Son of God?

   _____

   _____

_____

_____

_____

2. Where do we come from according to the Bible?

    _____

    _____

    _____

    _____

    _____

3. How can we become, children of God, born of His Holy Spirit?

    _____

    _____

    _____

    _____

    _____

CHAPTER 7

Summaries and Conclusion

"But the word is very nigh unto thee, in thy mouth,
and in thy heart, that thou mayest do it."
- DEUTERONOMY 30:14

Introduction

This book was admittedly written with the desire to reach out to the "Jews" of this world, as well as the whole world. God has His chosen people, Israel, and the tribe of Judah in particular, through whom our Saviour came to us. But now we live in a time, as Jesus said, that we ought to worship our Creator "...in spirit and in truth." (John 4:24). This is the key to understanding and having a relationship with the true Potter. We are the clay; God is the true Potter (Isa. 64:8). It may seem at times that the molding and the fiery furnace of trials may be more than we can handle, but our Master Potter knows what is required to turn us into a fine piece of pottery, by the working of His Holy Spirit in us, through us and amongst us. This chapter has the general summaries and conclusions from each chapter and a final word for the book as a whole. As I have mentioned throughout this book and in my other writings, a relationship with your Creator starts first and foremost with accepting His Holy Spirit, repenting of our sins, giving our life and burdens over to Jesus Christ of Nazareth for the forgiveness of our sins and following Him. Praying, reading God's written Word, thanksgiving, praise and fellowship with other believers are all great ways of developing, redeveloping and/or maintaining our relationship with God, the Father, Almighty, and Jesus Christ of Nazareth, God's only begotten Son, through His Holy Spirit, here on earth and with others forever more. Alleluia and praise the LORD. Amen and Amen.

Chapter One Summary

Chapter one was an introduction to Jesus Christ of Nazareth, as fulfilment of the prophecies of the Old Testament. The chapter also spoke about Jesus' ancestry according to New Testament accounts, and in comparison to Old Testament genealogical records. And the chapter went into greater detail of Jesus fulfilling the role of a true Prophet, as well as our Saviour (Deut. 18:15, John 7:40). Alleluia and praise the LORD. Amen and Amen.

Chapter Two Summary

Chapter two spoke about how Jesus was prophesied of in the prophecies of the tribe of Judah, as Jesus was a physical descendant of the tribe of Judah, from His mother, Mary (Gen. 49:8-12, Deut. 33:7, Luke 3:23-38, Rev. 5:5). The chapter also spoke about Jesus' prophetic fulfilment in the Hebrew annual Holydays, namely in Passover, and in the wilderness experience, that the Israelites experienced for forty years, and Jesus experienced a trial of forty days in the wilderness after His baptism in later 27 A.D., just prior to His three and a half year earthly ministry, before His crucifixion at Passover in 31 A.D. (Lev. 23:5, Num. 14:33, Matt. 4:1-11, 26:2). Jesus is and was the eternal Passover lamb, whom died on the cross for the forgiveness of our sins, at Passover in 31 A.D., shedding His Holy and righteous blood, He was buried and the third day He arose to give us the hope and promise of eternal life in His Holy name. Alleluia and praise the LORD. Amen and Amen.

Chapter Three Summary

Chapter three speaks of the two or three witnesses required to establish a matter (Deut. 19:15, Matt. 18:16). And in this case, it is the witnesses of Moses, King David, and the other prophets, that have prophesied of Jesus Christ of Nazareth, as the true Messiah, and Saviour of the whole world. Alleluia and praise the LORD. Amen and Amen.

Chapter Four Summary

Chapter four was about the "key of David", and that relationship we can all have with our Creator, through His only begotten Son, Jesus Christ of Nazareth (Isa. 22:22, Rev. 3:7). Although, King David was not perfect, His descendant, Jesus Christ of Nazareth, conceived by the Holy Spirit in and born to the virgin, Mary, espoused to Joseph, also of the tribe of Judah, was and is perfect (Matt. 1, Rev. 5:5). Jesus is the root and the offspring of David (Rev. 22:16). This chapter also spoke of Jesus' relationship with Jerusalem, and the prophecies of the Bible, that even Jesus prophesied of regarding the city, including the "Great Tribulation", and the "Messianic Age", that may still be yet to come, as of the date of writing this book in 2019 A.D. (Matt. 24, Rev. 20:4, 6). Chapter four also spoke about the New Covenant, Jesus Christ of Nazareth, came to make with us. That is He suffered and died on the cross for the forgiveness of our sins, spilling His Holy and righteous blood on the cross, He was buried and the third day He arose to give us the hope and promise of eternal life in His Holy name. Alleluia and praise the LORD. Amen and Amen.

Chapter Five Summary

Chapter five spoke about Jesus' and the physical temple in Jerusalem, His earthly body as the temple of God, and the Body of Christ, that is, Jesus and the people of His Church, the Church of God. Nehemiah 8:3 says of Ezra and the people, "And he read therein before the street that was before the water gate from the morning until midday, before the men and the women, and those that could understand; and the ears of all the people were attentive unto the book of the law.". This says that Ezra read to both men, women and also to any others that could understand, possibly the younger generation, as Jesus says to suffer the little children to come to Him, "…for of such is the kingdom of heaven." (Matt. 19:14). The point here is that when the "Body of Christ" comes together, we are not called to separate ourselves based on gender at the least, and any whom can understand ought to be allowed to listen to God's Word. That is, God is no respecter of persons (Acts 10:34). Alleluia and praise the LORD. Amen and Amen.

Chapter Six Summary

The reason why Jesus was not likely recognized as Messiah by some religious authorities and laymen at the time of His earthly ministry and even today is because of the curses that came upon Israel, by God, because of their disobedience (Deut. 28:28, 29). Daniel 9:7 and 8 say, "O Lord, righteousness *belongeth* unto thee, but unto us confusion of faces…". Also, blindness in part has happened to Israel, spoken of by the apostle, Paul, in order to bring into the Church of God, the fullness of the gentile believers (Rom. 11:25). This is likely the same reason, this world and the lost sheep of Israel have not fully accepted Jesus Christ of Nazareth as the true Messiah and Saviour of the whole world completely yet, as of the date of writing this book in 2019 A.D. (John 10:15, 16). But this does not have to be you. Jesus Christ of Nazareth indeed is the Messiah and Saviour of us all. To God be the Glory in Jesus Christ of Nazareth's Holy name. Repent and believe on the gospel of Jesus Christ of Nazareth and the Kingdom of God, the Father, Almighty, here on earth and in heaven above forever more, through His Holy Spirit. Alleluia and praise the Lord. Amen and Amen.

Conclusion

Jesus Christ of Nazareth was before the world began (John 17:5, 24). God made us in His image, He said, "…Let us make man in our image, after our likeness…" (Gen. 1:26). Jesus Christ of Nazareth, whom was before the world began, came into this world, conceived by the Holy Ghost in the virgin, Mary, espoused to Joseph (Matt. 1:18-25, John 1:1-3). He was born of the virgin, Mary, espoused to Joseph and raised up as a child of Israel, with brothers and sisters (Matt. 1:18-25, Luke 2:41-52). Micah 5:1 and 2 say, "…they shall smite the judge of Israel with a rod upon the cheek. But thou, Bethlehem Ephratah, *though* thou be little among the thousands of Judah, *yet* out of thee shall he come forth unto me *that is* to be ruler in Israel; whose goings forth *have been* from of old, from everlasting.". John confirms these claims at the beginning of his gospel writing. John 1:1-3 says, "In the beginning was the Word, and the Word was with God, and the Word was God. The same was in the beginning with God. All things were made by him; and without him was not any thing made that was made.".

Malachi speaks of the "…Sun of righteousness…" (Mal. 4:2). The apostle, Peter, speaks of the "…day star…" arising in our hearts (2 Pet. 1:19). And the book of Revelation calls Jesus, the "…morning star…" (Rev. 22:16). Jesus Christ of Nazareth with God, the Father, created the sun and the moon and the stars in the beginning (Gen. 1:14-19). Before there was the sun, there was light, and before there was light, God's Holy Spirit moved on the face of the deep (Gen. 1:2-5, 14-19). Jesus Christ of Nazareth was before all other creation with God, the Father, in the beginning (Rev. 1:8, 3:14, 21:6, 22:13). All of this creation is a sign and ultimately points to the LORD, whom is greater than all of His creation. Alleluia and praise the LORD. Amen and Amen. The point is, we are not to worship creation, but to understand God is living in all of us, through His Holy Spirit. That is, we ought to worship the Creator, God, the Father, in the name of His only begotten Son, Jesus Christ of Nazareth, through His Holy Spirit. Alleluia and praise the LORD. Amen and Amen.

In Jesus Christ of Nazareth we are no longer debtors to the flesh (Rom. 8:12). We have been crucified with Christ Jesus of Nazareth unto death, but have also been raised with Him unto eternal life (Romans 6:20-23, Col. 2:10-12). If we live in the Spirit, the Holy Spirit of God, we are the children of God (Rom. 8:13-17). It is no longer this world and its sinful ways that have dominion over us, but Christ Jesus of Nazareth, the living begotten Son of God, Saviour of the whole world, and Redeemer of all of mankind (Rom. 6:9, 14). If we believe and accept the free gift of eternal life in the life saving blood of Jesus Christ of Nazareth, the only begotten Son of God; God, the Father, has redeemed us from the sins of our flesh, and the fallen nature of this world by the blood of Jesus Christ of Nazareth (Eph. 2:8, 9). Alleluia and praise the LORD. Amen and Amen. And last, we must remember, that Jesus came to forgive us our sins, He died on the cross at Passover in 31 A.D., shedding His Holy and righteous blood, He was buried and arose the third day to give us the hope and promise of eternal life in His Holy name. Alleluia and praise the LORD. Amen and Amen.

Discussion: The Word of God

"...greater is he that is in you, than he that is in the world."
- 1 John 4:4

The reality is Jesus Christ of Nazareth has given us a gift of freedom in His Holy name. He did not come to give us a yoke or burden greater than what we already have, but He came to give us a light yoke (Matt. 11:29, 30). As He says of Himself, "Come unto me, all *ye* that labour and are heavy laden, and I will give you rest. Take my yoke upon you, and learn of me; for I am meek and lowly in heart: and ye shall find rest unto your souls. For my yoke *is* easy, and my burden is light." (Matt. 11:28-30). He did not come to condemn, judge or give us heavier burdens, but to lighten the load of sin we have accumulated from our natural birth into a sinful world (John 1:29). He has given us the Holy Spirit, a promissory note of sort, for eternal life in Jesus Christ of Nazareth's Holy name (Gal. 3:14). We have received God's Holy Spirit unto eternal life in the name of Jesus Christ of Nazareth, God's only begotten Son. Praise the LORD God, the Father, Almighty and His only begotten Son, Jesus Christ of Nazareth. Alleluia and praise the LORD. Amen and Amen. When reading through this chapters discussion question, consider what this "new life", means for you. How do you move forward with God, the Father, Almighty, His only begotten Son, Jesus Christ of Nazareth, and His Holy Spirit, and with others here on earth? Alleluia and praise the LORD. Amen and Amen.

Discussion Question

1. How can you and I move forward in our relationship with God, the Father, Almighty through His only begotten Son, Jesus Christ of Nazareth, with His Holy Spirit and others here on earth?

   _____

   _____

   _____

   _____

   _____

AFTERWORD

To attempt to speak about all that Jesus has done in this world; would seem to be a nearly impossible task. The apostle, John, wrote in the gospel according to John, "And there are also many other things which Jesus did, the which, if they should be written every one, I suppose that even the world itself could not contain the books that should be written. Amen." (John 21:25). So this book in general is my own attempt to reason through the Scriptures both Old and New Testament about how they speak of Jesus Christ of Nazareth. No doubt there are infinite ways in which Jesus Christ of Nazareth, God, the Father, and the Holy Spirit could be understood, as the Holy Bible says, God's "…understanding *is* infinite." (Ps. 147:5). But as Jesus said, "Enter ye in at the strait gate: for wide *is* the gate, and broad *is* the way, that leadeth to destruction, and many there be which go in thereat: Because strait *is* the gate, and narrow *is* the way, which leadeth unto life, and few there be that find it." (Matt. 7:13, 14). Alleluia and praise the LORD. Amen and Amen.

Some influence of the latter stages of writing this book have come through the writings of Uri Yosef, a well-educated man, born in Israel, according to the website reference, http://thejewishhome.org/counter-index.html, retrieved 16/09/2018. His writings seem to attempt to deride "Christian Missionaries" attempts to use Old Testament references to prove Jesus Christ of Nazareth's Messianic fulfilment. But he does seem to admit Jesus, "at best", is a spiritual Son of God, as we also have the opportunity to be, through His Holy Spirit (Matt. 1:18-25, John 1:12-14). I will say, in his defence, that he provokes the question of how is Jesus' Messianic fulfilment relevant to us today? This brings the gospel message to the present, and how it needs to be relevant today. He also speaks about the understanding of the "Messianic Era", as I have referred to, as the "Messianic Age" in my writing, as being part of what is written regarding the Messianic prophecies spoken of in the Old Testament. Although many of his claims are that "Christian" use of Old Testament proofs of Jesus' authenticity as Messiah, are not relevant because many of the verses used are speaking of Old Testament historical events, which in part is true, I believe they still have prophetic significance, as God does not change (Amos 3:6). Also, God's understanding is infinite, as mentioned above (Ps. 147:5). The Holy Bible also says, "…Cursed be the man that trusteth in man…" (Jer. 17:5). That is why I have said in my writings, not to trust in my own understanding, or anyone else's for that matter, but to "Prove all things; hold fast that which is good." (1 Thess. 5:21).

The fruit of the Holy Spirit is "…love, joy, peace, longsuffering, gentleness, goodness, faith, Meekness, temperance: against such there is no law." (Gal. 5:22, 23). One of the fruits, temperance, seems to have a root meaning of, self-control, Strong's number 1466 (Gal. 5:23). This is where Jesus says, "…the truth shall make you free." (John 8:32). The reality is that we do all indeed have freedom in God, the Father, and Jesus Christ of Nazareth, His only begotten Son, through His Holy Spirit, given to us (Matt. 10:8). Because Jesus Christ of Nazareth did indeed die on the cross for the forgiveness of our sins, He was buried and the third day He arose to give us the hope and promise of eternal life in His Holy name. Alleluia and praise the LORD. Amen and Amen.

God, the Father's, only begotten Son, Jesus Christ of Nazareth, is the only way to eternal salvation (John 1:14). There is no other name under heaven whereby we can be saved (Acts 4:12). And God has given us the freedom to choose what we believe (Matt. 10:8). Mr. Yosef may also have had some spiritual blindness, at least in His writings, of when Jesus was crucified, amongst some other details of Jesus' life. It is my understanding that Jesus Christ of Nazareth was crucified on a Wednesday, in 31 A.D., at Passover, as I have mentioned the like subject briefly in this book, and in some of my other writing and I will go into greater detail of this proof and other ideas like it in my seventh book. Again, the Scriptures say that we have been and are blind for various reasons, namely because of our sins and for God's greater purposes of bringing the "gentiles" into the simple understanding of Salvation in God's only begotten Son, Jesus Christ of Nazareth, before the "Messianic age", the final one thousand years here on this present earth's history, and before the "New Heavens and a New Earth" come, spoken of in the Holy Bible, and as I have spoken of in my other writing, and will mention again in my seventh book (Deut. 28:28, 29; Isa. 65:17, Ezek. 40-48, Rom. 11:25, 2 Pet. 3:13, Rev. 20:4, 6; 21:1). Whatever the truth of all of these things, let them be to the glory of God, the Father, in the name of His only begotten Son, Jesus Christ of Nazareth. Alleluia and praise the LORD. Amen and Amen.

APPENDICES

APPENDIX A

MESSIAH

Introduction

In early 2013, after being released from imprisonment in late 2012 A.D., I was given the opportunity to volunteer at a small newly opened local museum, dedicated to military history during the 20th century mostly, and some domestic history in general during that time. One day when I was working at one end of the museum hall corridor, which was an old armoury from the first world war, I saw a figure at the opposite end about fifty feet away, near the front entrance. He was walking sort of from one side of the front lobby area to the other. I say sort of, because He appeared as flames like. He had a robe sort of draped to the ground, and He had long hair, and He appeared to be a man in His early thirties about. I would say if this was true what I saw, it could have been none other than Jesus Christ of Nazareth. The Holy Bible does describe Him in many places with the attributes of fire, in His eyes, feet, face, etc. (Matt. 17:2, Rev. 2:18, 10:1, 19:12, 22:16). So if this was a manifestation of Jesus Christ of Nazareth, which I am inclined to believe that it was, this was indeed confirmation that Jesus Christ is alive, if I ever needed any more proof. Just like "doubting" Thomas had the opportunity to feel Jesus' wounds, so that seeing, he would believe (John 20:24-29). Jesus Christ of Nazareth, and God, the Father, Almighty are no respecter of persons, so He will reveal Himself to you, and I as often and in whatever fashion needed to give us the hope and assurance that He is indeed alive and well (Acts 10:34, 35). Alleluia and praise the LORD. Amen and Amen. This is the good news we have in Jesus Christ of Nazareth, that we serve a living God, whom created all of us, and all things, and has a purpose for each and every one of us, here on earth and in eternity, life everlasting (Jer. 29:11, Rev. 4:11). Alleluia and praise the LORD. Amen and Amen. Nevertheless, the remainder of this appendix is about the Messiah, Jesus Christ of Nazareth, speaking of some prophecies of Him in comparison to things that have been, are and are yet to come. So if you are interested in learning a little more about Jesus Christ of Nazareth, and the possibilities of how He has and will continue to fulfill the historic, present, and prophetic Scriptures of the Holy Bible of God, read on to learn more. To God be the glory in the truth of all of these things. Alleluia and praise the LORD. Amen and Amen.

Can there be more than one?

Messiah, in the Hebrew means "anointed", the word is used in many places in the Old Testament to refer to the anointed priests, kings and prophets, including King Saul and King David (Lev. 4:3, 1 Sam. 2:10, 24:6; 2 Sam. 22:51). Also, the elect, saints and anointed of God, maybe considered "gods", better put children of God (Ps. 82:6). But they are not the Messiah, Saviour of the whole world, Emmanuel, God with us (Isa. 45:21). Jesus Christ of Nazareth has this title and He will keep it forever (Isa. 7:14, Matt. 1:23)! There are multiple and likely tens of thousands of anointed since the beginning of this world (Rev. 7, 14). But there is only one, Jesus Christ of Nazareth, there is only one Saviour of all of mankind, there is only one begotten Son of God, conceived by the Holy Spirit, in the womb of the virgin, Mary, whom shed His Holy and righteous blood and died on the cross for the forgiveness of our sins, He was buried and He arose three days later to give us the hope and promise of eternal life in His Holy name. Alleluia and praise the LORD. Amen and Amen. If we miss this one point and wait for some other "anointed" to come, we are only fooling ourselves. It is God who saves in Jesus Christ of Nazareth's Holy name, God's only begotten Son, He came in the flesh, and with God and in God in the Holy Spirit (John 14:10-12). The Bible suggests that Jesus was with God and is God from the beginning, there are multiple places in the Bible that show a conversation going on between God and Himself, using "us" and "we" (Gen. 1:26, Isa 41:22-26, 43:9; John 1:1-3, 14). So Jesus and God are either two separate, but Holy Spirit related lives, or He has someone else with Him in the clouds He speaks to about us! No matter the case of this "mystery" of God's relationship with us and Jesus Christ of Nazareth through the Holy Spirit, Jesus is indeed the Messiah and Saviour of all of mankind. Alleluia and praise the LORD. Amen and Amen.

The main two witnesses of life, truth, and everlasting life, no doubt, are God, the Father, and Jesus Christ of Nazareth, His only begotten Son, two men (John 8:17, 18). The book of Revelation speaks of two witnesses prophesying during a three and a half year period, during the great tribulation (Rev. 11:3). This could very literally be two people to come, but also I have heard a few other interpretations, that it is, Jesus and the Church or Elijah and Moses, or some other similar ideas (John 17:22, 23; 1 Cor. 12:27). The truth of the matter is, it could be literal, and still to come, or it could be figurative, as much of the book of Revelation can be interpreted as a parable or similitudes, as I have interpreted much of it in a few of the books I have written (Hos. 12:10). But there also seems to be some literal interpretation to the entire Holy Bible of God. Nevertheless, let us look at these two witnesses from Jesus and the Church's perspective, namely at His crucifixion, during His burial, at His resurrection and then His revealing of His resurrected body to His disciples in 31 A.D.. If He was crucified on a Wednesday morning and died at the 9th hour about 3 p.m. that afternoon, buried that late afternoon, and resurrected three days later on Saturday afternoon, that would be three days, but the disciples did not see Him resurrected until Sunday morning, so that would be three and a half days (Matt. 12:40, 28:1).[6] The same amount of time the two witnesses are said to be laying in the streets dead, spiritually called Sodom and Egypt, where also our Lord was crucified (Rev. 11:8). From this perspective, we could interpret it as the Church laying "dead" spiritually, in the street, that is walking aimlessly without their Messiah during this time (Mark 16:10, 11; Luke 24:11). This can be seen when Jesus visited two men literally walking in the street, lamenting the death of Jesus (Luke 24:13-27). In my book "Time, Times and a Dividing of Time – What did John really see?", regarding the Great Tribulation, I wrote it as if I was one of these two witnesses, I must confess, writing from the perspective of somebody whom would have to endure the "great tribulation" (Matt. 24:21). And it could be true that I am a witness, but the reality is in Christ, and even the apostle, Paul, speaks of us being surrounded by a great cloud of witnesses, and other parts of the Holy Bible mention anyone who testifies of Jesus Christ of Nazareth and His promise for us of eternal life, as being a witness of His (John 15:26, 27; Heb. 12:1). Again though, I will leave it up to you to decide what you believe about these things. To God be the glory in the truth of all these things. Alleluia and praise the LORD. Amen and Amen.

Last, there is a section of this prophecy as mentioned in chapter four, "…to anoint the most Holy.", that may include in this, the saints (Dan. 9:24). As Jesus Christ of Nazareth is the head of the Church; and the Church, even of the saints, is His body (1 Cor. 14:33). If the saints are the same as the 144 000, then God has a plan to "anoint" and resurrect all of His saints, at the beginning of the "Messianic age" (Rev. 20:4). Why this is important to understand is that, the other reason, why people may not believe that Jesus is the Christ, is that His "saintly" body, the church of saints, may not be completely finished yet (Eph. 1:15-23). This is likely the key, to understanding the challenge of why some people have not accepted Jesus Christ of Nazareth as the unmistakable Messiah yet, as of the date of writing this book in 2019 A.D.. They are either knowingly or ignorantly waiting for the remainder of prophecy to be fulfilled regarding His body of the church, in His saints (1 Cor. 6:2). Once all of the saints have been perfected through their birth, growth, testimony; and then death, either naturally or martyred and finally spiritually resurrected, then the Scriptures may be fulfilled regarding "…to anoint the most Holy." (Dan. 9:24). To understand what I am explaining in this paragraph takes Spiritual discernment, but if you ask God, He will reveal the truth to you (1 Cor. 2:12-16). This is not to ignore the millions and billions of faithful followers of Christ whom are a part of the Church, here on earth and will receive their resurrection promise as well, likely at the final resurrection of all of mankind (Rev. 20:11-15). But the Holy Bible of God does seem to indicate some separation between the "saints" and the "people of the saints", the "elect" and the "great multitude", etc. (Rev. 20:4-6). In the end whatever the truth of this matter, the result is that we are called to be one body in Christ Jesus of Nazareth's Holy name, with Him as the Head of all things (Eph. 4:15, 16). As the apostle, Paul, says, "Now therefore ye are no more strangers and foreigners, but fellowcitizens with the saints, and of the

[6] http://www.wrcog.net/biblelight_crucifixion2.html, retrieved 18/03/2022

household of God…" (Eph. 2:19). The saints may have a "special" reward in this life and the resurrection, but ultimately eternity is everlasting, and God is not a respecter of persons, so we will all likely receive the same or similar opportunities that the saints of this time have, in the "…new heavens and a new earth…" (Acts 10:34, 35; 2 Pet. 3:13). No matter, the reality is in Christ Jesus of Nazareth; He shed His righteous and holy blood and died on the cross for the forgiveness of our sins, He was buried and He arose the third day to give us the hope and promise of eternal life in His Holy name. Alleluia and praise the LORD. Amen and Amen.

Christ, Messiah and Daniel's prophecy

This 70 week prophecy of Daniel, where the Messiah is cut off in the middle of the week, likely includes the temple and walls being rebuilt in Ezra and Nehemiah's time, Jesus' physical ministry, possibly the destruction of the temple in 70 A.D. and finally the "Great Tribulation", just prior to the "Messianic Age" (Ezra, Neh., Dan. 9:25-27, John 2:19, Matt. 24:21, Rev. 2:22, 7:14). The first part of this prophesy, the sixty nine weeks, was likely fulfilled in and around Daniel's time when King Cyrus commanded that the Israelites return to Jerusalem and build the temple (2 Chr. 36:22, 23; Ezra 1:1, 2; Dan. 9:25). As well as this, Nehemiah built the walls of Jerusalem in "…troublous times.", under King Artaxerxes, which was prophesied by Daniel (Neh. 4:8, 16-18; 6:15, Dan. 9:25). All of this took place in and around 500-400 B.C., 483 years or 69 weeks before Christ started His three and a half year earthly ministry, based on the day for a year principle (Dan. 9:25; Ezek. 4:6). Depending on the person, you could take it from the time of Jesus Christ of Nazareth's birth, likely in September 4 B.C., or the time of the beginning of His ministry in the fall of 27 A.D.. Although secular history books and online references do record these historical facts, the dates are not all exactly the same, 457 B.C. seems to be the date that works for the decree of Artaxerxes, http://dedication. www3.50megs.com/457.html, retrieved 17/08/2018. A letter was sent to Artaxerxes early in his reign, that the Jews were rebuilding the wall (Ezra 4). But the successive kings, first Cyrus, then Darius, and finally Artaxerxes, seem to be mentioned in the involvement of building the temple, supplying the temple and building the walls of Jerusalem (Ezra 6:14). These kings reigned from at least approximately 486 to at least 445 B.C., so based on Scripture, and with some faith, I would say, that this interpretation and these dates are a good approximation for the prophecy (2 Chr. 36:22, 23; Ezra 6:15, Neh. 5:14). See appendix E for a proposed timeline of the Daniel prophecy of seventy weeks with milestone events noted (Dan. 9). Nevertheless, only God knows for sure the certainty of the interpretation of prophecy, as the Bible says, "…no prophecy of the scripture is of any private interpretation." (2 Pet. 1:20). And the testimony of Jesus is the spirit of prophecy (Rev. 19:10). So Jesus Christ of Nazareth must be mentioned in spirit and in truth when someone is prophesying, otherwise the prophecy may be in doubt to say the least (John 4:23). Alleluia and praise the LORD.

The second part of this prophecy that has been interpreted in two separate ways, that of Daniel's prophecy of the Messiah being "…cut off…", and "…in the midst of the week he shall cause the sacrifice and the oblation to cease…" (Dan. 9:26, 27). Jesus did cause the "sacrifice" and the "oblation" to cease by offering up His own sinless body on the cross for the forgiveness of our sins at Passover in 31 A.D. (Heb. 4:15, 7:27). Daniel 9 is the only place that I know of, that the term "Messiah" is used in the Old Testament, at least of the King James Version of the Holy Bible, although in the Hebrew, originally it is used in many places, where it says "anointed", referring to the Levitical priests in many cases and the Kings of Israel and Judah (Lev. 4:5, 1 Sam. 24:6, 2 Sam. 22:51). Some have said that this is related to a seven year tribulation period with the "beast" or "antichrist" breaking some sort of peace contract in the middle of the seven year period, starting the final "Armageddon" like war spoken of throughout the Holy Bible, namely in the book of Revelation (Rev. 16:16). Although this prophecy is likely associated with the "Great Tribulation", as the Bible calls it, including the "…day of the Lord…", or "…year of recompenses…", the prophecy was likely at least half fulfilled during Jesus' earthly ministry (Isa. 2:12, 34:8; Matt. 24:21). Jesus was "…cut off…" from His ministry three and a half years into it, a sinless man taking on our sins, and dying on the cross for the forgiveness of our sins (Dan. 9:26). Not only that, but He was literally crucified in the middle of the week, Wednesday morning at about 9 a.m. dying on the cross that afternoon at 3 p.m. during Passover in 31 A.D., He was buried and He arose the third day for our hope and promise of eternal life in His Holy name. At least two references suggest that the 6th hour John was speaking about regarding the time just prior to Jesus' crucifixion was a Roman time keeping method, equivalent to 6 a.m. (John 19:14). This would then help agree with Mark's account of a third hour crucifixion according to the Hebrew time keeping method of 6 a.m. starting the day, therefore 9 a.m. being the crucifixion time (Mark 15:25, 33-37). See the following reference for more details on the discussion; https://www.apologeticspress. org/apcontent.aspx?category=6&article=4759, retrieved 16/07/2018. Although this was also prophesied to take place, the other part of the interpretation is that, this final three and a half year "Great Tribulation", is the continuation of Jesus' ministry in spirit form no doubt, on disobedient mankind and ultimately Satan (Rev. 2:22, 7:14). After that, as is written in the Holy Bible, and I have written about in other books, a final earthquake will take place with a crack forming in the earth near the temple mount, and will issue out "living waters", representing Jesus' presence and fulfillment of these prophecies, God willing (Zech. 13:1, 14:4-8). Aside from this, there is only one Jesus Christ of Nazareth, Saviour of the entire world (Acts 4:12). Jesus Christ is the first fruits of the saints (1 Cor. 15:20). All of the people of God have received the "anointing" in Jesus Christ of Nazareth's Holy name (Rev. 1:4-6). In the end, we can have "rulers" over us, and they may even be considered "anointed" to their position, but there is only One, Jesus Christ of Nazareth, the only begotten Son of God, King of Israel and the whole earth. Creator of all things and the Word become flesh. Alleluia and praise the LORD. Amen and Amen.

It is no wonder that some do not believe that Jesus Christ of Nazareth is the Messiah, as this prophecy if interpreted correctly may not be completely fulfilled yet, as of the date of writing this book in 2019 A.D. (Ezek. 39:25-29, Rom. 11:25). That would include "...to anoint the Most Holy.", that is Jesus Christ of Nazareth and God, the Father, Almighty, in the Holy Spirit, through the body of His Church (Dan. 9:24). This is in no doubt part of the reason why some "Jews" may not believe that Jesus is the Messiah, at least in full yet; this is also likely the reason why all on earth do not whole heartedly follow Jesus, the Messiah of God, yet, as of the date of writing this book in 2019 A.D. (Rev. 17:17). This does not however mean that we as individuals cannot have a relationship with Jesus Christ of Nazareth, as the Messiah, and anointed of God, it only means that some of the prophecies of Christ, through the body of His Church, may not be completely fulfilled yet. The fact of the matter is Jesus is eternal, and His physical life here on earth, although only for a time, was not His entire life. Jesus lives, and the prophecy of Him and His faithful followers will continue to be fulfilled unto the ends of the earth (Matt. 5:18, Rev. 14:6, 7). Jesus did say, "Think not that I am come to destroy the law, or the prophets: I am not come to destroy, but to fulfil." (Matt. 5:17). And He and other witnesses testified to Him being the Messiah (John 1:41, 4:25, 26). So there is no doubt in my mind that He will fulfill this prophecy of the Messiah in Daniel 9:24-27, if for some reason He has not completely fulfilled it yet. He was already witnessed to be resurrected and came to His disciples and said about Himself, "...All power is given unto me in heaven and in earth." (Matt. 28:18). Even on the cross He said, "...It is finished..." (John 19:30). Meaning, He has done the work God sent Him to do, teaching the gospel message of the kingdom of God and repentance for the forgiveness of our sins, through belief in Him, Jesus Christ of Nazareth (John 6:29). He has already died on the cross for the forgiveness of our sins, taking our sins upon Himself as a sinless man, shedding His righteous and holy blood for us, He was buried and He arose the third day to give us all the hope and promise of eternal life in His Holy name. Alleluia and praise the LORD. So what are we really waiting for? Should we wait for some heavenly sign or earthly sign that Jesus is indeed the Messiah? If this is required by some, I have no doubt God will give it. But the signs that are to come, especially the "Great Tribulation", may not necessarily be the best time to start a relationship with your Creator, through Jesus Christ of Nazareth (Matt. 24, Mark 13, Luke 21, Rev. 6-19). If you are in doubt of this prophecy and its relationship with Jesus Christ, ask God Almighty for yourself. Do not put your trust in my interpretation; put your trust in God Almighty and the Holy Spirit, through Jesus Christ of Nazareth. Alleluia and Praise the LORD. Amen and Amen.

Messianic Age

In general, some have suggested that we are heading for a time of relative peace, where the Holy Spirit of God and general rest from war and evils of all kind will be the norm (Isa. 2:4, Mic. 4:3, Rev. 20:2). I have written a book about this time, called "The Day Star and Us". But one particular interpretation that seems to be up for discussion is how Jesus is going to manifest Himself during this time if it is literal. I had said in the book that there are many Scriptures indicating that it will be God's Holy Spirit that will be the "main character" during that age, not necessarily Jesus' literally walking amongst us, "ruling" over us with His saints (Rev. 20:4). One of the major signs of all of this is a river issuing forth from the temple mentioned in Ezekiel's vision (Ezek. 47:1-12). Also prophesied by Zechariah, although Zechariah speaks of two rivers issuing out, one to the west and one to the east, where I interpreted the river issuing to the west as a spiritual river, representing God's Holy Spirit and the people whom would visit the temple in that so called "Messianic age" (Zech. 14:4-8, Isa. 48:18, 49:10). Isaiah 33:21 confirms this overall interpretation, it says, "But there the glorious LORD *will be* unto us a place of broad rivers *and* streams; wherein shall go no galley with oars, neither shall gallant ship pass thereby.". The point being in all of this is that God's Holy Spirit is what Jesus said would be sent to us, in these "latter days" (Joel 2:28, 29; John 14:16, 17, 26; Acts 2:15-21). It came fully at Pentecost in 31 A.D. and continues to be poured out, working in and through faithful followers, as we accept Him and unbelievers alike, whether we recognize it or not (Acts 2:15-21). This is why Jesus said, you can speak against the Son of man and be forgiven, but if you blaspheme the Holy Ghost you are in danger of eternal damnation (Mark 3:28, 29; Luke 12:10). The Holy Spirit is the last and only relationship we have or need between us and God. As Jesus said Himself, "It is the spirit that quickeneth; the flesh profiteth nothing…" (John 6:63). If we give up the Holy Spirit, then it is like giving up on life! As Jesus gave up the ghost on the cross, for the forgiveness of our sins, He was buried and then He arose the third day to give us the hope and promise of eternal life in His Holy name (Matt. 27:50). Alleluia and praise the LORD. Amen and Amen.

But Jesus Christ of Nazareth said of Himself, "And whosoever liveth and believeth in me shall never die." (John 11:26). This is the gift of eternal life we have in Jesus Christ of Nazareth's Holy name no matter what happens here on earth, "Messianic Age" or not, "Great Tribulation" or not. Jesus Christ of Nazareth said of Himself, "…Before Abraham was, I am." (John 8:58). This is the nature of God with us, Immanuel; Jesus Christ is with you and in you today, through His Holy Spirit. Alleluia and praise the LORD. We commune with Him by obeying His commandments, we love Him by obeying His commandments (John 18:21). But more importantly we serve a God who gives, He is seeking us, not the other way around, this is the grace of our God in Jesus Christ of Nazareth, by His Holy Spirit (Matt. 18:11-14). Alleluia and praise the LORD. The Bible says there is, "…none that doeth good…" (Ps. 14:3, 53:3). If this is the truth then the only way we can have a true relationship with God, the Father, is by His works, His righteousness and Holiness, in His only begotten Son, Jesus Christ of Nazareth, accepting Him, allowing Him into our life, through His Holy Spirit, to fill and fulfill our body, soul and spirit. This is where freedom of choice comes in; we can either receive Him and His gift of eternal life or reject Him and become separated from His life and creation forever. God willing you do not choose the latter. God is loving, kind, merciful, longsuffering, and forgiving. He does not desire to see you perish forever. He has no pleasure in the destruction of our souls (Ezek. 18:32). He desires us to live forever, like Him, this is His commandment (John 12:50). And we can receive this everlasting life, becoming the adopted children of the living God, by receiving His only begotten Son, Jesus Christ of Nazareth, and repenting, receiving forgiveness of our sins and receive His Holy Spirit to dwell with us and in us forever! Alleluia and praise the LORD. What are you waiting for? Jesus says of Himself, "Behold, I stand at the door, and knock: if any man hear my voice, and open the door, I will come in to him, and will sup with him, and he with me." (Rev. 3:20). Alleluia and praise the LORD. Amen and Amen.

Conclusion

Regarding time, and determining whom God, through the revelation to John, is speaking of when referencing "two witnesses" (Rev. 11:3). It may be helpful to consider God's sovereignty over time, and even His willingness to give us some amount of authority over it (Jos. 10:12-14, 2 Kings 20:8-11). There is at least a couple of Old Testament examples of this, one was when God was asked to move the sun back ten degrees for a sign to King Hezekiah of his healing (2 Kings 20:8-11). And another is when there was a battle, and the sun and the moon stood still for the entire time, that was likely twenty four hours (Jos. 10:12-14). These of course may be extreme examples of God's abilities and perfect sovereignty over all of His creation, and even His willingness to listen to our own desires regarding these things (Jos. 10:12, 2 Kings 20:10). As Jesus said, "...If ye have faith as a grain of mustard seed, ye shall say unto this mountain, Remove hence to yonder place; and it shall remove; and nothing shall be impossible unto you." (Matt. 17:20). He also said, "...With men this is impossible; but with God all things are possible." (Matt. 19:26). King David also was given as a witness for us, as said in Isaiah 55:4, and he did indeed say in a Psalm, "My God, my God, why hast thou forsaken me?", but he died of natural causes in his old age (Ps. 22:1, Ps. 37:25). But it was Jesus Christ of Nazareth ultimately, whom spoke these words on the cross as He was about to give up His sinless life, taking on all of our sins, for the forgiveness of our sins (Matt. 27:46, Mark 15:34). So we still have Jesus' example to follow, as He asks us to follow Him (Matt. 4:19, 8:22, 9:9). Jesus Christ of Nazareth is the way, the truth and the life (John 14:6). He died on the cross for the forgiveness of our sins, He was buried and He arose the third day to give us the hope and promise of eternal life in His Holy name. Alleluia and praise the LORD. Amen and Amen. As the Holy Bible says, "...there is none other name under heaven given among men, whereby we must be saved." (Acts 4:12). Alleluia and praise the LORD. Amen and Amen.

Another reference to these "two witnesses", and the likelihood of whom they are, is that Jesus spoke to His disciples regarding preaching in the streets, and spoke against it (Matt. 6:2, 5; 11:16, 17; 12:19). He even said at one point not to mention whom He was, that is, that He is the Son of God, Christ, the Saviour (Matt. 16:20). He did indeed overthrow the tables of the moneychangers in the temple, and accused them of turning the temple into a den of thieves, when it ought to be a house of prayer, but He was generally discrete in His ministry, and He admonished His followers to be also (Mark 11:15-17, 12:34). Nevertheless, Isaiah 51:23 says, speaking of the cup of God's trembling and fury, "...I will put it into the hand of them that afflict thee; which have said to thy soul, Bow down, that we may go over: and thou hast laid thy body as the ground, and as the street, to them that went over.". Isaiah 59:14-16 says, "And judgement is turned away backward, and justice standeth afar off: for truth is fallen in the street, and equity cannot enter. Yea, truth faileth; and he *that* departeth from evil maketh himself a prey: and the LORD saw *it*, and it displeased him that *there was* no judgement. And he saw that *there was* no man, and wondered that *there was* no intercessor: therefore his arm brought salvation unto him; and his righteousness, it sustained him.". This is speaking of Jesus Christ of Nazareth, and His sacrifice made for all of mankind on the cross, because we cannot save ourselves (Ps. 22:29). He died for the forgiveness of our sins, His arms spread wide, bringing salvation, He spilt His Holy and righteous blood and died on the cross, He was buried and the third day He arose, to give all whom believe in Him, the hope and promise of eternal life in His Holy name. Alleluia and praise the LORD. Amen and Amen. The other thing to be said about these "two witnesses" is that Jesus said, "And no man hath ascended up to heaven, but he that came down from heaven, *even* the Son of man which is in heaven." (John 3:13). In order for this scripture to stay true, these witnesses would have to be Jesus Christ of Nazareth, and God, through the Holy Spirit (Rev. 11:11, 12). Actually, albeit not at the same time, the Holy Spirit was given up by Jesus on the cross and I suppose, did ascend back to God in heaven, as Jesus said, "...Father, into thy hands I commend my spirit: and having said thus, he gave up the ghost." (Luke 23:46). And then three days later, He had His bodily resurrection, and then about forty days after that, He did indeed ascend to heaven into a cloud (Acts 1:2, 3). So this could be the "two witnesses" in that respect. Alleluia and praise the LORD. Amen and Amen.

Last, the scriptures say that the Holy Spirit is the witness of God, and Jesus Christ of Nazareth is the faithful and true witness, and we have that witness of the Holy Spirit in us, if we believe, and receive Him by faith in the name of God's only begotten Son, Jesus Christ of Nazareth (1 John 5:6, 8-10; Rev. 1:5, 3:14). Alleluia and praise the LORD. Amen and Amen. Jesus said that the Holy Spirit, the Comforter, would be sent to reprove the world of sin, and righteousness and judgement (John 16:7-14). The prophet Joel prophesied of the Holy Spirit being poured out unto all in the "last days", and this was confirmed at Pentecost 31 A.D. (Joel 2:28, Acts 2:1-21). I will admit, when I first thought about the idea of the "two witnesses", being literal and a prophecy that was still to come, I thought that it would be purposeful to show the world that the resurrection of the dead is true, and it has, does and will take place (Rev. 11:11, 12). But that being said, Jesus even spoke a parable regarding this, speaking about the rich man in hell and Lazarus, the poor man, in the bosom of Abraham after their decease (Luke 16:19-26). In the parable, the rich man was convinced that if someone were raised from the dead, his family, whom were still living would believe, but in the parable Abraham said, that even if someone spoke to them whom was raised from the dead they would not believe (Luke 16:27-30). Nevertheless, Abraham said, in this parable that Jesus was speaking, that they have Moses and the prophets to teach them, if they do not believe them they will not believe if someone was raised from the dead (Luke 16:29, 31). So regarding these "two witnesses", it may be the same, we have Moses, the Old Testament prophets, and the New Testament witnesses, that is the gospel books, the epistles, and the book of Revelation as a witness to the testimony of Jesus Christ of Nazareth. And we have the faithful witnesses whom followed and follow Jesus Christ of Nazareth, in history, today, and no doubt until the end of this world to show us that there is a faith in the true God, and His only begotten Son, Jesus Christ of Nazareth. Jesus Christ of Nazareth died on the cross for the forgiveness of our sins, by spilling His holy and righteous blood, as a sinless man taking on our sins, He was buried and He arose the third day, to give us the hope and promise of eternal life in His Holy name. Alleluia and praise the LORD. Amen and Amen.

APPENDIX B

JESUS CHRIST OF NAZARETH AND DAVID'S THRONE

Introduction

Although David, his son, Solomon, and other successive kings sitting on David's throne had sinned against God (2 Sam. 12:1-24, 1 Kings 11:1, 2). The throne of David remained in Jerusalem until the final phase of the Babylonian exile of Judah from Jerusalem, from approximately 525 to 500 B.C. (2 Kings 25, Jer. 32-34, 38, 40, 41-44, 52). Around this time Jeremiah is said to have brought one of the king's daughters to Ireland, likely via Egypt, to maintain the throne, and literally meet with other Israelites in this area of the world, whom had gone into captivity centuries earlier (Jer. 41-44).[7] This was all part of prophecy that included the descendants of Jacob living at the four corners of the earth in the "latter days", prophesied of first by God to Abraham for his descendants (Gen. 22:15-18). Nevertheless, the more important part of these prophesies and others, is that Jesus Christ of Nazareth, the Messiah, Son of David, born in the city of David, Bethlehem, the root and offspring of David, even King David's Lord, came into this world, born of a virgin, Mary, espoused to Joseph, of the house of David, conceived by the Holy Spirit of God, to redeem Israel, and forgive the world for all of our sins (Matt. 1:18-25, Luke 2:4, 11; Acts 2:34, 36; Rev. 22:16). Alleluia and praise the LORD. Amen and Amen. The remainder of this appendix will go into some greater detail regarding the prophecies of David, His throne, and how Jesus Christ of Nazareth has fulfilled them. Read on to learn more about David's throne, where it may exist today, and how Jesus Christ of Nazareth, the Saviour of the whole world is seated on it ultimately with God, the Father, through His Holy Spirit, first and foremost above all principalities and governments here on earth (Col. 1:12-20). Alleluia and praise the LORD. Amen and Amen.

What is David's throne?

Although I will not go into the Biblical accounts of David's throne in detail here, as the Holy Bible does a sufficient job of it, and I have written at least one other book that expands on the

---

[7] https://www.cbcg.org/booklets/america-britain/chapter-twelve-the-prophet-jeremiah-s-mysterious-royal-commission.html, retrieved 20/03/2022

subject, "Origin of Mankind". In our time and into the future, as I had suggested, there will likely continue to be kings, plural, sitting on David's throne, this obviously means succession, as mentioned in Jeremiah 22:4 (1 Kings 2:12, Ps. 132:12). Also, Jeremiah 23:3-8, is proof of God's method of reigning over us, it says, "And I will gather the remnant of my flock out of all countries whither I have driven them, and will bring them again to their folds; and they shall be fruitful and increase. And I will set up shepherds over them which shall feed them: and they shall fear no more, nor be dismayed, neither shall they be lacking, saith the LORD. Behold, the days come, saith the LORD, that I will raise unto David a righteous Branch, and a King shall reign and prosper, and shall execute judgment and justice in the earth. In his days Judah shall be saved, and Israel shall dwell safely: and this *is* his name whereby he shall be called, THE LORD OUR RIGHTEOUSNESS. Therefore, behold, the days come, saith the LORD, that they shall no more say, The LORD liveth, which brought up the children of Israel out of the land of Egypt; But, The LORD liveth, which brought up and which led the seed of the house of Israel out of the north country, and from all countries whither I had driven them; and they shall dwell in their own land.". The righteous Branch came in Jesus Christ of Nazareth, and Jesus is now sitting with God on His throne (Rev. 3:21). He is "…THE LORD OUR RIGHTEOUSNESS." (Jer. 23:6). Just like God revealed Himself to Moses in the burning bush, brought the Israelites out of Egypt and was present with them in the pillar of the cloud by day, and pillar of fire by night (Ex. 3:2, 13:9, 21, 22). He has been and will continue to lead His people through His divine powers, in signs and wonders and especially through our relationship with His Holy Spirit, in us and working through us and with us in our relationship with Him in prayer, praise and in the study of His Word, the Holy Bible of God and with mankind in fellowship, as God wills it.

Hosea 3:5 says, "Afterward shall the children of Israel return, and seek the LORD their God, and David their king; and shall fear the LORD and his goodness in the latter days.". The latter days are the days we are in and will be in until the final judgement, hence the "latter days" (Ezek. 38:16, Dan. 2:28, 10:14; Hos. 3:5). But I think what God is saying through this passage and others like it, is that, we should seek what David represented, read, learn and follow his righteous example, but not his sin. The Bible says in 1 Samuel 13:14, "…the LORD hath sought him a man after his own heart…", and He found that man in David, the seventh son of Jesse, a descendant of the tribe of Judah, one of the tribes of Israel (1 Sam. 16:1-13, 1 Chr. 2:1-15). Of course, as I have mentioned and will continue to believe, David is an early example of the fruit of the true knowledge of Jesus Christ of Nazareth, the root and offspring of David, and that ultimately Jesus Christ of Nazareth has inherited King David's throne, forever (Isa. 11:1, 10; Rev. 5:5, 22:16). Because Jesus Christ of Nazareth is the Creator of all things, but also was born into this world, conceived by the Holy Spirit in a descendant of King David, through His earthly mother, Mary, a virgin at the time, espoused to Joseph, also a descendant of King David (Matt. 1, Luke 3:23-38). So we can learn from King David in the psalms, and through some of the trials that are mentioned of him, such as his fight with the Philistine, Goliath, but we ultimately have that perfect example of a King sitting on King David's throne in Jesus Christ of Nazareth. Alleluia and praise the LORD. Amen and Amen. Even the Old

Testament mentions God, the LORD, as the King of Israel (Isa. 44:6, Zeph. 3:15). This also may be a call to submit to the earthly authority of the descendant of David, whom likely sits on a literal throne today here on earth. As we are called to obey government even in the New Testament, as it is ordained by God, as God Almighty wills it of course, however we are not to worship men, men's works, or follow the traditions of men, but we are called to follow God, the Father, Almighty, in Christ Jesus of Nazareth's Holy name, through His Holy Spirit, first and foremost (1 Pet. 2:13, 14). Alleluia and praise the LORD. Amen and Amen.

It has been suggested that the "Stone of scone" or "Jacob's pillar", that has travelled through the succession of monarch's in the British Isles, was indeed the stone that Jacob slept on and dreamed his dream on and then anointed the stone after the dream (Gen. 28:10-22). The historical account is that this stone was carried unto the Isles, like the heraldry of David's line, through a daughter of a King of Judah, during the Babylonian exile around approximately 500 B.C. (Jer. 41-44). This stone, at least at one point in time, was recorded to have been resting under the coronation chair of the Kings and Queens at the Westminster Abbey in London, England. At least a few books have been written on this subject and various scholars have commented on this being the case. "Symbols of our Celto-Saxon Heritage" by W.H. Bennett, is at least one reference. What did David do, that no other king did? He was the first king of Israel from the tribe of Judah (1 Sam. 16:1-13, 1 Chr. 2:3-15). Saul was the first physically anointed King of Israel, a Benjamite in tribal ancestry, before King David of Judah (1 Sam. 9-11). Judah was prophesied to keep the sceptre, as a sign of authority, until Shiloh come (Gen. 49:10). Shiloh came in Jesus Christ of Nazareth, and the "Messianic Age", may fulfill the tranquil, restful nature of Jesus Christ of Nazareth, which the word Shiloh can be interpreted as, Strong's number 7886 (Gen. 49:10). But most important, Jesus did indeed fulfill Shiloh, we can rest in Jesus, as He was and is the atoning sacrifice for the forgiveness of our sins, He is the Prince of peace and He is Lord of the Sabbath day (Rom. 3:25, Isa. 9:6, Matt. 12:8). The point is that in Jesus Christ of Nazareth we have Shiloh and "...unto Him shall the gathering of the people be..." (Gen. 49:10). Jesus is the Shepard of Israel, He says to us, of Himself, "Come unto me, all *ye* that labour and are heavy laden, and I will give you rest." (Matt. 11:28). Jesus came for the lost sheep of Israel and the world; even King David admitted that he was a lost sheep (Matt. 15:24, Ps. 119:176, Jer. 50:6). The point is that we need Jesus Christ of Nazareth, the root and offspring of David, and inheritor of David's throne as King over Israel and the entire earth in order to live a good, abundant and healthy life, here on earth and forever more in Jesus Christ of Nazareth's Holy name (Rev. 22:16). Alleluia and praise the LORD. Amen and Amen.

Jesus Christ of Nazareth

Luke 1:31-33 explains through a message from an angel to Mary, whom Jesus is and what authority He is given. It says, "And, behold, thou shalt conceive in thy womb, and bring forth a son, and shalt call his name JESUS. He shall be great, and shall be called the Son of the Highest: and **the Lord God shall give unto him the throne of his father David:** And **he shall reign over the house of Jacob for ever**; and of his kingdom there shall be no end.". This message and prophecy has and will continue to fulfill any prophecy regarding King David, and His family lineage forever more! In Zechariah 12:8 it says, "In that day shall the LORD defend the inhabitants of Jerusalem; and he that is feeble among them at that day shall be as David; and the house of David *shall be* as God, as the angel of the LORD before them.". Jesus Christ of Nazareth fulfilled this prophecy in that He is the Son of God, the angel of the Lord, and God (John 1:1-5, 14, 17). And He has given everyone who accepts His gift of eternal life, the opportunity to be "like David", that is, a child of God; so we can all receive our crown of glory (1 Peter 5:4, Rev. 17:14)! Through Jesus Christ, we are God's children, and a "royal priesthood", with the promise of resurrection and ruler ship with Christ Jesus over all of His creation (1 Peter 2:9, Rev. 2:26, 3:5, 3:12). This is the gift of God in the name of Jesus Christ of Nazareth, inheriting **all things**, and **eternal life** (Rev. 3:21, 21:7). Alleluia and praise the LORD. Amen and Amen. Jesus did not mention that David would be coming back to sit on his earthly throne. Jesus did however accept that He, Himself, was the King of Israel (Mark 11:10, John 1:49, 12:13). Alleluia and praise the LORD. Amen and Amen. How could both Jesus and David be kings over Israel? The only way is if Jesus is the spiritual king and David's physical lineage as long as God wills it, maintains the physical throne status here on earth. Alleluia and praise the LORD. Amen and Amen. Nevertheless, Jesus said, "My kingdom is not of this world: if my kingdom were of this world, then would my servants fight, that I should not be delivered to the Jews: but now is my kingdom not from hence." (John 18:36). That is we must remember that God's true kingdom is a spiritual one first and foremost, as Jesus said, "But the hour cometh, and now is, when the true worshippers shall worship the Father in spirit and in truth: for the Father seeketh such to worship him." (John 4:23). That is, God is a Spirit, the Holy Spirit (John 4:24). Alleluia and praise the LORD. Amen and Amen.

More proofs of Jesus' position on the throne of David are mentioned by the angel at Jesus' birth and to John in vision in the Book of Revelation. Luke 2:11 says, "For unto you is born this day in the city of David a Saviour, which is Christ the Lord.". And as a testimony is established with two or three witnesses, the "…wise men…" confirmed Jesus' authority and position as King of Israel, as well as Simeon and Anna, at the temple during Jesus' dedication to the LORD as the firstborn in Joseph and Mary's family according to Hebrew law (Matt. 2:2, 11; Luke 2:25-32, 2:36-38). And Revelation 5 does a great job of describing Jesus as the Lamb of God and whom and what tribe He comes from. Revelation 5:5 says, "And one of the elders saith unto me, Weep not: behold, the Lion of the tribe of Juda, the Root of David, hath prevailed to open the book, and to loose the seven seals thereof.". Also, at the cross Jesus said, "…My God, my God, why hast thou forsaken me?" (Matt. 27:46, Mark 15:34). This was also written in a psalm, by David, king of Israel, in about 1000 B.C. (Ps. 22:1). The relationship between the Spirit of God in King David and Jesus Christ of Nazareth are unmistakable. The point is that the same spirit that ruled in David and gave David all that he had, conceived

Jesus Christ of Nazareth in the womb of the virgin, Mary, espoused to Joseph, and ruled in Jesus Christ of Nazareth's earthly life, He gave up that ghost by dying on the cross for the forgiveness of our sins, as a sinless man taking all of our sins upon Himself, shedding His righteous and holy blood, He was buried and He arose the third day by that same Holy Spirit unto eternal life, also giving us the hope and promise of eternal life in His Holy name (Matt. 27:50, Mark 15:37, Luke 23:46, John 19:30). Alleluia and praise the LORD. Amen and Amen. This same spirit, the Holy Spirit of God, can and does dwell in us, as we receive Him, through repentance, and the forgiveness of our sins in Christ Jesus of Nazareth's Holy name (Luke 11:13, Eph. 1:13, 14). It is the Spirit of life, that same spirit that breathed life into Adam and gave Eve life a few millennia ago! This is the Spirit that communes with our spirit, the Spirit that relates all the living unto God Almighty and Him, the Father, to us in Christ Jesus of Nazareth's Holy name. The same Spirit will resurrect all flesh at the final judgement, some to everlasting life and possibly some to the second death (Rev. 20:11-15). Do you believe that Jesus Christ of Nazareth is your Maker, your life giver? If so, you can receive the same everlasting gift He has received, that is everlasting life in Jesus Christ of Nazareth's Holy name. Alleluia and praise the LORD. Amen and Amen. As the Holy Bible of God says, "…there is none other name under heaven given among men, whereby we must be saved." (Acts 4:12). Alleluia and praise the LORD. Amen and Amen.

Present to the Future

Ezekiel 34:23-25 says, "And I will set up one shepherd over them, and he shall feed them, *even* my servant David; he shall feed them, and he shall be their shepherd. And I the LORD will be their God, and my servant David a prince among them; I the LORD have spoken *it*. And I will make with them a covenant of peace, and will cause the evil beasts to cease out of the land: and they shall dwell safely in the wilderness, and sleep in the woods.". It should be said, that often, when the Bible refers to a person spoken of beforehand in the Bible, especially after they have passed, it may be referring to that person's descendants as well, especially in prophecy. A perfect example of this is in Jeremiah 31:11, it says "For the LORD hath redeemed Jacob and ransomed him from the hand of *him that was* stronger than he.". I am certain God can be talking about Jacob, when he was alive and going through trials, but in this instance, He is also likely talking about Jacob's descendants, the descendants of the tribes of Israel, Jacob's name being changed to Israel, after wrestling with a man all night for a blessing, whom turned out to be God (Gen. 32:24-30). In the case of David, God may either be talking about his descendants, or in the case of the spiritual realm, certainly Jesus Christ of Nazareth has fulfilled all of these prophecies of the maintenance of the throne of King David, as has been mentioned, forever! In regards to the Bible and King David and the other contributors to it through the inspiration of the Holy Spirit, no doubt, these messengers still maintain an influence over this world and a level of "ruler ship" through the scriptures that they helped create. We are judged through God's message to and through those people in the Holy Bible! We are judged by the word of God, which these saints' partook in producing and maintaining throughout the centuries and millennia. Alleluia and praise the LORD. Amen and Amen.

Ezekiel 37:24 and 25 say, "And David my servant *shall be* king over them; and they all shall have one shepherd: they shall also walk in my judgments, and observe my statutes, and do them. And they shall dwell in the land that I have given unto Jacob my servant, wherein your fathers have dwelt; and they shall dwell therein, *even* they, and their children, and their children's children for ever: and my servant David *shall be* their prince for ever.". The key to understanding the future and even present perspective of these two verses is to understand and accept the prophecy given to Jesus by the angel in Luke 1:31-33, mentioned earlier. If indeed Jesus has been given the throne of David and Jesus is everlasting, then this scripture in Ezekiel 37:24 and 25 has been fulfilled in Jesus Christ of Nazareth. After His resurrection, He said that all power had been given to Him in heaven and in earth (Matt. 28:18). The fact of the matter is, David indeed will be resurrected someday and He will be given his reward, just like the other saints (Rev. 20:6). Are all of the rewards going to be the exact same? I do not know. But in the end, we will all receive our reward from God Almighty, the Father, and Jesus Christ of Nazareth, His only begotten Son, through His Holy Spirit, for the works we have either done for Him, or against Him in this lifetime (Matt. 16:27). Will David rule on this earth again, in the flesh over the descendants of Israel? Of course it is possible, the Bible says, "…with God all things are possible." (Matt. 19:26). But I would suggest that the more likely scenario is that Jesus has inherited the throne of David, and rules over all of Israel and mankind for that matter in the Spiritual realm, and quite frankly in the natural or fleshly realm as well. As the Bible says, "…*it is* not in man that walketh to direct his steps." (Jer. 10:23). The point is that Jesus Christ of Nazareth is King of Kings and Lord of Lords, and David will receive his lot or reward, when the time comes, whatever, wherever and whenever that may be, here on earth or in the heavenly, "New Jerusalem", in a "new heaven and a new earth" (Rev. 19:16, 21:1-5). Alleluia and praise the LORD. Amen and Amen.

Conclusion

To put this idea to rest, we can look at a couple Scriptures again. First, Zechariah 12:8 says, "In that day shall the LORD defend the inhabitants of Jerusalem; and he that is feeble among them at that day shall be as David; and the house of David *shall be* as God, as the angel of the LORD before them.". As mentioned earlier, this was fulfilled in Jesus Christ of Nazareth, as He is God, and is the angel of the LORD (John 1:1). And we are all Jesus' disciples, as God wills it, and draws us to Him; it is God whom calls and brings us to Jesus Christ of Nazareth, through the Holy Spirit of God, and chooses us to do whatever He desires here on earth, and in the "world to come", eternal life (John 15:16). Alleluia and praise the LORD. Amen and Amen. Secondly, regarding Jeremiah 22:4 briefly referenced earlier, it says, "For if ye do this thing indeed, then shall there enter in by the gates of this house kings sitting upon the throne of David, riding in chariots and on horses, he, and his servants, and his people.". Jesus in a way did indeed fulfill this scripture when He entered into Jerusalem, lowly, and meek riding upon an donkey's colt (Zech. 9:9, Matt. 11:29, 21:5; John 12:15). The people before and behind Him, worshipped Him, and praised God, recognizing Him as the King of Israel, and no doubt, God was with Him, so that I suppose would fulfill the plural "kings", sitting upon the throne of David (Matt. 21:9, Mark 11:9, 10; Luke 19:37, 38; John 12:13). No matter the interpretations of prophecy, to put it simply, Jesus Christ of Nazareth said of Himself, "Search the scriptures; for in them ye think ye have eternal life: and they are they which testify of me." (John 5:39). This arguably is the point to me writing this entire book, that is to prove, in my own feeble attempt, hopefully led by the Holy Spirit of God, by His grace working in me, that indeed all the Scriptures, have, do and always will be fulfilled in the Holy name of Jesus Christ of Nazareth, the Word of God, the Word become flesh (John 1:1-3, 14; Rev. 4:8). Conceived of the Holy Spirit in and born of the virgin, Mary, espoused to Joseph, raised as a child of Israel, a child of the tribe of Judah, of the maternal lineage of King David, through His earthly mother, Mary, with brothers and sisters (Matt. 1, Luke 2). He spilt His holy and righteous blood on the cross for the forgiveness of our sins, a sinless man taking all of our sins upon Himself, He died, He was buried and on the third day He arose to give us the hope and promise of eternal life in His Holy name. Alleluia and praise the LORD. Amen and Amen.

Last, regarding ruler ship or judgement over the twelve tribes of Israel, this responsibility was given to the founding apostles of Jesus Christ of Nazareth's New Covenant Church, the New Testament Church, the Church of God (Matt. 19:28, Luke 22:30). That is, it is the apostles of Jesus Christ of Nazareth whom continued the gospel message of salvation in the Holy name of Jesus Christ of Nazareth, through the forgiveness of sins, after their witnessing of His spilt holy and righteous blood and death on the cross for the forgiveness of our sins and His burial, then His miraculous resurrection three days later for the hope and promise of eternal life in His Holy name. Alleluia and praise the LORD. Amen and Amen. After His resurrection He revealed Himself the next morning, the first day of the week, first to Mary Magdalene, and then to others, and finally to His chosen apostles, where they were assembled, doors shut, for fear of the Jews, and finally to, Thomas, with them eight days later (Matt. 28:1-9, Mark 16:9, Luke 24:13-31, John 20:11-16, 20:19-21, 20:24-28). These are the men whom, two wrote their gospel accounts, namely John and Matthew, John also wrote the book of Revelation by inspiration of the Holy Spirit of God in Christ Jesus of Nazareth, and some others, including John, wrote epistles to the churches of God, namely, Peter, James, and Jude. This does not include the other New Testament writers, whom likely were also apostles, but not of the original twelve, namely the apostle, Paul, but also Luke and Mark, whom wrote their own accounts of the gospel of Jesus Christ of Nazareth. Jesus even said it would be by His words and ours that we would be judged (Matt. 12:36, 37; John 12:47, 48). So it is the very words of the Holy Bible, namely in the New Testament, for believers in Jesus Christ of Nazareth, that judge us (John 12:47, 48). And it is by our own actions, words and deeds, that we are judged, as Jesus said we would be (Matt. 12:36, 37). Alleluia and praise the LORD. Amen and Amen. Nevertheless, we must remember that Jesus came full of grace and truth, and it is indeed by the grace of God that we are saved, through faith, and it is a gift of God, not by works, so that no man can boast of one's own efforts (John 1:17, Eph. 2:8, 9). Jesus did not come to condemn, but to save (John 3:17). As the Scripture says, "For God so loved the world, that he gave his only begotten Son, that whosoever believeth in him should not perish, but have everlasting life." (John 3:16). Alleluia and praise the LORD. Amen and Amen.

APPENDIX C

REFERENCES

Books

1. Foxe's Book of Martyrs by John Foxe, edited by W. Grinton Berry, Baker Publishing Group, 1998
2. Symbols of our Celto-Saxon Heritage by W.H. Bennett, Covenant Publishing Co. Ltd., July 1998

Websites

1. https://www.ccel.org/ccel/josephus/complete.toc.html, retrieved 08/01/2018
2. http://www.bethlehemstar.com/starry-dance/westward-leading/, retrieved 25/08/2017

Articles

1. John Reid suggests approximate time of Jesus birth to be between September 16 and 29, 4 B.C. http://www.sabbath.org/index.cfm/fuseaction/Library.sr/CT/ARTB/k/568/When-Was-Jesus-Born.htm, retrieved 03/01/2018
2. Herod's Death, Jesus' Birth and a Lunar Eclipse - Biblical Archaeology Society - https://www.biblicalarchaeology.org/daily/people-cultures-in-the-bible/jesus-historical-jesus/herods-death-jesus-birth-and-a-lunar-eclipse/, retrieved 04/01/2018
3. https://eclipse.gsfc.nasa.gov/LEcat5/LE0001-0100.html, retrieved 08/04/2018
4. Skyviewcafe.com settings Jerusalem, 11pm on the 25th of April in 31 A.D., seem to confirm an eclipse, referencing the ecliptic tab, http://skyviewcafe.com/#/ecliptic, retrieved 08/04/2018.

Note: The author does not guarantee the availability of all references, especially websites, as organizations from time to time change names, addresses and discontinue services. Nor does the author guarantee the accuracy of the references. As the Bible says, "Prove all things; hold fast that which is good." (1 Th. 5:21). That being said, God willing, you will be brought to the proof and references you are seeking. As Jesus said, "…seek, and ye shall find…" (Matt. 7:7).

APPENDIX D

Proposed timeline of Jesus Christ of Nazareth's earthly life

~June 5 B.C.
- John, the baptist, conceived
- Luke 1:24

~Dec. 5 B.C.
- Jesus Christ of Nazareth, conceived
- Matt. 1:18
- Luke 1:31,

~Mar. 4 B.C.
- John, the baptist, born
- Luke 1:57

~Sept. 4 B.C.
- Jesus Christ of Nazareth, born
- Matt. 2:1
- Luke 2:7

~Jan. - Dec. 1 B.C.
- Herod dies
- Joseph, Mary and Jesus return from "exile" in egypt
- Matt. 2:19, 20

~Apr. 10 A.D.
- Jesus, 12, at temple
- Luke 2:42, 43

~Oct./Nov. 27 A.D.
- Jesus ministry starts
- John 1

~Apr. 31 A.D.
- Jesus Christ of Nazareth, crucifixion at Passover, burial and resurrection three days later
- John 19
- John 20

Note: not to "scale" regarding proposed linear time, only in order of proposed linear time.

APPENDIX E

Proposed Daniel 9, 70 week proph   y timeline

69 weeks — 3.5 days — | — — | — 3.5 days |

Cyrus decree
486 B.C.
2 Ch. 36:22, 23
Ezra 1:1, 2

Artaxerxe   lecree
457 B.C.
Ezra 7, Ne   miah

Jesus Ministry
begins in fall
of 27 A.D.
Luke 3:23

Jesus crucifixion
at Passover, burial
and resurrection
three days later in
31 A.D.
Matt. 27, 28

Great Tribulation
begins
some time A.D.
Matt. 24:21
Rev. 2:22

"Messianic Age"
begins
some time plus
3.5 years A.D.
Rev. 7:14, 20:6
Ezek. 39:8-39
Ezek. 40-48

Note: There was an initial dec   given by Cyrus, then again by
Darius after him (Ezra 1:1,2;   But it seems that the decree of
Artaxerxes is the one that hel   fast for the account of
Nehemiah, whom Ezra is also   entioned by (Neh. 9).

Also, the time between the "   ssiah" being cutoff and the final
3.5 days or three and a half ye   of the "Great Tribulation", is
not known with any certainty,   Jesus said, our Father in
Heaven knows, but we can kn   the times we are in by
watching and praying (Matt. 2   6-51). Repenting and accepting
forgiveness for our sins, and t   indwelling of the Holy Spirit in
the name of Jesus Christ is th   first steps, our need for
salvation in Jesus Christ of N   reth comes before the need to
understand any other prophec   s of the Bible. Because Jesus'
testimony is the spirit of prop   cy (Rev. 19:10).

Using day for a year principle in Bible (Ezek. 4:6)

69 weeks = 483 years

3.5 days + 3.5 days = 3.5 years + 3.5 years

Total = 490 years
     = 490 days   Using day for a year principle to
                         convert back to days or weeks.
     = 70 weeks

APPENDIX F

TALES, LEGENDS, AND
THE GOLDEN RULE

Introduction

This appendix has much of its root in my education during University in my early 20's. Albeit I owe credit to having a proper foundation in order to learn these things in University and ultimately God deserves the glory in all of this, as without Him, I am nothing. To God be the glory in the name of His only begotten Son, Jesus Christ of Nazareth's Holy name. Alleluia and praise the LORD. Amen and Amen. Matthew 6:22 and 23 say, "The light of the body is the eye: if therefore thine eye be single, thy whole body shall be full of light. But if thine eye be evil, thy whole body shall be full of darkness. If therefore the light that is in thee be darkness, how great *is* that darkness!". This verse is important to understand because Jesus said do not judge by the appearance, but in righteousness judge (John 7:24). This world, it's "education" system, and even professing followers of God can seem to be deceived from time to time, and I am no exception. In the conclusion of this appendix, I bring up some examples in the New Testament of some of these concerns. That being said, Jesus Christ of Nazareth is the answer, He is the way, the truth and the life, no one comes to God, the Father, accept by Jesus Christ of Nazareth, through His Holy Spirit (John 14:6). Alleluia and praise the LORD. Amen and Amen. Hebrews 12:2 says, "Looking unto Jesus the author and finisher of *our* faith; who for the joy that was set before him endured the cross, despising the shame, and is set down at the right hand of the throne of God." This ought to be the reality of our life here on earth, regardless of what we have learned, read about, think we know and the like. The reality is in Jesus Christ of Nazareth, whom overcame this world and all that is in it, to give us the hope and promise of eternal life in His Holy name. Alleluia and praise the LORD. Amen and Amen. Nevertheless, read on to learn about God and His only begotten Son, and their involvement in both the "secular" and Biblical accounts of world history, and other tales told from the past, concluding with the knowledge of the common salvation we all have in the name of Jesus Christ of Nazareth (Jude 1:3). Because He died on the cross for the forgiveness of our sins, spilling His Holy and righteous blood, a sinless man taking all of our sins upon Himself, He was buried and the third day He arose to give us the hope and promise of eternal life in His Holy name. To God be the glory in the truth of all of these things, in the name of His only begotten Son, Jesus Christ of Nazareth. Alleluia and praise the LORD. Amen and Amen.

Tales

Lives like a tale told (Ps. 90:6). In Psalm 90, the Hebrew word for tale is hegeh, meaning muttering, thought as thunder, mourning, sound, tale, Strong's number 1899. Interestingly, Jesus Christ said He compared His coming to lightening and Satan was compared to falling from heaven like lightening, albeit, thunder is a product of lightening, not the lightening itself (Matt. 24:27, Luke 10:18). That being said, God spoke everything into existence, and the Bible would suggest that the thunder comes first, then the lightening; even God's voice is compared to thunder (Gen. 1:3, Job 28:26, 37:4, 5; 38:25, 40:9; Rev. 8:5, 11:19, 16:18). In John 12:28, before His crucifixion, burial and resurrection, Jesus said, "Father, glorify thy name. Then came there a voice from heaven, *saying,* I have both glorified *it,* and will glorify *it* again.", whom some when they heard thought they had heard thunder (John 12:28-30). And I do not think that it is a coincidence that Jesus renamed John and James, the sons of thunder, whom were the sons of their earthly father, Zebedee, a fisherman (Mark 3:17). As I was told early on in my grown-up years of conversion, that the gospel according to John is a good place to start reading, to become a student of the Holy Bible of God, and namely a disciple of Jesus Christ of Nazareth, and His life works here on earth, according to Biblical accounts (Matt., Mark, Luke, John, etc.). Jesus' coming again, no doubt, was fulfilled at least partially when the angel of the Lord, whose countenance was like lightening rolled back the stone of the tomb Jesus' had been resurrected from three days after His crucifixion at Passover in 31 A.D. (Matt. 28:2, 3). Alleluia and praise the LORD. Amen and Amen. In High school, in English class, we read at least a few Shakespeare classics. I am very thankful now that we did, as I have decided to use the King James version of the Holy Bible for most of my studies in recent years, and probably will for most of my Biblical study the rest of my God given life here on earth. Shakespeare and his literary works, I have heard, have been given a certain amount of credit due for the existence of our modern English grammar and vocabulary. I do not know how true this is, but certainly if you can understand Shakespeare, understanding the King James version of the Holy Bible, with its; thy, thou, ye, and some verbs, such as wont, and wantonness, etc., would almost seem to be a welcome relief from the sometimes challenging descriptive language of Shakespeare's works (Matt. 1:20, 2:8, 27:15, Rom. 13:13).

I have heard, that the Holy Bible of God today is said to be the most published and sold book in all of world history and continues to maintain this status, for how long, God only knows. But how did we arrive at the versions that we have currently? Well, as mentioned above, as far as the English language versions, namely the King James Version; Shakespeare's works may have influenced the language of the time at the least, which was in about 1600 A.D.. But there were other versions, even of the English translated Bible, being created around this time, namely previously by John Wycliff, 1384 A.D., and William Tyndale, 1525 A.D., http://biblemanuscriptsociety.com/Bible-resources/English-Bible-History, retrieved, 24/01/2018. So which translation is best suited for the student of the Holy Bible today? Well, when I was attending a church of God congregation, in 2010 A.D., they suggested the King James Version of the Holy Bible was suitable. I stuck with it, as I have said, if it is good enough for a king, it is good enough for me. But there are even at least a few popular "modern" translations, as of the 20th century. We have the New International Version, which I also have read from. There is the Revised Standard Version, the Good News translation, and again the list can go on. So no matter what translation you decide to use, as the Scriptures admonish, "Prove all things; hold fast that which is good." (1 Thess. 5:21). The scriptures also admonish us to try the spirits; we need to discern, by God's Holy Spirit, what translation best suits us (1 John 4:1). Alleluia and praise the LORD. Amen and Amen.

Last, let us talk about Jesus Christ of Nazareth, the Holy Bible, and Biblical idea's in popular culture. I suppose the list could be endless, but I will speak about a few musical and theatrical influences of the 20th century. The first that comes to mind of all the ideas is, "To Everything There Is a Season" by the Byrds. This song has a direct influence from Ecclesiastes 1:1-8, interesting and simple enough. Other songs, include, "Spirit in the sky" by Norman Greenbaum and more popularly, Elvis Presley's extensive gospel music recordings. In movies and theatre, there is "the Ten Commandments", "Jesus Christ Superstar", and "Joseph and the Amazing technicolour dream coat", etc.. But I will say that all of these do not necessarily portray the Historical Biblical account of whatever events they may be depicting with 100% accuracy, at least from my experience in watching them, regarding movies and theatre. But they are a form of entertainment and creative expression, which the Holy Bible is a very good example of, with parables, similitudes and signs and wonders. And as the Holy Bible does admonish us, we are to try and/or discern the spirits, because not every spirit is Holy of God, there is the spirit of error, which is of the tree of knowledge of good and evil, and the spirit of Truth, which is of God, the Holy Spirit, in the name of Jesus Christ of Nazareth (1 John 4:1, 6). Alleluia and praise the LORD. Amen and Amen. Ultimately, God has given us freedom of choice of what to consume by our eyes and listen to with our ears, etc.. This is where our relationship with our Creator and with Him in the world around us becomes very real and intimate. Alleluia and praise the LORD. But we must place our trust in Him first and foremost for all things, through accepting His only begotten Son, Jesus Christ of Nazareth, whom died on the cross for the forgiveness of our sins, shedding His righteous and holy blood. He was buried and He arose the third day to give us the hope and promise of eternal life in His Holy name. Alleluia and praise the LORD. Amen and Amen.

The Epics, God's Chosen People and Church History

The Epic of Gilgamesh, accounts of a flood event, likely that of Noah and the ark, and the Epic's author(s), may be associated with Nimrod, the tower of Babel, Mesopotamia and the Babylonian empire in general, approximately 2250 B.C. - 500 B.C. (Gen. 6-8, 10:8-10, 11:1-9). Homer's Odyssey and Iliad, and Virgil's Aeneid may be related to the Israelites early exploration, during the time of judges, 1400 B.C.-1100 B.C., and after going into captivity and fulfilling greater prophetic plans spoken of by the prophets of Israel in the Holy Bible, approximately 700 B.C. (Jud. 18, 2 Kings 15:29, 17:4-41, 18:9-12). The book of Revelation speaks of other books being opened, this may include various religious books and even "fiction" books, plays, movies, etc., that can have life lessons in them (Rev. 20:12). It is what we do with the information that the book of Revelation, of the Holy Bible, is speaking of (Rev. 20:12). But this is likely talking about the various books of the Holy Bible, first and foremost, with the most important books being the four gospel books according to Matthew, Mark, Luke and John, as well as our own life testimony of the living God, His only begotten Son, Jesus Christ of Nazareth and the Holy Spirit of God. Alleluia and praise the LORD. Amen and Amen. Regarding New Testament Church history, the book of Revelation does a good description of the seven churches, which also seem to be referenced by the prophet Zechariah in the Old Testament. Revelation 1:20 says, "The mystery of the seven stars which thou sawest in my right hand, and the seven golden candlesticks. The seven stars are the angels of the seven churches: and the seven candlesticks which thou sawest are the seven churches.". Zechariah speaks of a stone with seven eyes, Zechariah 3:9 says, "For behold the stone that I have laid before Joshua; upon one stone *shall be* seven eyes: behold, I will engrave the graving thereof, saith the LORD of hosts, and I will remove the iniquity of that land in one day.". This is fulfilled in Christ Jesus of Nazareth dying on the cross for the forgiveness of our sins at Passover in 31 A.D., He was buried and He arose three days later to give us the hope and promise of eternal life in His Holy name. Alleluia and praise the LORD. Amen and Amen. Revelation 5:6 says, "And I beheld, and, lo, in the midst of the throne and of the four beasts, and in the midst of the elders, stood a Lamb as it had been slain, having seven horns and seven eyes, which are the seven Spirits of God sent forth unto all the earth.". This no doubt is Jesus Christ of Nazareth, and represents His headship and Sovereignty over the entire church of God, no matter when and where we congregate and dwell. Alleluia and praise the LORD. Amen and Amen. In the next two paragraphs, I will give a brief description of the Churches of God, throughout recent history starting with Jesus Christ and His disciples in the early first century A.D., using the descriptions of the churches in the book of Revelation as the template, as some other Biblical scholars have done similarly. Alleluia and praise the LORD. Amen and Amen.

The church at Ephesus was the opening era of the Church of God, during Jesus' life and after Jesus Christ of Nazareth, our Saviour, was crucified at Passover 31 A.D., He was buried and He arose three days later, and then visited with the disciples, confirming His words and the Scriptures that prophesied of Him, ascending to heaven about forty days after that (Matt. 27:35, 58-60; John 20, 21; Acts 1:1-9). And then the Holy Spirit, promised by Jesus to be given to His faithful followers was poured out on the apostles, and three thousand congregants baptized, receiving the Holy Spirit, with the twelve apostles, namely Peter, witnessing of the event, with the subsequent acts of the apostles and the other epistles confirming the beginning of this era (Acts 2:1-36, the Epistles, etc.). Revelation 2:1-7 says, "Unto the angel of the church of Ephesus write; These things saith he that holdeth the seven stars in his right hand, who walketh in the midst of the seven golden candlesticks; I know thy works, and thy labour, and thy patience, and how thou canst not bear them which are evil: and thou hast tried them which say they are apostles, and are not, and hast found them liars: And hast borne, and hast patience, and for my name's sake hast laboured, and hast not fainted. Nevertheless I have *somewhat* against thee, because thou hast left thy first love. Remember therefore from whence thou art fallen, and repent, and do the first works; or else I will come unto thee quickly, and will remove thy candlestick out of his place, except thou repent. But this thou hast, that thou hatest the deeds of the Nicolaitanes, which I also hate. He that hath an ear, let him hear what the Spirit saith unto the churches; To him that overcometh will I give to eat of the tree of life, which is in the midst of the paradise of God.". Alleluia and praise the LORD. Amen and Amen. The Church in Smyrna and it's persecution is likely related to the general persecution of the Church of God, by the condensed power of the Church at Rome by the Council of Nicaea in 325 A.D. and the years of the development of Islam in the 6th century A.D., as well (Rev. 3:9).[8] Revelation 3:8-11 says, "And unto the angel of the church in Smyrna write; These things saith the first and the last, which was dead, and is alive; I know thy works, and tribulation, and poverty, (but thou art rich) and *I know* the blasphemy of them which say they are Jews, and are not, but *are* the synagogue of Satan. Fear none of those things which thou shall suffer: behold, the devil shall cast *some* of you into prison, that ye may be tried; and ye shall have tribulation ten days: be thou faithful unto death, and I will give thee a crown of life. He that hath an ear, let him hear what the Spirit saith unto the churches; He that overcometh shall not be hurt of the second death.". Alleluia and praise the LORD. Amen and Amen.

The church in Pergamos, no doubt, is related to the era of history which had the crusading "Christians" coming against Muslims of the Middle East in the Middle Ages, speaking of the seat of Satan, where Satan dwells (Rev. 2:13). Revelation 3:12-17 says, "And to the angel of the church in Pergamos write: These things saith he which hath the sharp sword with two edges; I know thy works, and where thou dwellest, *even* where Satan's seat *is:* and thou holdest fast my name, and hast not denied my faith, even in those days wherein Antipas *was* my faithful martyr, who was slain among you, where Satan dwelleth. But I have a few things against thee, because thou hast there them that hold the doctrine of Balaam, who taught Balac to cast a stumblingblock before the children of Israel, to eat things sacrificed unto idols, and to commit fornication. So hast thou also them that hold the doctrine of the Nicolaitanes, which thing I hate. Repent; or else I will come unto thee quickly, and will fight against them with the sword of my mouth. He that hath an ear, let him hear what the Spirit saith unto the churches; To him that overcometh will I give to eat of the hidden manna, and will give him a white stone, and in the stone a new name written, which no man knoweth saving he that receiveth *it*.". Alleluia and praise the LORD. Amen and Amen. The Church in Thyatira is likely related to the Enlightenment era and the seemingly infamous "Illuminati".

---

[8] https://rcg.org/books/thogtc.html, chapter 7, retrieved 24/03/2022

Strangely enough, I had heard about the "Illuminati" in recent years, and when I was doing my research, I found a website in plain site dedicated to the organization.[9] Truly, I never thought it would be that easy to find. Nevertheless, in general the "Illuminati" movement, has its roots in Germany by a man named, Adam Weishaupt, during the Thyatira era of the Church, mentioned in the book of Revelation, whom have the "…morning star." (Rev. 2:28).[10] It should be no surprise then that the Thyatira era of the Church of God, is associated with the Enlightenment movement of the 1700's, because of the reference to light, the "…morning star." (Rev. 2:28). And Jesus Christ of Nazareth is the true Light and Morning Star mentioned in the Holy Bible (John 1:1-14, 8:12, 9:5; Rev. 22:16). Revelation 2:18-29 says, "And unto the angel of the church in Thyatira write: These things saith the Son of God, who hath his eyes like unto a flame of fire, and his feet *are* like fine brass; I know thy works, and charity, and service, and faith, and thy patience, and thy works; and the last *to be* more than the first. Notwithstanding I have a few things against thee, because thou sufferest that woman Jezebel, which calleth herself a prophetess, to teach and to seduce my servants to commit fornication, and to eat things sacrificed unto idols. And I gave her space to repent of her fornication; and she repented not. Behold, I will cast her into a bed, and them that commit adultery with her into great tribulation, except they repent of their deeds. And I will kill her children with death; and all the churches shall know that I am he which searcheth the reins and hearts: and I will give unto every one of you according to your works. But unto you I say, and unto the rest in Thyatira, as many as have not this doctrine, and which have not known the depths of Satan, as they speak; I will put upon you none other burden. But that which ye have *already* hold fast till I come. And he that overcometh, and keepeth my works unto the end, to him will I give power over the nations: And he shall rule them with a rod of iron; as the vessels of a potter shall they be broken in shivers: even as I received of my Father. And I will give him the morning star. He that hath an ear, let him hear what the Spirit saith unto the churches.". Alleluia and praise the LORD. Amen and Amen.

The church in Sardis, I am rather convinced is associated with the many denominations, especially of the west that were developed in the 1800's, namely the Seventh day Adventists, and the Jehovah's Witnesses, as Sardis is commanded to be watchful, and the Jehovah's Witnesses have a magazine named the "Watchtower" (Rev. 3:2). Revelation 3:1-6 says, "And unto the angel of the church in Sardis write; These things saith he that hath the seven Spirits of God, and the seven stars; I know thy works, that thou hast a name that thou livest, and art dead. Be watchful, and strengthen the things which remain, that are ready to die: for I have not found thy works perfect before God. Remember therefore how thou hast received and heard, and hold fast, and repent. If therefore thou shalt not watch, I will come on thee as a thief, and thou shalt not know what hour I will come upon thee. Thou hast a few names even in Sardis which have not defiled their garments; and they shall walk with me in white: for they are worthy. He that overcometh, the same shall be clothed in white raiment; and

[9] https://www.illuminatiofficial.org/, retrieved 02/02/2018

[10] https://en.wikipedia.org/wiki/Illuminati, retrieved 02/02/2018

I will not blot out his name out of the book of life, but I will confess his name before my Father, and before his angels. He that hath an ear, let him hear what the Spirit saith unto the churches.". Alleluia and praise the Lord. Amen and Amen. The Philadelphian era of the church has been associated with the 1900's, namely the Radio Church of God, and its subsequent organization, the Worldwide Church of God, until about the 1980's. This era is said to have an open door that no man can close (Rev. 3:7, 8). Revelation 3:7-13 says, "And to the angel of the church in Philadelphia write; These things saith he that is holy, he that is true, he that hath the key of David, he that openeth, and no man shutteth; and shutteth, and no man openeth; I know thy works: behold, I have set before thee an open door, and no man can shut it: for thou hast a little strength, and hast kept my word, and hast not denied my name. Behold, I will make them of the synagogue of Satan, which say they are Jews, and are not, but do lie; behold, I will make them to come and worship before thy feet, and to know that I have loved thee. Because thou hast kept the word of my patience, I also will keep thee from the hour of temptation, which shall come upon the world, to try them that dwell upon the earth. Behold, I come quickly: hold that fast which thou hast, that no man take thy crown. Him that overcometh will I make a pillar in the temple of God, and he shall go no more out: and I will write upon him the name of my God, and the name of the city of my God, *which is* new Jerusalem, which cometh down out of heaven from my God: and *I will write upon him* my new name. He that hath an ear, let him hear what the Spirit saith unto the churches.". Alleluia and praise the LORD. Amen and Amen.

This brings us to the Laodicean era of the church, and the fulfillment of prophecy of the "falling away", albeit, the "falling away" from God, has been happening since the beginning of time (Gen 4:6, Isa. 14:12, 2 Th. 2:3). And these church eras were actually physical churches of God in these actual places in now western Turkey, when John wrote to these churches from the nearby island of Patmos in his book of Revelation, inspired by the Holy Spirit of God, in Christ Jesus of Nazareth's Holy name, no doubt (Rev. 1:9). And the church in Laodicea is encouraged by God, in Christ Jesus of Nazareth to "...buy of me gold tried in the fire, that thou mayest be rich; and white raiment, that thou mayest be clothed, and *that* the shame of thy nakedness do not appear; and anoint thine eyes with eyesalve, that thou mayest see." (Rev. 3:18). This, no doubt, is in reference to marriage, which of course, the definition of true marriage between a man and woman is challenged in this day, as of the date of writing this book in 2019 A.D.; but again, this is not a new challenge (Eccl. 1:9). This also makes clear, where true and enduring riches come from, that is, within the institution of the Biblical definition of a lasting marriage between one man and one woman (Gen. 2:24, Matt. 19:5, 6; Mark 10:7, 8). Alleluia and praise the Lord. Amen and Amen. And we are encouraged to anoint our eyes with eye salve, that is, seek the truth and keep it (Rev. 3:18). Revelation 3:14-19 says, "And unto the angel of the church of the Laodiceans write; These things saith the Amen, the faithful and true witness, the beginning of the creation of God; I know thy works, that thou art lukewarm, and neither cold nor hot, I will spue thee out of my mouth. Because thou sayest, I am rich, and increased with goods, and have need of nothing; and knowest not that thou art wretched, and miserable, and poor, and blind, and naked: I counsel thee to buy of me gold tried in the fire, that thou mayest be rich; and white raiment, that thou mayest be clothed, and *that* the shame of thy nakedness do not appear; and anoint thine eyes with eyesalve, that thou mayest see. As many as I love, I rebuke and chasten: be zealous therefore, and repent.". Alleluia and praise the LORD. Amen and Amen. Last, Revelation 3:20-22 says of Jesus, "Behold, I stand at the door, and knock: if any man hear my voice, and open the door, I will come in to him, and will sup with him, and he with me. To him that overcometh will I grant to sit with me in my throne, even as I also overcame, and am set down with my Father in his throne. He that hath an ear, let him hear what the Spirit saith unto the churches.". This is an invitation from Jesus Christ of Nazareth, to dwell with Him, in Him and Him in us, through His Holy Spirit. We do this by accepting His life saving work, finished for us on the cross at Passover in 31 A.D. (John 19:30). He died on the cross for the forgiveness of our sins, He was buried, and He arose the third day to give us the hope and promise of eternal life in His Holy name. Alleluia and praise the LORD. Amen and Amen.

Golden Rule and Faith

Matthew 7:12 says, "Therefore all things whatsoever ye would that men should do to you, do ye even so to them: for this is the law and the prophets.". Ultimately, we are not all called necessarily to die on the "battle field" or on a literal cross, but Jesus is calling us to take these steps forward in faith, regardless of where they might lead (Luke 11:22). We are not to be afraid of our "future", but to put our trust in Jesus Christ of Nazareth for it (Matt. 12:21). He is calling us to be obedient unto death, everyday (Luke 9:23). We die to our old self daily (Rom. 6:6, 1 Cor. 15:31). The nature we took on after our ancestors, Adam and Eve, ate from the tree of knowledge of good and evil, became sinful (Gen. 3). You may be able to feel in your flesh the struggle between doing good and evil (Gal. 5:17). But ultimately, in the name of Jesus Christ of Nazareth, we can and will overcome our sinful nature. God has given us all an appointed time here on earth (Eccl. 3:2). Jeremiah said that we have "…an expected end." (Jer. 29:11). You may or may not have an idea of when your time is going to be up here on earth, but you can be rest assured in Jesus Christ of Nazareth, your life will continue forever, wherever Jesus Christ is, you are and will be (Matt. 28:20, John 14:16-18, Heb. 13:5). The apostle, Paul, says in Romans 4:5, "But to him that worketh not, but believeth on him that justifieth the ungodly, his faith is counted for righteousness.". If you were looking for a God that does not justify us by works, you have found Him in this one simple verse. And the ungodly are justified in the name of Jesus Christ of Nazareth, a sinless man taking all of our sins upon Himself, He spilled His Holy and righteous blood on the cross and died on the cross for the forgiveness of our sins, He was buried and the third day He arose to give us the hope and promise of eternal life in His Holy name. Alleluia and praise the LORD. Amen and Amen.

Hebrews 11:4-19 says, "By faith Abel offered unto God a more excellent sacrifice than Cain, by which he obtained witness that he was righteous, God testifying of his gifts: and by it he being dead yet speaketh. By faith Enoch was translated that he should not see death; and was not found, because God had translated him: for before his translation he had this testimony, that he pleased God. But without faith *it is* impossible to please *him:* for he that cometh to God must believe that he is, and *that* he is a rewarder of them that diligently seek him. By faith Noah, being warned of God of things not seen as yet, moved with fear, prepared an ark to the saving of his house; by the which he condemned the world, and became heir of the righteousness which is by faith. By faith Abraham, when he was called to go out into a place which he should after receive for an inheritance, obeyed; and he went out, not knowing whither he went. By faith he sojourned in the land of promise, as *in* a strange country, dwelling in tabernacles with Isaac and Jacob, the heirs with him of the same promise: For he looked for a city which hath foundations, whose builder and maker *is* God. Through faith also Sara herself received strength to conceive seed, and was delivered of a child when she was past age, because she judged him faithful who had promised. Therefore sprang there even of one, and him as good as dead, *so many* as the stars of the sky in multitude, and as the sand which is by the sea shore innumerable. These all died in faith, not having received the promises, but having seen them afar off, and were persuaded of *them,* and embraced *them,* and confessed that they were strangers and pilgrims on the earth. For they that say such things declare plainly that they seek a country. And truly, if they had been mindful of that *country* from whence they came out, they might have had opportunity to have returned. But now they desire a better *country,* that is, an heavenly: wherefore God is not ashamed to be called their God: for he hath prepared for them a city. By faith Abraham, when he was tried, offered up Isaac: and he that had received the promises offered up his only begotten *son,* Of whom it was said, That in Isaac shall thy seed be called: Accounting that God *was* able to raise *him* up, even from the dead; from whence also he received him in a figure.". And the account continues with other examples of the faithful of God throughout the Old Testament generations. Alleluia and praise the LORD. Amen and Amen.

With faith of a mustard seed we can move mountains; we can move trees (Matt. 17:20, Luke 17:6). Faith is defined, by Paul, an apostle of Christ Jesus of Nazareth, as "… the substance of things hoped for, the evidence of things not seen. For by it the elders obtained a good report. Through faith we understand that the worlds were framed by the word of God, so that things which are seen were not made of things which do appear." (Heb. 11:1-3). In the Old Testament, the word faith is associated with belief, as if the words are interchangeable, and Moses is called faithful by God (Gen. 15:6, Num. 12:7). The Hebrew word for faithful and belief is 'aman, meaning; to build up or support; to foster as a parent or nurse; figuratively to render (or be) firm or faithful, to trust or believe, to be permanent or quiet; morally to be true or certain; once (Isaiah 30:21; interchangeable with 541) to go to the right hand: — hence, assurance, believe, bring up, establish, + fail, be faithful (of long continuance, stedfast, sure, surely, trusty, verified), nurse, (-ing father), (put), trust, turn to the right; Strong's number

539. Strong's number 541, 'aman, literally says, to take the right hand road: — turn to the right. Of course, Jesus admonishes this in the New Testament gospel accounts as He says, "… seek ye first the kingdom of God, and his righteousness…" (Matt. 6:33). He says to take the strait gate and narrow way (Matt. 7:14). Isaiah 30:21 says, "And thine ears shall hear a word behind thee, saying, This *is* the way, walk ye in it, when ye turn to the right hand, and when ye turn to the left.". This is in reference to the Holy Ghost, the Holy Spirit of God, given to us as our Comforter in Christ Jesus of Nazareth's Holy name, whom will never leave us, even until the end of this world and unto everlasting life in Christ Jesus of Nazareth's Holy name, through His resurrection promise to us and all whom believe in His Holy and lifesaving name (Matt. 28:20, John 14:16-18, Heb. 13:5). Alleluia and praise the LORD. Amen and Amen. The point of all of this is that, Jesus Christ of Nazareth, came in the flesh, He was conceived of the Holy Spirit in and born of the virgin, Mary, espoused to Joseph, raised as a child of Israel, of the tribe of Judah, He ministered for three and a half years, starting at the age of about thirty, He took all of our sins upon Himself as a sinless man, shedding His Holy and righteous blood on the cross for us, He died on the cross for the forgiveness of our sins, He was buried and He arose the third day to give us the hope and promise of eternal life in His Holy name. Alleluia and praise the LORD. Amen and Amen. He is the faithful and true witness, and the Amen (Rev. 3:14). Amen.

Conclusion

Jesus was given a command by His Father, God, that Jesus had authority over His own life, that He could lay it down and take it up again (John 10:17, 18). All faithful followers of Jesus Christ of Nazareth have this same reward from God, that is, we have full authority over our own life, death and resurrection, in Christ Jesus of Nazareth's Holy name. This is the power of God, and the gift of eternal life in the name of God's only begotten Son, Jesus Christ of Nazareth. Alleluia and praise the LORD. No person here on earth can force us to lose our life, or else God would be a liar, which is not the case. If you are afraid of man, and what he can do to you, it is in vain, because God is in authority over all things (Rev. 4:11). Alleluia and praise the LORD. Jesus said, "And fear not them which kill the body, but are not able to kill the soul: but rather fear him which is able to destroy both soul and body in hell." (Matt. 10:28). And even at that, God does not ultimately desire us to fear Him. Alleluia and praise the LORD. God is Love after all (1 John 4:18). This is why Jesus Christ of Nazareth came, to show us God's love (John 15:13). John speaks in one of his epistles, that love is not that we love God, but that God loves us (1 John 4:10). We are the sinners and He is the righteous One (Matt. 19:17). We need forgiveness and He offers us forgiveness by the blood of His dearly beloved Son, Jesus Christ of Nazareth (Matt. 17:5). Alleluia and praise the LORD. Amen and Amen. We overcome this world and all its evil, seen and unseen by the blood of Jesus Christ of Nazareth, shed on the cross for the forgiveness of our sins and the whole world's sins, a sinless man taking on all of our sins on the cross at Passover 31 A.D., He died on the cross, He was buried and He arose after three days in the grave to give us the hope and promise of eternal life in His Holy name. Alleluia and praise the LORD. Amen and Amen. Do you believe all of this? Have faith in your God and my God, in your Christ and my Christ, in Christ Jesus of Nazareth, the only begotten Son of God, born of the virgin Mary, espoused to Joseph in the late last century B.C., and raised up as a child of Israel, of the tribe of Judah, a son of David (Matt. 1:18-25). Alleluia and praise the LORD. Jesus Christ of Nazareth is the only person here on earth that can save you, myself or anyone else, whom has ever lived, lives or ever will live from our sin that brings about death (Acts 4:12). Alleluia and praise the LORD. Amen and Amen. But do not take my word for it, ask Him for yourself whom He is, where He is, and what He is. He will reveal to you all things by the knowledge given through His Holy Spirit, given to us, and truly, given to all of mankind as was prophesied by the Old Testament prophet, Joel, and confirmed at Pentecost in 31 A.D. by the apostle, Peter (Joel 2:28-32, Acts 2:1-21). Alleluia and praise the LORD. Amen and Amen.

I will say, that the Bible says two things that have caught my attention, regarding prophecy. One of which I know was fulfilled in Jesus Christ of Nazareth for certain, but both have been fulfilled in other ways and I suppose will be fulfilled for some amount of time until God desires otherwise. The first is that the Holy Bible of God prophesies of God doing a strange thing, and a new thing, and a woman shall compass a man (Isa. 28:21, 42:9, 43:19, 48:6; Jer. 31:22, Hos. 8:12). Witnesses of Jesus' works spoke of the strangeness of what He was doing, because of the simple fact that the works He did had never been heard of, nor seen before here on earth (Luke 5:26). Of course, God also spoke of these things in prophecy of new things happening that have not been spoken of beforehand, I suppose this may include Jesus turning water into wine and walking on water (Isa. 48:6-9, John 2:1-11). As far as the woman compassing a man, Jesus' mother, Mary, encouraged Him to start His miracle working ministry with changing the water into wine at a wedding feast, because they had run out of wine (John 2:3-5). And the second prophesy that has received my attention is that of God sifting the nations with the sieve of vanity (Isa. 30:28). Now Jesus in and of Himself is not a vain person, by God. He is perfect, but the people, the disciples and apostles whom wrote about Him, by themselves, including you and I, are vain, if we do not have Christ Jesus of Nazareth and His life giving blood shed for us on the cross, dying on the cross for the forgiveness of our sins, being buried and arising the third day to give us the hope and promise of eternal life in His Holy name (Heb. 2:9, 10; 1 Pet. 1:17-21). Now regarding this sifting of the nations with "...the sieve of vanity...", the word vain can mean emptiness or outright lies (Isa. 30:28). My point is, that some people have pointed out seeming errors or contradictions in the New Testament regarding the various accounts of Jesus Christ of Nazareth's life and His works. And to be honest with you, I have had my challenges with scripture, but they are not errors and contradictions, they are actually fulfillment of prophecy first and foremost, but they are more than this, they are also proof that man, no matter an apostle of Jesus Christ of Nazareth or not, can be rather imperfect in this life, because of our sinful flesh and blood (John 2:24, 25). But thanks be to God, that we are imperfect that God may be glorified through us, in His beloved Son, Jesus Christ of Nazareth's Holy name (John 13:31, 32; 15:8). Alleluia and praise the LORD. I will not list all of these cases, but a few are, whether His robe was purple or scarlet at the judgement, albeit I have seen with my own eyes colours can change by the change in the reflection angle and amount of light shone on them (Matt. 27:28, Mark 15:17, John 19:2). The other may be was there a donkey and a colt, the foal of a donkey, that Jesus rode triumphantly into Jerusalem upon, as King of Israel and the whole world, or just the foal (Matt. 21:1-11, Mark 11:1-10, Luke 19:28-40, John 12:12-17)? And was there two devil possessed men that Jesus cast the legion out of into the swine, whom subsequently ran into the water, or was there just one, or was one left out of the one account or was there two separate occasions even (Matt. 8:28-32, Mark 5:1-13, Luke 8:26-33)? And there may be others like this including the anointing of the feet of Jesus by the woman, did it happen a week before the crucifixion, or in Luke's account, was it earlier than this, or was Luke's account accurate, but the written account out of chronological order, or did it happen twice (Luke 7:37-48, John 11:2, 12:1-3)? Well, my friend, now you know, I do not have all of the answers. But I do know one thing. God does. And by His Holy Spirit, He will reveal to you and I all things, as He wills it and as we faithfully obey Him, in Christ Jesus of Nazareth's Holy name. Alleluia and praise the LORD. Amen and Amen. To God be the glory in His only begotten Son, Jesus Christ of Nazareth's Holy name. Amen and Amen.

What should we do? God has given us the freedom of choice, and this has been since the beginning, where He gave Adam and Eve the freedom to choose between life and death, the tree of life or the tree of knowledge of good and evil (Gen. 2:9, 16, 17). This again was the choice given to the Israelites whom came out of Egypt, when they had the choice to follow God's commands and law, or they could go after their own way (Deut. 30:15-20). So now again I say to you, what will you do? I encourage you to accept Jesus Christ of Nazareth as your Lord and Saviour of your life. But I cannot ultimately, as this is in God's hands. Even Jesus said that God, the Father, draws us to Him, and gives us to His only begotten Son, Jesus Christ of Nazareth (Matt. 20:16, John 6:44). So maybe a better question would be; is God calling you? And if so, what is He calling you to do? To simply put it, if He is calling you, and no doubt He is, He desires you to follow Him, and be obedient to Him alone (Matt. 22:37, 38). Alleluia and praise the LORD. Some years ago, I had a "word" from God that said to me, evil will be cast from earth by praising God. Jesus said to worship God in spirit and in truth, not necessarily in a specific place or at a specific time (John 4:23). Albeit we are to fellowship with other believers as well to strengthen our faith, to grow in the body of Christ and to enjoy the abundant life God has given us here on earth in general (Rom. 10:13-17). However, in general, the Holy Bible of God asks us to watch, pray, sing psalms and hymns, and go about our own business, working with our hands and to rest (Matt. 26:41, Eph. 5:18-21, 1 Thess. 4:10-12). The prophecy of the tribe of Judah was that their hands would be sufficient for them to work, I suppose this is why the Jewish people have been successful in this world, even if they have not accepted Jesus Christ of Nazareth as their Messiah fully yet, as of the date of writing this book in 2019 A.D. (Deut. 33:7). And I suppose then that this blessing would rest on all of the disciples of Jesus Christ of Nazareth, if He is indeed the Lion of the tribe of Judah, and Saviour of the whole world (John 4:42, Rev. 5:5). This would explain why the true Church of God has not failed throughout the centuries and even millennia, because we have our Creator, in Christ Jesus of Nazareth, watching over us, leading us, and guiding us, with His mercifully guiding hand, as a true Shepherd leads His flock (John 10:11). Alleluia and praise the LORD. Amen and Amen.

Last, pray to God for His Holy Spirit to dwell in you; to comfort you, to help you, to teach you, and to provide for you, and pray to God for all things (John 14:26, 1 Thess. 5:17). As the apostle, John, says in his epistle, "But the anointing which ye have received of him abideth in you, and ye need not that any man teach you: but as the same anointing teacheth you of all things, and is truth, and is no lie, and even as it hath taught you, ye shall abide in him." (1 John 2:27). This is that anointing of the Holy Spirit of God; we receive by faith, which is a gift from God, not by our own works, but by the grace of God that is in Jesus Christ of Nazareth's Holy name (Eph. 2:8, 9). God's Holy Spirit is good and free, paid in full by the blood of Jesus Christ of Nazareth, shed on the cross for the forgiveness of our sins, He died on the cross, He was buried and He arose the third day to give us all the hope and promise of eternal life in His Holy name (Neh. 9:20, Ps. 51:12). Alleluia and praise the LORD. Amen and Amen.

APPENDIX G

JERUSALEM AND ANTICHRIST; GOD AND CHRIST JESUS OF NAZARETH; SATAN AND THE DEVILS; GOOD AND EVIL

Introduction

Jesus mentioned in His prophetic warning on the Monday of the final week of His earthy ministry, before His resurrection, about the abomination of desolation standing in the Holy Place, that Daniel also spoke of and He admonishes us to understand what He is saying about it (Dan. 11:31, 12:11; Matt. 24:15, Mark 13:14, Luke 21:20). This happened in 70 A.D., when Jerusalem was destroyed by the Roman occupiers, including the temple, which Jesus did indeed prophecy of (Matt. 24:2, Mark 13:2, Luke 21:6). This could also be any number of other things, including devil possession in our mind, or general slavery of man, including taking the mark of the beast, etc. (Rev. 13). But of course, Jesus Christ of Nazareth says to love your enemy, pray for them that persecute you and bless them that curse you (Matt. 5:44). And ultimately the Holy Bible of God says of God, that "I have overthrown *some* of you, as God overthrew Sodom and Gomorrah and ye were as a firebrand plucked out of the burning: yet have ye not returned unto me, saith the LORD. Therefore thus will I do unto thee, O Israel: *and* because I will do this unto thee, **prepare to meet thy God**, O Israel. For, lo, **he** that formeth the mountains, and createth the wind, and **declareth unto man what** *is his thought*, that maketh the morning darkness, and treadeth upon the high places of the earth, **The LORD, The God of hosts, *is* his name.**" (Amos 4:11-13). The reality is that no matter how hard we try to understand something, rebel against God, etc.; God indeed is sovereign over all things (John 1:1-3, Rev. 4:11). Alleluia and praise the LORD. And has been and always will be, in the name of His only begotten Son, Jesus Christ of Nazareth. Alleluia and praise the LORD. And we can all overcome the works of Satan, the Devil, the dragon, that old serpent, whom deceives the whole world, and is a murderer and liar, and the father of them, and was one from the beginning (John 8:44, Rev. 12:9). We can all overcome evil, by the blood of Jesus Christ of Nazareth, shed for us on the cross at Passover in 31 A.D., He was buried, and He arose the third day, overcoming death for us and the whole world (Matt. 12:40, 27:33-50, 27:57-60, 28:1-10). Alleluia and praise the LORD. And now sits at the right hand of the true Father, God Almighty, until all of His enemies are made His footstool (Heb. 10:12, 13). Alleluia and praise the LORD. Amen and Amen. Nevertheless, read on to learn more about the differences between God and the wicked, the difference between good and evil. And overcome evil by the life giving blood of Jesus Christ of Nazareth, the only begotten Son of God, and the testimony of His eternal life, and His Holy life in us, through His Holy Spirit given to us, as we accept Him. Alleluia and praise the LORD. Amen and Amen.

Jerusalem

The place

Jerusalem was originally a city of the Jebusites, descendants of Canaan, Son of Ham; but they were cut off from the city by God and Israel, namely through King David, albeit, at least two scriptures indicate they dwell with Judah and Benjamin in Jerusalem (Gen. 10:6, 15, 16; Ex. 23:23, Deut. 20:17, Jos. 15:63, Judges 1:21, 2 Sam. 5:6). Later, God came to smote King David and Jerusalem for his rebellion against God in numbering the children of Israel (2 Sam. 24:1-10). God, through the prophet Gad, gave King David three ultimatums for punishment for David's sin, David chose pestilence from the Lord, and it continued three days, where seventy thousand men in Israel died (2 Sam. 24:11-15). Then, the LORD repented Him of the evil, and King David saw the angel of the LORD, that smote the people by the threshing floor of Araunah (2 Sam. 24:16, 17). David bought the threshing floor of the Jebusite, Araunah, to give an offering to the LORD on and the Lord's anger turned from the city and Israel (2 Sam. 24:16-25). This same threshing floor is likely where Abraham attempted to offer up Isaac, about one thousand years earlier, and is known as mount Moriah (Gen. 22:1-18, 2 Chr. 3:1). This is also where the Temple of the Lord was built by David's son, King Solomon, and then destroyed by the Babylonians, and then subsequently the second temple was built by the remnant whom came out of captivity from Babylon, decreed by King Cyrus of Persia, and then King Darius, and finally furnished by decree of Artaxerxes (2 Chr. 3:1, 2 Kings 25:9, Ezra 5:13, 6:1-12, 7). The same place that Jesus Christ of Nazareth was taken to, as a young child, to be consecrated as a firstborn child of Israel, a son, of the tribe of Judah (Luke 2:22-38). And where He visited as a child at twelve years old, staying behind during the feast of unleavened bread, when His parents had already begun to travel back to Galilee without noticing Jesus' absence from the group of travellers (Luke 2:42-52). And where Jesus did miracles during His ministry (Matt. 21:14). Also, Jesus prophesied of the destruction of the temple, the Monday of the final week of His ministry, before His crucifixion on the Wednesday of that week, His death on the cross, His burial of three days in a grave and His resurrection that Saturday afternoon (Matt. 24). Jesus also spoke of His own body as the temple (John 2:21). This is the reality for all of us in Christ Jesus of Nazareth's Holy name (1 Cor. 6:19, 20). The true tabernacle of God, is that of our body, which God created and

He desires to dwell in us, through His Holy Spirit, given to us as a promise, by our Lord, Jesus Christ of Nazareth, whom died on the cross for the forgiveness of our sins, offering to us eternal life in His Holy name, He was buried and He arose three days later, giving us the hope and promise of eternal life in His Holy name. Alleluia and praise the LORD. Jerusalem is called to be a place of truth (Zech. 8:3). And if God intends to bring a literal "Messianic Age", that is, one thousand years of Christ's rule with His saints, Satan being chained until the final judgement, then the temple mentioned in the prophecies of Ezekiel, in the Holy Bible, can be taken as literal, which I am rather certain they are (Ezek. 40-48, Rev. 20:1-4). And various Biblical scholars have written about, including myself, and some have even built models of its prospective form (Ezek. 43:11). Nevertheless, our reality of Jerusalem must be in Jesus Christ of Nazareth, as He said to a Samaritan woman, "…the hour cometh, when ye shall neither in this mountain, nor yet at Jerusalem, worship the Father. …the hour cometh, and now is, when the true worshippers shall worship the Father in spirit and in truth…" (John 4:21, 23). That truth is in Jesus Christ of Nazareth, and that true Spirit, is the Holy Spirit of God, given to us by God, through accepting His only begotten Son, Jesus Christ of Nazareth, as our Saviour and the Saviour of the whole world. Alleluia and praise the LORD. Amen and Amen.

The people

Jerusalem means city of Peace, and Jesus Christ of Nazareth is the Prince of peace (Isa. 9:6). Psalm 125:2 says, "As the mountains are round about Jerusalem, so the LORD is round about his people from henceforth even for ever.". This is the greater reality we have in our relationship with God through Jesus Christ of Nazareth. The king, David, in Psalm admonishes us to pray for the peace of Jerusalem and another Psalmist was encouraged to remember the city, when in captivity in Babylon (Ps. 122:6; 137:1, 5, 6). This is speaking of the physical place, but most importantly it is speaking of the people, that is, the institutions, families, nations and the like, that make up the descendants of the tribes of Israel, that went into captivity, grew as nations in the 1st millennia B.C., were visited by their Messiah and King, Jesus Christ of Nazareth, physically born into this world from 4 B.C. to 31 A.D., and the gospel of the Kingdom of God has been preached to these nations and the whole world since then (Matt. 4:23, 24:14). This includes the "lost" sheep of Israel in the west and scattered throughout the world that the Holy Bible speaks of (Matt. 15:24, Jam. 1:1). This means you and I. Alleluia and praise the Lord. But Jesus did not only come for the "…lost sheep of the house of Israel…", He came to save the whole world (John 10:16, 1 John 2:2). Alleluia and praise the LORD. Amen and Amen. I have written about the descendants of Israel and the general demographic makeup of the world we live in today in another book, "Origin of Mankind", and the Old Testament does a good job of describing mankind's migrations and disbursements, first after the flood at the tower of Babel, and then Abraham's migration to the "promised land", and then Israel's sojourning in Egypt, Exodus and establishment as a nation in the "promised land" (Gen. 10,

11:1-9, 12:1-5, 46, 47; Ex., Jos., Jud., etc.). And then subsequent captivity and migration to other parts of this world, especially in the west today, namely the Judea Christian people of the west, whom generally have their roots in the Israelites of the Holy Bible of God (Gen. 28:14, 2 Kings 17:6, 24:1-25:11; Isa. 43:5, 6). Alleluia and praise the LORD. Amen and Amen. Jeremiah 9:11 says, "And I will make Jerusalem heaps, *and* a den of dragons...". This was fulfilled when the people of Jerusalem went into captivity to Babylon in about 600-500 B.C. and the first temple burned and also when the Romans destroyed Jerusalem and the second temple in 70 A.D. (2 Kings 24:1-25:11, Matt. 24:2). But Jesus also called the religious authorities in Jerusalem of His time, a generation of vipers, serpents, hypocrites, wolves in sheep's clothing, etc. (Matt. 6:2, 7:15, 10:16, 12:34; 23:13-15, 33; Luke 10:3). And this may have some prophetic warning regarding the future, during the "Great Tribulation", I do not know for certain, as of the date of writing this book in 2019 A.D. (Zech. 14:2, 14; Matt. 24:21, Luke 21:20). Nevertheless, this is why we need Jesus Christ of Nazareth to heal us from this world and the evils in it, as He is the true Jerusalem, and temple of God, as mentioned in the book of Revelation (John 2:21, Rev. 21:22). Although there is a physical place here on earth, that God indeed has chosen to dwell in, we must remember that God has created each and every one of us, Jew and Gentile alike in His image, in His likeness from the beginning (Gen. 1:26, 27; Zech. 12:5, 6; Gal. 3:28). And we all have the opportunity to receive the inheritance of the new Jerusalem, that is spiritual first and foremost in the name of Jesus Christ of Nazareth, the only begotten Son of God, by His Holy blood shed on the cross for the forgiveness of our sins, He was buried and the third day He arose to give us the hope and promise of eternal life in His Holy name. Alleluia and praise the LORD. Amen and Amen.

The Spirit

King David said of God, "Whither shall I go from thy spirit? or whither shall I flee from thy presence? If I ascend up into heaven, thou art there: if I make my bed in hell, behold, thou art there. If I take the wings of the morning, and dwell in the uttermost parts of the sea; Even there shall thy hand lead me, and thy right hand shall hold me. If I say, Surely the darkness shall cover me; even the night shall be light about me." (Ps. 139:7-12). This is a similar description that God gives regarding the New Jerusalem spoken of in the book of Revelation. Revelation 21:23 says, "And the city had no need of the sun, neither of the moon, to shine in it: for the glory of God did lighten it, and the Lamb is the light thereof.". In my book, "Heaven, Hell and the Resurrection", I described the "New Jerusalem" in terms of encompassing the entire earth, as it presently stands, using the size and shape of it today, and the volume of the "New Jerusalem" described in the book of Revelation (Rev. 21:16). I figured that the "New Jerusalem" encompasses the entire earth, up to the Stratosphere, about 17 miles into the atmosphere comparing the dimensions of the volume of the city with the earth's surface. Of course, this is an interpretation based on some mathematical calculations, but the reality is in Jesus Christ of Nazareth, the only begotten Son of God. He has given us His Holy spirit, a

FREE spirit, and His GOOD spirit, to dwell in us and with us no matter where we are or go here on earth, or anywhere else, as God wills it, in this life and in the "world to come" (Neh. 9:20, Ps. 51:12, John 14:16-18). Alleluia and praise the LORD. Amen and Amen. God is no respecter of persons, so the Holy Spirit has been given to all whom receive it (Acts 10:34). It was poured out on Pentecost in 31 A.D., as was prophesied by the prophet, Joel, of the Old Testament, and God's Holy Spirit continues to do His work through us, in us and with us as God wills it in the name of His only begotten Son, Jesus Christ of Nazareth (Joel 2:28, 29; Acts 2:1-24). Jesus Christ of Nazareth died on the cross for the forgiveness of our sins at Passover in 31 A.D., He was buried in the grave for three days, and He arose the third day, to give us the hope and promise of eternal life in His Holy name. Alleluia and praise the LORD. Amen and Amen. God is the God of the spirits of all flesh (Num. 27:16). And He forms the spirit in man (Zech. 12:1). He has created all things (John 1:3). So no matter our cultural, ethnic, physical, socioeconomic, etc., background in this life, we can all receive of His Holy Spirit freely, that is, it is a gift, not by works, but by grace (Eph. 2:8, 9). Jesus Christ of Nazareth shed His own blood on the cross for the forgiveness of our sins, any and all of them, He was buried and He arose the third day to give us the hope and promise of eternal life in His Holy name. Alleluia and praise the LORD. Amen and Amen.

Antichrist

Whom or what is it?

To put it simply, it is those who deny Jesus Christ of Nazareth has come in the flesh, and deny He is the Messiah and the only begotten Son of God (1 John 2:22, 4:3; 2 John 1:7). Judas, a son of perdition, is the architype of the New Testament Antichrist, the apostle, Peter, even denied he knew Jesus (Matt. 26:47, 48; Matt. 26:34, 69-75; John 17:12). And Jesus, Himself, even told His disciples not to mention whom He was at one point during His earthly ministry (Matt. 16:20). In general, the "antichrist", is or are the betrayers of Jesus Christ of Nazareth and the false witnesses against the testimony of the true Jesus Christ of Nazareth (Matt. 26:59-61, 1 John 2:22, 2 John 1:7). In some of my other writing I have gone into greater detail about the prophecies of the "antichrist", but ultimately, it is the spirit of disobedience and rebelliousness, that has influenced mankind throughout the ages. And was typified in the Garden of Eden, with Adam and Eve disobeying God and listening to the serpent, eating from the tree of knowledge of good and evil, and then in their descendants, in subsequent history in the Holy Bible and throughout earth's recorded history in general, and will continue until God, subdues this spirit of disobedience in mankind, once and for all! John put it simply, "For many deceivers are entered into the world, who confess not that Jesus Christ is come in the flesh. This is a deceiver and an antichrist." (2 John 1:7). But Jesus Christ of Nazareth has come in the flesh, conceived by the Holy Spirit in the virgin, Mary, born of the virgin, Mary, espoused to Joseph (Matt. 1:18). He was raised as a child of Israel, with brothers and sisters (Luke 2:42-52, Matt. 13:55, 56). Jesus started His earthly ministry in the fall of 27 A.D., He did miracles, taught, healed and ultimately gave His life up on the cross at Passover in 31 A.D. for the forgiveness of our sins, He died on that cross and He was buried and He arose the third day to give us the hope and promise of eternal life in His Holy name. Alleluia and praise the LORD. Amen and Amen.

What should you do?

At all cost, including losing your own life, you should not deny Jesus Christ of Nazareth is the Lord and Saviour of all of mankind (Matt. 10:32, 33). This is what Jesus ultimately called His disciples to do. Deny themselves and take up their cross daily and follow Him (Matt. 16:24, Mark 8:34, 10:21; Luke 9:23). He is still asking us, His disciples today, to do the same thing (John 17:20, 21). Although, Peter denied Jesus three times during His final trial and must have been forgiven for it (Matt. 26:34, 69-75; 1 Pet. 1:3-5). Jesus does say that God will forgive us if we speak against the Son of man, but if we blaspheme the Holy Spirit, this is the unforgiveable sin, that puts us in danger of eternal damnation (Mark 3:28, 29; Luke 12:10). Ultimately, we need to accept the Holy Spirit into our mind, soul and body. We need to accept the sacrifice Jesus Christ of Nazareth made for mankind approximately 2000 years ago, as of the date of writing this book in 2019 A.D.. He died on the cross for the forgiveness of our sins, He was buried and He arose the third day to give us the hope and promise of eternal life in His Holy name. Alleluia and praise the LORD. Amen and Amen. He came to show us the kingdom of God, and to forgive us of our rebellious ways, our sin. He did not come to condemn, but to save (John 3:17). Alleluia and praise the LORD. Amen and Amen.

The outcome

The Holy Bible says constantly that those who follow God will be blessed and provided for abundantly in this life, and in the "world to come", eternal life (Deut. 30:19, 20; Mark 10:29, 30; 3 John 1:2). It even says that obedience to God brings the pleasures that mankind seeks (Job 36:11). The world and Satan have deceived mankind; convincing them that pleasure comes from sin and disobedience to God (Heb. 11:25). The perfect example of this is the serpent beguiling Adam and Eve in the garden of Eden (Gen. 3). But the fact of the matter is; that old serpent, the devil is a liar (John 8:44, Rev. 12:9). Satan is said to be the father of lies from the beginning (John 8:44). Whether it is another person, an evil spirit or some thoughts in our own mind that are telling us untruthful things; these "powers" can and will be conquered in the name of Jesus Christ of Nazareth. Alleluia and praise the LORD. Amen and Amen. If you are having doubts about this, accept the blood of Jesus Christ of Nazareth into your life for the forgiveness of your sins, and accept the Holy Spirit of God into your heart, mind and soul to teach you and be with you forever in Christ Jesus of Nazareth's Holy name. Alleluia and praise the LORD. Amen and Amen. God gives us a sound mind, He gives us peace and He gives us rest in the name of His only begotten Son, Jesus Christ of Nazareth (2 Tim. 1:7). Alleluia and praise the LORD. As the Holy Bible says, "...there is none other name under heaven given among men, whereby we must be saved." (Acts 4:12). Place your trust in the name of Jesus Christ of Nazareth and submit your life; spirit, body and soul to Him, you will not regret it. Alleluia and praise the LORD. Amen and Amen.

Satan and devils

Satan

The Hebrew root word means, to attack, accuse, resist, be an adversary, Strong's number 7853 (Ps. 38:20, etc.). The Hebrew word used for Satan according to Strong's concordance says, an opponent, the arch-enemy of good, adversary, withstand, Strong's number 7854. The word Satan is used nineteen times in the Old Testament (1 Chr. 21:1, Job 1:6, 7, 8, 9, 12; 2:1, 2, 3, 4, 6, 7; Ps. 109:6, Zech. 3:1, 2). Interestingly, Satan is described in 1 Chronicles 21:1 to have provoked David to number Israel and in another account of what I believe to be the same event, the Scripture speaks of God in anger moving David to number Israel (2 Sam. 24:1). You can draw your own conclusions as you will. But David ultimately takes the blame for the evil done, that is, numbering the Israelites (2 Sam. 24:10, 1 Chr. 21:8). This may have been considered evil because David was not putting his trust in God for the increase, but David's own understanding (2 Sam. 24:3, 1 Chr. 21:3). This could very well have been a test by God, using Satan also, but ultimately God and Satan must not be the same person as will be shown in the trial of Job (Job 1:6). One day, among the sons of God, Satan also came to present himself before God, speaking to God about his doings and God points out His servant Job to Satan (Job 1:1-8). In the book of Job, Satan can be shown to have authority over people, weather, and physical health (Job 1:12-19, 2:4-7). This of course ultimately was authority given by God though (Job 1:12, 2:6). Alleluia and praise the LORD. The prophet Zechariah again shows the difference between Satan and God. He says, "And he shewed me Joshua the high priest standing before the angel of the LORD, and Satan standing at his right hand to resist him. And the LORD said unto Satan, The LORD rebuke thee, O Satan; even the LORD that hath chosen Jerusalem rebuke thee: is not this a brand plucked out of the fire? Now Joshua was clothed with filthy garments, and stood before the angel." (Zech. 3:1-3).

Jesus was in the wilderness forty days fasting and after Satan came to tempt Jesus (Matt. 4:1-11). Satan is named by Jesus Christ of Nazareth as a murderer, a liar and a thief (John 8:44). A liar and the father of it (John 8:44). This can be seen by the serpent in the garden of Eden, starting the first lie given to Eve, saying that if she ate from the tree of knowledge of good and evil, they would not die, but would be like gods knowing both good and evil (Gen. 3:1-5). Of course this was a lie, because Adam and Eve died, at the least the Bible indicates

Adam died and he ate from the same fruit of the tree of knowledge of good and evil that Eve gave to him to eat (Gen. 3:6, 19; 5:5). But ultimately we have forgiveness of our sins, and eternal life in the only begotten Son of God, Jesus Christ of Nazareth, whom died on the cross for the forgiveness of our sins, He was buried and He arose the third day to give us the hope and promise of eternal life in His Holy name. Alleluia and praise the LORD. Amen and Amen. Jesus was also accused of being Beelzebub, prince of the devils (Matt. 12:24). Jesus even said this, He said if the master of the house is accused of being the prince of the devils, how much the more those of His household (Matt. 10:25)? Beelzebub seems to be a god of Ekron (2 Kings 1:2). And idol gods, as the true God considers them end up being wood and stone in the end; except for Jesus Christ of Nazareth, the true Stone of the corner, the chief Cornerstone of the Church of God (2 Kings 19:18, Matt. 21:42, Acts 4:10, 11; Eph. 2:20). Dagon, a god of the Philistines, was a statue and when the ark of the LORD was taken by the Philistines and brought to this god's temple, the next morning the Dagon statue had fallen on its face to the ground before the ark of the LORD. So they set the statue in his place again, and then the following morning it had fallen again face to the ground with the head and palms of his statues hands cut off, only the stump of Dagon was left (1 Sam. 5:1-4). No doubt this was done by the true God, that is, the God of Abraham, Isaac and Jacob, personified in His only begotten Son, Jesus Christ of Nazareth (Ex. 3:6, Mark 12:26, John 8:58). Alleluia and praise the LORD. Amen and Amen.

The apostle, Peter, was rebuked as if being Satan (Matt. 16:23). I am not suggesting that Peter and his efforts as an apostle of Christ should be ignored, and considered evil, far from it, but I am suggesting, that if an apostle of Christ could be called Satan, how much the more you and I? The apostle, Paul, experienced a messenger from Satan, acting as a thorn in the flesh to humble him, and God said, His grace was sufficient for Paul (2 Cor. 12:7-9). The apostle, Paul, in one of his epistles actually says, "But be it so, I did not burden you: nevertheless, being crafty, I caught you with guile." (2 Cor. 12:7). This seems to be an attribute of Satan, that is guile, so I wonder if that was the thorn in the flesh manifesting itself in Paul at that time (Gen. 3:13, 2 Cor. 11:3, 12:16)? I do not know. Later on in another epistle he seems to say, "For our exhortation *was* not of deceit, nor of uncleanness, nor in guile…" (1 Thess. 2:3). But the apostle, Paul, also said, "…let God be true, but every man a liar…" (Rom. 3:4). So I will leave the interpretation of these matters up to you to decide. But the truth is in Christ Jesus of Nazareth's Holy name. Alleluia and praise the LORD. Amen and Amen. The apostle, Peter, admonishes us to lay aside guile; he says, "Wherefore laying aside all malice, and all guile, and hypocrisies, and envies, all evil speakings…" (1 Pet. 2:1). Jesus Christ of Nazareth had no guile in His mouth according to the apostle, Peter, he says, "For even hereunto were ye called: because Christ also suffered for us, leaving us an example, that ye should follow his steps: Who did no sin, neither was guile found in his mouth…" (1 Pet. 2:21, 22). The apostle, Peter, again admonishes us not to have guile in our mouth, if we desire to live a good life; he says, "For he that will love life, and see good days, let him refrain his tongue from evil, and his lips that they speak no guile: Let him eschew evil, and do good; let him seek peace, and ensue it." (1 Pet. 3:10, 11). Of course the Scriptures also say to love your enemy (Matt. 5:44). So I will leave it for you to decide how to live your life here on earth and in the world to come, forever more. To God be the glory, in the name of His only begotten Son, Jesus Christ of Nazareth. Alleluia and praise the LORD. Amen and Amen.

Devils

One Hebrew word for devils is sa`iyr and means shaggy, a he-goat, a faun, devil, goat, hairy, kid, rough, satyr, Strong's number 8163 (Lev. 17:7, 2 Chr. 11:15). Similarly, Strong's number 8164 means a shower, or small rain (Deut. 32:2). A root word of sa`iyr is sa`ar meaning storm, wind, shiver, fear, afraid, a whirlwind, Strong's number 8175 (Deut. 32:17, Job 27:21, Ps. 50:3, 58:9; Jer. 2:12, Ezek. 27:35, 32:10; Dan. 11:40). The word devil, singular, does not seem to be used in the Old Testament of the King James Version of the Holy Bible. And the word devils, plural, is only used four times in the Old Testament of the King James Version of the Holy Bible (Lev. 17:7, Deut. 32:17, 2 Chr. 11:15, Ps. 106:37). The goat sent into the wilderness was used in the Old Testament to signify that God's peoples sins were being forgiven and sent away (Lev. 16:8-10). As the scripture says, "As far as the east is from the west, so far hath he removed our transgressions from us." (Ps. 103:12). Jesus is the ultimate sacrifice for the forgiveness of our sins (Heb. 10:10). He was the atonement, overcoming evil in His earthly life and dying on the cross for the forgiveness of our sins, He was buried and He arose the third day to give us the hope and promise of eternal life in His Holy name. Alleluia and praise the LORD. Amen and Amen. Regarding the appearance of people and comparing them to a goat, hairy, shaggy, etc. or any other judgement for that matter, God looks at the heart of a man or woman (1 Sam. 16:7). This was shown when choosing a king for Israel, after Saul (1 Sam. 16:1). David was chosen, not because of his physical stature, but God considered what was in his heart, first and foremost (1 Sam. 16:11-13). God desires us to be the same. Alleluia and praise the LORD. Amen and Amen. Jesus said, "Judge not according to the appearance, but judge righteous judgment." (John 7:24). And ultimately in Jesus Christ of Nazareth we have no condemnation, neither ought we to condemn others (John 3:17, 1 John 3:20, 21). Alleluia and praise the LORD. Amen and Amen. Jesus stilled the wind; He rebuked it (Mark 4:37-41). And God said He was not in the wind, earthquake or fire that came to Elijah when Elijah was standing on mount Horeb in the cave before the LORD, but God was the still small voice after these things, that Elijah came out to the entering of the cave to speak with (1 Kings 19:11, 12). Alleluia and praise the LORD. Amen and Amen.

The other Hebrew word for devils is shad, meaning a daomen (as malignant), devil, Strong's number 7700 (Deut. 32:17, Ps. 106:37). Similarly, a Hebrew word shuwd is the root word of shad, meaning to swell up, devastate, waste, Strong's number 7736 (Ps. 91:6). Deuteronomy 32:17 also makes clear that devils are not God, it says, "They sacrificed unto devils, **not to God**; to gods whom they knew not, to new *gods that* came newly up, whom your fathers feared not.". In the apostle, James', epistle, he says, "Thou believest that there is one God; thou doest well: the devils also believe, and tremble." (Jam. 2:19). The Holy Bible says we are "…fearfully and wonderfully made…" (Ps. 139:14). It also tells us to work out our own salvation with fear and trembling (Phil. 2:12). Nevertheless, ultimately, God does not give us the spirit of fear, but of peace and of a sound mind (John 14:27, 2 Tim. 1:7). Jesus cast out devils (Mark 1:34). Judas Iscariot was called a devil by Jesus (John 6:70, 71). In the Old Testament, there is an account of Judas' betrayal, but it sounds like Jesus is the one doing it (Zech. 11:12, 13; Matt. 27:3-5). Of course He did give command to Judas, saying, "…That thou doest, do quickly." (John 13:27). This is not to suggest Jesus is evil, quite the opposite, what it does suggest though is that Jesus and God, through the Holy Spirit were fully in control of the situation and the betrayal process (John 1:1-3, Rev. 4:11). This, Jesus indicated when speaking with Pontius Pilate during Jesus' trial (John 19:11). He also said to God, "…Father, forgive them; for they know not what they do." (Luke 23:34). Also, it seems that Judas did repent, albeit he still killed himself in the process, hanging himself on a tree (Matt. 27:3-5). These things were all part of Old Testament prophecy of Jesus' betrayal and crucifixion, death on the cross for the forgiveness of our sins and His burial. Not only this but also His glorious resurrection three days later with the hope and promise that we can and will receive the same, when our time comes, in Jesus Christ of Nazareth, God's only begotten Son's, Holy name. Alleluia and praise the LORD. Amen and Amen.

Good and Evil

Good

God and Jesus Christ of Nazareth; God is good to all, God is good (Ps. 144:2, 145:9; Matt. 19:17). This is proved ultimately in the life, death and resurrection of His only begotten Son, Jesus Christ of Nazareth, whom died on the cross for the forgiveness of our sins, He was buried, and He arose the third day to give us the hope and promise of eternal life in His Holy name. Alleluia and praise the LORD. Amen and Amen. The light is good; Jesus Christ of Nazareth is the Light of this world, and the life of the light of men (Gen. 1:4, John 1:4, 9). In the book of Revelation, in the "New Jerusalem", we have no need of the light of the sun or even a candle and there is no night there (Rev. 22:5). That is because God is our true life and light, in Christ Jesus of Nazareth's Holy name. Alleluia and praise the LORD. Amen and Amen. He created the light after all, in the beginning (Gen. 1:2). And we must remember first and foremost that God is a Spirit, as Jesus Christ of Nazareth, said of His Father, God, the LORD (John 4:24). Alleluia and praise the LORD. Amen and Amen. Jesus said, "It is the spirit that quickeneth; the flesh profiteth nothing…" (John 6:63). This is why the Holy Spirit of God, the Spirit of truth, is so important for us to receive (John 14:16, 17). It is the true Spirit, the good and pure Spirit of God that provides for us, and gives to all abundantly, from His endless storehouse of riches, in Christ Jesus of Nazareth's Holy name. Alleluia and praise the LORD. Amen and Amen. Everything God created in the beginning was good, very good indeed (Gen. 1:31). Alleluia and praise the LORD. Amen and Amen. And after finishing His creation in six days, He rested on the seventh day, and blessed it, and made it holy (Gen. 2:2, 3). This is God's good nature, working, but not as a slave driver, He gives us weekly rest (Mark 2:27). Alleluia and praise the LORD. Amen and Amen. And in Christ Jesus of Nazareth we have this true and good rest from all evils and sin (Matt. 11:28). He has forgiven us of all of our sins, by dying on the cross for the forgiveness of our sins, shedding His Holy and righteous blood for us on the cross, then He was buried and on the third day He arose out of His grave, giving us the hope and promise of eternal life in His Holy name. As there is no other name under heaven whereby we can be saved (Acts 4:12). Alleluia and praise the LORD. Amen and Amen.

Evil

One Hebrew word for evil is ra`, meaning adversity, affliction, bad, calamity, displease(-ure), distress, grief(-vous), harm, heavy, hurt(-ful), ill (favoured), + mark, mischief(-vous), misery, naught(-ty), noisome, + not please, sad(- ly), sore, sorrow, trouble, vex, wicked(-ly, -ness, one), worse(-st), wretchedness, wrong, Strong's number 7451 (Gen. 2:9, 17; 3:5, 22; 6:5, etc.). Ra` has a root word, ra`a`, properly, to spoil (literally, by breaking to pieces); figuratively, to make (or be) good for nothing, i.e. bad (physically, socially or morally): — afflict, associate selves (by mistake for 7462), break (down, in pieces), + displease, (be, bring, do) evil (doer, entreat, man), show self friendly (by mistake for 7462), do harm, (do) hurt, (behave self, deal) ill, do mischief, punish, still, vex, (do) wicked (doer, -ly), be (deal, do) worse, Strong's number 7489 (Gen. 19:7, 9; 31:7, etc.). Reference to Strong's number 7489 regarding association is Strong's number 7462, ra`ah, meaning to tend a flock; i.e. pasture it; intransitively, to graze (literally or figuratively); generally to rule; by extension, to associate with (as a friend): companion, keep company with, devour, eat up, evil entreat, feed, use as a friend, make friendship with, herdman, keep (sheep) (-er), pastor, + shearing house, shepherd, wander, waste (Gen. 4:2, 13:7, 8, 26:20, 29:7, 9, 30:31, 36, 36:24, 46:32, 34, etc.). Of course, Jesus warns us of wolves in sheep's clothing, false prophets coming, and false Christs, and hired servants that do not tend to the sheep when trouble comes (Matt. 7:15, 24:24; John 10:12, 13). Jesus Christ of Nazareth is the good and true Shephard of the sheep (John 10:11, 14, 15). The sheep know His voice, and they do not listen to another voice (John 10:4, 5). And He is the true Lamb of God (John 1:29, 36). He gave His life up for the sheep, that is us, the whole world, dying on the cross for the forgiveness of our sins, He was buried and He arose the third day to give us the hope and promise of eternal life in His Holy name. Alleluia and praise the LORD. Amen and Amen. The Holy Bible of God says; God formed the crooked serpent (Job 26:13). God sent the evil angels (Ps. 78:49). God created evil (Isa. 45:7). That is, ultimately God takes full responsibility for all evil that ever has, does or evil will exist (Isa. 45:7, John 1:1-3). And He has done this by sending His True and Holy, only begotten Son, Jesus Christ of Nazareth to earth to save us from our sin (John 3:16). He was conceived by the Holy Spirit of God in, as God is a Spirit, and born of the virgin, Mary, espoused to Joseph (Matt. 1:18, John 4:24). Jesus was raised a child of Israel, of the tribe of Judah, He had brothers and sisters (Matt. 13:55, 56; Luke 2:40, 42-52; Rev. 5:5). He started His ministry in the fall of 27 A.D., and for three and a half years, healed, did miracles and taught about the kingdom of God, and salvation through belief in God's only begotten Son, Jesus Christ of Nazareth, whom God sent (Luke 3:23, John 13:1). He died on the cross for the forgiveness of our sins, not only your sins and mine, but for the whole world's sins, He was buried and He arose the third day to give us the hope and promise of eternal life in His Holy name (John 19, 20). Alleluia and praise the LORD. Amen and Amen.

Conclusion

The tree of knowledge of good and evil, why did it or does it exist (Gen. 2:9)? Simply put God created it to give us freedom of choice, to give us freedom to choose between life and death, good and evil, blessings and cursings (Jos. 24:15). Alleluia and praise the LORD. Amen and Amen. Ultimately, we are not even called to judge evil (Matt. 7:1, John 8:15, 1 Cor. 4:5). The apostle, Jude, says that Michael, the archangel, brought not a railing accusation against Satan when contesting over the body of Moses, all he said was, "…The Lord rebuke thee." (Jude 1:9). This is exactly what Jesus did during His own earthly ministry (Matt. 4:10, 16:23). And we ought to follow the same example. Do not get caught up in temptations, wars, battles, fighting, etc., in the flesh, but give your efforts to God, the Father, Almighty in Jesus Christ of Nazareth's Holy name. Pray, read God's Word, the Holy Bible of God and trust in Him and Him alone for all things. Alleluia and praise the LORD. Amen and Amen. The Holy Bible admonishes us to overcome evil with good (Rom. 12:21). The good news is that the tree of knowledge of good and evil; did indeed have good in it (Gen. 3:6). Alleluia and praise the LORD. Amen and Amen. And the Holy Bible says, "…if a kingdom be divided against itself, that kingdom cannot stand." (Mark 3:24). Jesus said, "…if Satan rise up against himself, and be divided, he cannot stand, but hath an end." (Mark 3:26). Alleluia and praise the LORD. Amen and Amen. Jesus said of Himself, He is building His church and the gates of hell will not prevail against it (Matt. 16:18). Alleluia and praise the LORD. Amen and Amen. Jesus said the kingdom of God does not come by observance, but it is within us (Luke 17:20, 21). When we have received Jesus Christ of Nazareth and His shed blood on the cross for the forgiveness of our sins, from that first time, our first Love, we have been saved from that day forward (1 John 4:19, Rev. 2:4). Alleluia and praise the LORD. Amen and Amen. He asks us to strengthen ourselves in the things that we have learned of Him (Rev. 3:2). He calls us to keep our lamp filled with oil (Matt. 25:4). These are all admonishments to continue in the faith of Christ Jesus of Nazareth, as our Lord and Saviour, until the "end", whenever and however that comes about (Matt. 10:22, 24:13). This is our daily task in this world, and in the "world to come" eternal life, to take up our cross daily and follow Jesus Christ of Nazareth, as there is no other name under heaven whereby we can be saved (Acts. 4:12). Jesus came into this world, conceived by the Holy Spirit, in the virgin, Mary. He was born of the virgin, Mary, espoused to Joseph (Matt. 1:18). He was raised as a child of Israel, of the tribe of Judah, and He had brothers and sisters (Matt. 13:55, 56; Luke 2:40, 42-52; Rev. 5:5). He began His earthly ministry in autumn of 27 A.D., and ministered, healed, taught and did miracles for three and a half years (Matt. 4:23, 5:2, 20:28; Luke 3:23, John 2:22, 13:1). And at Passover in 31 A.D., He gave His life up for us on the cross for the forgiveness of our sins, He was buried and the third day He arose to give us the hope and promise of eternal life in His Holy name (John 19, 20). Alleluia and praise the LORD. Amen and Amen.

READER'S GUIDE

This book was written with the idea of revelation in mind. There may be some subjects in the end that are of more interest, or need more clarification, where you may desire to review them for a better understanding. Part of the reason why the "appendices" exist is to expand on some of the topics written about in this book, so referring to them may be preferred. When writing the book I had in mind I was reaching out to a "lost" generation, but the truth of the matter is we are all children of God, no matter what age we are. Some of the topics discussed are not usually talked about at least commonly, weekly, in Church or in the home, at least that I know of, so they may be new to the reader. And it may take some time to discern how to apply them to each of our daily lives.

The question section attempts to do this, at least in part, by opening back up the readers mind to the Holy Spirit of God. So that you can pray about, meditate on and discuss with others the subjects spoken about. Although the topics in this book have been spoken about and continue to be spoken about by various students of the Holy Bible, the reality of the subjects will only be fully known in God's timing. In order to better understand our place with God, in life, family and in this world, we need to grow in our understanding of somethings. Hopefully, most of the subjects will be simple enough to understand that not much contemplation is needed, because God does desire us to become like little children in our relationship with Him and others (Matt. 18:3). So with that being said, pray about, meditate on and discuss the ideas that interest you with whom God wills and see if you can come to some peace in these matters. God bless and keep the faith!

CHAPTER ONE
That prophet…

Discussion: Messiah

"But his bow abode in strength, and the arms of his hands were made strong by the hands of the mighty *God* of Jacob; (from thence *is* the shepherd, the stone of Israel:)"
- Genesis 49:24

Some have suggested that there will be a "Messiah" ben Joseph, a messiah coming from the tribe of Joseph, aside from the "Messiah" ben David, Jesus Christ of Nazareth, son of David (Gen. 49:22, 24; Ps. 89:20, 21; Matt. 1:1, Rev. 5:5).[11] Messiah meaning anointed one, as many have been anointed, like King David, of the tribe of Judah (1 Sam. 16:13). However, the reality is that Jesus Christ of Nazareth was the son of Joseph, of the tribe of Judah, "Messiah" ben Joseph, and "Messiah" ben David, Messiah, Son of David (Matt. 1:1, 16; John 1:45). His earthly father's name was Joseph, and His mother's ancestors were of the tribe of Judah, through King David (Luke 3:23-38). Nevertheless, this "idea", may have its roots in the "Messianic Age", and the "prince" of the Israelites during the "Messianic Age" (Ezek. 40-48, Rev. 20:2, 6). The reality is; Ephraim, son of Joseph, received the birthright from his grandfather Jacob, also known as Israel (Gen. 48, Jer. 31:9). Joshua, a descendant of Ephraim did "rule" for a time when the "ancient" Israelites were brought into the promised land by God through Joshua's leadership, but Ephraim's position did not last, as a "leader" so to speak (Gen. 49:22-26, Num. 27:17-19, Deut. 33:13-17). The reality is that, in the "Messianic Age", a descendant of Ephraim, may very well hold the position of "prince" for the purposes of worship at the temple during the "Messianic Age", but this would be like other positions of this world, where God is still the ruler above us all (Num. 27:17-19, Ps. 80:2, 89:18; Ezek. 44:3). The quote above if read alone, could even suggest that the "Shepherd" would come from

by the God of thy father, who shall help thee; and by the Almighty, who shall bless thee with blessings of heaven above, blessings of the deep that lieth under, blessings of the breasts, and of the womb:". Even if it was literal, it was fulfilled through Joshua, son of Non, of the tribe of Ephraim, the son of Joseph, at least once, but even he bowed down to the "…captain of the host of the LORD…", on the way to the "promised land", which was likely Jesus Christ of Nazareth, the great I am (Num. 27:17-19, Jos. 5:13-15, John 8:58, Heb. 2:10). It is clear from this verse that the prophecy is speaking of the Shepherd coming from God, the Father, Almighty, not the descendants of Joseph, son of Israel, first and foremost (Ps. 23:1, 80:1; Eccl. 12:11). And this is why we have Jesus Christ of Nazareth whom is born seemingly with little

---

[11] https://www.britam.org/messiah.html, retrieved 16/03/2022

expectation from the "ruling" Jews at His time, from the tribe of Judah, to save the world from our sins (Ps. 80:1, Eccl. 12:11, Isa. 31:4). Alleluia and praise the LORD. It is He whom is the "Good Shepherd" over us all forever more (Ps. 23:1, John 10:11, 14; Heb. 13:20, 1 Pet. 2:25, 5:4). Regardless of a "Messianic Age" earthly "prince" or not (Ezek. 44:3, Rev. 20:4, 6). That being said, this "prince" of the "Messianic Age", if literal, will fulfill his role, along with his descendants, as God wills it, regardless of my or any other person's interpretation of the matter (Num. 27:17-19, Ps. 80:2). Thanks be to God, the Father, Almighty, and His only begotten Son, Jesus Christ of Nazareth. Praise God and worship Him, in the name of Jesus Christ of Nazareth, through His Holy Spirit. Alleluia and bless Him and let Him receive all of the glory. Amen and Amen.

Discussion Questions

1. What about Jesus as Messiah?
    a. He has clearly fulfilled all of the requirements of the Messiah (Isa. 7:14, Matt. 1:18-25).
    b. The only portion that has not likely been fulfilled completely yet, as the date of writing this book in 2019 A.D., is "…to anoint the Most Holy…", as I have mentioned in chapter four and in appendix A (Dan. 9:24). This is related with the "Body of Christ", the fulfillment of God choosing, developing, perfecting and resurrecting His elect, the saints, with those whom are still alive, whom will "change" at the onset of the "Messianic Age" (1 Thess. 4:13-18, Rev. 20:4, 6). This may be one of the main reasons, if not the only reason, that some "Jews", may have not accepted Jesus Christ of Nazareth as their Messiah yet, as of the date of writing this book in 2019 A.D..
    c. This all being said, this should not stop anyone from having a relationship with Jesus Christ of Nazareth, as our Messiah and Saviour today, Jew or Gentile alike (Matt. 12:18, 21; John 4:22).

2. How can we worship God, believe in Jesus Christ of Nazareth as our Saviour and not be idolatrous according to the commands of the Old Testament?
    a. The commandment to have one God (Mark 12:29, 30)
    b. Jesus said, "…*there is* none good but one, *that is,* God…" (Matt. 19:17). So even Jesus said that there was one God, and that we ought to worship Him, the Father of us all (Mark 12:29, 30).
    c. He also said of Himself and God, "I and *my* Father are one." (John 10:30).

3. What about those whom worshipped Jesus?
    a. The apostle, Thomas, addressed Jesus as, God, after Jesus' resurrection (John 20:28).

b. Jesus said of Himself and God, the Father, "I and *my* Father are one." (John 10:30).

c. Elohim, in the Hebrew, is a plural form of a name for God, Strong's number 430 (Gen. 1:1). God said, "…Let us make man in **our** image, after **our** likeness…" (Gen. 1:26). This suggests God was not alone in the beginning, before the creation of man and woman in the flesh.

d. This is where I will say that we each have our own personal relationship with the Creator, and I will not judge others for how they worship Him. I do not have all of the answers obviously. I am not God, so in this case to each there own. Glory be to God, the Father, Almighty and His only begotten Son, Jesus Christ of Nazareth. Thanks and glory be to our God, forever and ever. Alleluia and praise the LORD. Amen and Amen.

e. Also, the apostle, Paul, did say that "…then shall the Son also himself be subject unto him that put all things under him, that God may be all in all.", when all is said and done (1 Cor. 15:28). Until then, Jesus Christ of Nazareth has a vital role and always will in the life of man, through His offering made for us on the cross, for the forgiveness of our sins, forever more. Thanks be to our God, the Father, in Jesus Christ of Nazareth, His only begotten Son. Alleluia and praise the LORD. Amen and Amen.

CHAPTER TWO

Prophecy and Similitudes in the tribe of Judah and the annual Holyday Feasts

Discussion: Prophecy

"But I will have mercy upon the house of Judah, and will save them by the LORD their God, and will not save them by bow, nor by sword, nor by battle, by horses, nor by horsemen."
- Hosea 1:7

Jesus Christ of Nazareth and His cross, are the best explanation of mercy and salvation for the "…house of Judah…", and all of Israel, and the whole world for that matter. He died on the cross at Passover, in 31 A.D., spilling His Holy and righteous blood on the cross, He was buried and the third day He arose to give us the hope and promise of eternal life in His Holy name. Alleluia and praise the LORD. Amen and Amen. Aside from this, it is possible that during the "Great Tribulation", this world may experience miracles similar to what the Israelites experienced during the plagues of Egypt, there exodus from Egypt, the crossing at the Red Sea, and their sojourn in the wilderness for forty years (Ex., Num., Matt. 24). The "Messianic Age" will likely be ushered in by a miraculous change in our spiritual and physical nature, as the New Testament would suggest, "…we shall be changed." (1 Cor. 15:52, 1 John 6, 8). Alleluia and praise the LORD. Amen and Amen.

Discussion Questions

1. Why do some "Jews" not believe in Jesus Christ of Nazareth, as their Saviour, fully yet?
   a. Aside from the answer in the chapter one discussion, there is at least one more reason for their "unbelief" at this time. The apostle, Paul, said that Israel is blind in part in order that the fullness of the gentiles be come in (Rom. 11:25). This is likely directly related to the "Great Tribulation", and then the onset of the "Messianic Age", as of the date of writing this book in 2019 A.D. (Matt. 24, Rev. 20:4, 6).
   b. Some of the descendants of Israel, and possibly most, are blind to their ancestry, as Jesus calls us, the "…lost sheep of the house of Israel…". But there is a purpose for this, as I have said, it is so that we "get along" easier with the gentiles, without having to worry about "the law" of the Bible and all sorts of other "issues", including interracial marriage, etc.. The point is that God has allowed the descendants of Israel to be blinded so that we can fulfill our part in prophecy, without being a stumbling block to the gentiles. That being said,

God still has full and sovereign control over all of mankind, the "…lost sheep of the house of Israel…", and the "…other sheep…not of this fold…", as Jesus said (Matt. 10:6, John 10:16).

c. If God is preparing this world for a period of one thousand years of Christ's rule with His saints, then He likely desires people from every nation, kindred, people and tongue, in this "age" to come (Rev. 7:9, 14). This would require protection of them, just like the "…lost sheep of the house of Israel…". So somehow the blindness in part of the "…lost sheep of the house of Israel…" is related to the protection and physical "salvation" of sorts for those from "…all nations, and kindreds, and people, and tongues…", the "…great multitude…", that will likely make it through the "Great Tribulation", into the "Messianic Age" (Matt. 24, Rev. 7:9, 14; 20:4, 6).

d. I suspect this, blindness in part, will not be completely healed until the onset of the "Messianic Age", as Ezekiel 39 would suggest (Ezek. 39:22-29). Praise the LORD God, the Father, Almighty and His only begotten Son, Jesus Christ of Nazareth. Alleluia. Amen and Amen.

CHAPTER THREE
Two or three witnesses of Jesus Messiah of Nazareth

Discussion: Witnesses

"Either his uncle, or his uncle's son, may redeem him, or *any* that is nigh of kin unto him of his family may redeem him; or if he be able, he may redeem himself."
- Leviticus 25:49

Understanding that God gave Jesus Christ of Nazareth the ability to resurrect Himself is very important, because it is by Jesus Christ of Nazareth's payment for our sins on the cross that we to can be resurrected unto eternal life someday. Jesus even said of faith in Himself, "And whosoever liveth and believeth in me shall never die. ..." (John 11:26). These again are powerful words, but the reality is in Jesus Christ of Nazareth. He died on the cross for the forgiveness of our sins, shedding His Holy and righteous blood, He was buried and He arose the third day, conquering death and giving us the hope of redemption of our own body, soul and spirit, someday unto eternal life in His Holy name. Glory be to God. Even King David, knew Jesus Christ of Nazareth as his Saviour. He said, "The LORD said unto my Lord, Sit thou at my right hand, until I make thine enemies thy footstool." (Ps. 110:1). How much more evidence do we need? Jesus said of Himself, "...Before Abraham was, I am." (John 8:58). He is the Rock of the Old Testament and the Lamb of God, the Son of God, whom gave His life up on the cross for the forgiveness of our sins. He spilt His Holy and righteous blood on the cross, He died on the cross, He was buried and the third day He arose to give us the hope and promise of eternal life in His Holy name. Praise the LORD God, the Father, Almighty and His only begotten Son, Jesus Christ of Nazareth, with His Holy Spirit. Alleluia and praise the LORD. Amen and Amen.

Discussion Questions

1. How did Jesus Christ of Nazareth have the ability to resurrect Himself?
   a. As mentioned above, Leviticus 25:49 says, "Either his uncle, or his uncle's son, may redeem him, or *any* that is nigh of kin unto him of his family may redeem him; or if he be able, he may redeem himself.".
   b. God, the Father, gave His only begotten Son, Jesus Christ of Nazareth, the ability, as He gives us the ability to choose life or death, in Jesus Christ of Nazareth's Holy name, as well (John 10:18).

2. Why does Jesus Christ of Nazareth have the ability to resurrect Himself?
   a. God, the Father, gave Jesus this ability (John 10:18).
   b. He said, "The Father loveth the Son, and hath given all things into his hand." (John 3:35). That includes life and life eternal.

3. What does this mean for us?
   a. We can have eternal life in the name of Jesus Christ of Nazareth.
   b. Jesus said of eternal life and God, the Father, "…this is life eternal, that they might know thee the only true God, and Jesus Christ, whom thou hast sent." (John 17:3).
   c. How simple is eternal life in Jesus Christ of Nazareth. Alleluia and praise the LORD. Amen and Amen.

CHAPTER FOUR
Key of David

Discussion: New Covenant

"…now is made manifest, and by the scriptures of the prophets, according to the commandment of the everlasting God, made known to all nations for the obedience of faith…"
- Romans 16:26

Faith is required to believe in Jesus Christ of Nazareth. And this does not come by works, but is a gift from God, the Father, Almighty. We can search the scriptures all we desire, and listen to all the rabbis, preachers, teachers, and read all of the Bible study books, etc., but the reality is that we do not receive faith from God by doing, but it is a free gift (Eph. 2:8, 9). Jesus Christ of Nazareth calls us to wait for Him (Luke 12:35, 36). We grow our faith by doing all of the earlier mentioned things including worshipping God, and fellowshipping, but that initial "seed" of faith is not of this world. It is of God, this is the miracle of our adoption into the "…kingdom of God…", into the family of God (Matt. 6:33, Mark 10:29, 30; Eph. 3:14-19). God's kingdom is not of this world. Praise the LORD God, the Father, Almighty, and His only begotten Son, Jesus Christ of Nazareth. Alleluia and praise the LORD. Thanks be to God. Amen and Amen. When reading through this chapter's discussion questions, consider your faith, and where it comes from. Consider your "…first love…", where it all started, and turn to the true God that loves you, in Jesus Christ of Nazareth's Holy name (Rev. 2:4). You will not regret it. Jesus said we are to come to Him as little children (Matt. 18:3). Children are generally great in faith, and lack in knowledge, especially worldly knowledge (1 Kings 3:7). This may be the first step, to you realizing, whom your Saviour really is. He is not of this world (John 18:36). He was not known by this world (John 1:10). And He only reveals Himself truly, to those whom He loves, and desires to continue His relationship with. That means you and I. To God be the glory. But do not take my word for it, listen to the "…still small voice." for yourself (1 Kings 19:12). That is the Holy Spirit of God, in Jesus Christ of Nazareth. Alleluia and praise the LORD. Amen and Amen.

Discussion Questions

1. Where ought we to worship God?
    a. Jesus said, "But the hour cometh, and now is, when true worshippers shall worship the Father in spirit and in truth: for the Father seeketh such to worship him." (John 4:23).

b. This is part of, if not the entire, reason why you are reading this book, and why I wrote them.

c. It comes from my own spiritual walk with God, in Christ Jesus of Nazareth, and God willing is a part of yours.

d. But the reality is that God did create us to commune with each other. This is the life of Adam and Eve in the beginning, where there was no help meet for him. So God created Eve out of Adam's rib (Gen. 2:21, 22).

e. This brings another good point up regarding fellowship. Finding a spouse, from God, and starting a family of your own. As God, said "...Be fruitful, and multiply..." (Gen. 1:28). This is the other part of God's plan for us, to commune with Him, but also to love our spouse and raise up children that will follow in our footsteps and worship the true God and become His children as well (Mal. 2:15, John 1:13). All for His glory. Amen and Amen.

2. What about fellowship?

a. Jesus also did much fellowship, He fed five thousand and He fed four thousand people (Matt. 14:16-21, 15:32-38). He preached in the synagogues, and in the fields (Matt. 4:23, 14:38). He went to cities and healed, and met people in the streets (Matt. 9:1-8, Mark 6:56, Luke 10:1).

b. But we must also remember that He took time for Himself with God, through prayer in quite places, and in smaller groups with His disciples in houses, fields, mountains and on the water in ships (Matt. 14:23, 26:17-20, Mark 2:23, 4:35-41).

3. What about the "Messianic Age"?

a. The "Messianic Age" may very well come and even in "...this generation...", as of the date of writing this book in 2019 A.D. (Matt. 23:36).

b. But we must remember that God's kingdom is eternal and He inhabits eternity (Isa. 57:15). The Bible even says He inhabits our praise (Ps. 22:3).

c. He is the very breath of life in us (Gen. 2:7).

d. Also, Jesus said, "...The kingdom of God cometh not with observation...the kingdom of God is within you." (Luke 17:20, 21).

e. Again, I am not suggesting there will not be a "Messianic Age", according to the Ezekiel 40-48 account and Revelation 20:4 and 6, but we must remember that God's kingdom is a spiritual one first and foremost, as God, the Father, Almighty is a Spirit (John 4:24) And we ought to worship Him in spirit and in truth. Praise the LORD God, the Father, Almighty and His only begotten Son, Jesus Christ of Nazareth. Alleluia and praise the LORD. Thanks be to God, the Father, Almighty, and His only begotten Son, Jesus Christ of Nazareth, with His Holy Spirit. Alleluia and praise the LORD. Amen and Amen.

CHAPTER FIVE
The Temple, The Body, The Vine

Discussion: Holy Spirit

"And if thou wilt make me an altar of stone, thou shalt not build it of hewn stone: for if thou lift up thy tool upon it, thou hast polluted it."
- Exodus 20:25

This verse is actually quite revealing about our relationship with God, through Jesus Christ of Nazareth, God's only begotten Son. He was crucified on the cross, we polluted Jesus, by lifting up a hammer and nail against His body on the cross. But there is more to it than that. We can come up with so many different ideas of how the "future" is going to be and how mankind ought to live, with all of these fancy gadgets and technologies, but forget the Creator, whom gave us the ability to build all of these things. God is not looking for a fancy manmade altar for us to worship at. He just desires us to follow Him. He is a Spirit. That is what Jesus tells us (John 4:24). Jesus said, "...the hour cometh, and now is, when the true worshippers shall worship the Father in spirit and in truth: for the Father seeketh such to worship him." (John 4:23). Also, we must remember that this also points to Jesus Christ of Nazareth being conceived by the Holy Ghost, not by man's hands (Matt. 1:18-25). Another reason why Jesus was not polluted from the womb, was because He was conceived by the Holy Ghost, by God, the Father (Matt. 1:18-25) This all points to God's ability to prepare "works", materials, etc., ahead of time for us, as the Bible says is the case (Eph. 2:10). We must also remember that we were created in the womb, by God (Isa. 44:2). Our very existence is a miracle. Praise the LORD God, the Father, Almighty and His only begotten Son, Jesus Christ of Nazareth. The idea of "genetically modified organisms", "chemical" and "nuclear" weaponry, "cloning", man's interference in the natural birthing process and the like, maybe signs of our rebellion against the natural way God had intended for mankind to be fruitful and multiply from the beginning (Gen. 1:28). That all being said, He did indeed send His only begotten Son, Jesus Christ of Nazareth to die on the cross for the forgiveness of our sins, whatever they may be, at Passover in 31 A.D.. Thanks be to God. So whatever the truth is in all of this, we have an advocate with the Father in Christ Jesus of Nazareth, through His Holy Spirit, that has, will and does cleanse us of all of our sins, as we accept Jesus Christ of Nazareth and His truth into our life. We have freedom to learn and develop as children of God, in Christ Jesus of Nazareth. Praise the LORD God, the Father, Almighty, and His only begotten Son, Jesus Christ of Nazareth. This all being said, I will say, of course I am not perfect yet either, so I need God's forgiveness through Jesus Christ of Nazareth, as well as anyone else. So follow Him, all for God's glory. Praise Him. Alleluia. Amen and Amen.

Discussion Questions

1. How could Jesus Christ of Nazareth be conceived by the Holy Spirit?

    a. Adam was made of the dust and life was breathed into Him (Gen. 2:7). Eve was formed out of one of Adam's ribs (Gen. 2:21, 22). Of course if you do not believe this, then you may not likely believe that Jesus Christ of Nazareth was conceived of the Holy Spirit in and born of the virgin, Mary, espoused to Joseph (Matt. 1:18-25). Hopefully you believe that both are true, as they are. God's Word is truth.

    b. If you do not believe, you do not believe, but God willing you do. Alleluia and praise the LORD. Amen and Amen.

2. What about the "Messianic Age" temple?

    a. I have written another book on the subject, but to simplify it here. God, Jesus Christ of Nazareth and the saints, will likely be in spirit form during the "Messianic Age". One of the main references for this would be Psalm 90, where Moses says, "For a thousand years in thy sight *are but* as yesterday when it is past, and *as* a watch in the night." (Ps. 90:4). This would simply explain how God, the Father, Jesus Christ of Nazareth and the saints may very well experience the "Messianic Age".

    b. Regarding the temple in particular, it will be the descendants of the Levites that will have charge over it, like they have had in the past (Ezek. 44:10-16). Namely through the descendants of Zadok (Ezek. 44:15, 16). As well as the "prince", as mentioned in the chapter one discussion section (Ezek. 44:3).

    c. That all being said, as I have suggested in the other book I wrote about the "Messianic Age", God's Holy Spirit will likely be the "main character" during this time mentioned in the Holy Bible of God (Jer. 31:34). As this is the only true way mankind will experience a prolonged period of and everlasting peace (Gal. 5:22). It is only by the Holy Spirit of God that we experience true peace, as He is peace (Eph. 2:11-18). Praise the LORD God, the Father, Almighty, and His only begotten Son, Jesus Christ of Nazareth. Alleluia and praise the LORD.

    d. I will also say, as I had written in another book. That the palm tree, with the two cherubim on either side, could be a "new" memorial to God, the Father, Almighty, and His only begotten Son, Jesus Christ of Nazareth, as the "Tree of Life", which will be on the "Messianic Age" temple doors and walls (Ezek. 41:18-20). That being said, this is an interpretation, God only knows for certain the purpose of these signs. It could also be a sign of the marriage covenant between God and the "Body of Christ", and man and wife, as well (Gen. 2:24, Isa. 54:5). To God be the glory in the truth of the interpretation of all of this. Amen and Amen.

CHAPTER SIX
Jesus and His cross

Discussion: Miracles

"And it shall come to pass afterward, that I will pour out my spirit upon all flesh; and your sons and your daughters shall prophesy, your old men shall dream dreams, your young men shall see visions: And also upon the servants and upon the handmaids in those days will I pour out my spirit."
- Joel 2:28, 29

This was confirmed to have taken place at Pentecost in 31 A.D., but may very well have a greater fulfillment in the "Messianic Age". That being said, we can experience this "outpouring" of the Holy Spirit today, as we accept Jesus Christ of Nazareth as our Saviour and Redeemer. It is by His blood that we are healed. Jesus did wonderful miracles before God's miracle through Him on the cross. He multiplied fishes and loaves, He walked on water, He prophesied, and He healed the sick (Matt. 14:15-21, 22-33; 15:32-38; Mark 13, Luke 4:40). One of the notable miracles was that He healed the sight of the blind, which was a true sign of whom He is (John 9). This was a sign of what He has, is and will continue to do physically and spiritually to this world. He admonishes us to, "…anoint thine eyes with eye salve…" (Rev. 3:18). Jesus came to heal us from our blindness, which came through ours and our forefathers' sins, first in Adam and Eve (Rom. 5:14). He has come to show us that we were created to be like Him, sons and daughters of God, children of God, the Father, Almighty. We did not come from some evolutionary chain, or another planet, etc. (John 1:12, 13). We came from God, the Father, Almighty, through His Holy Spirit, in Christ Jesus of Nazareth's Holy name. Alleluia and praise the LORD. Amen and Amen.

Discussion Questions

1. Is Jesus really the only begotten Son of God?
   a. Yes
   b. Conceived by the Holy Spirit (Matt. 1:18-25).
   c. Voice from heaven, "…This is my beloved Son, in whom I am well pleased." (Matt. 3:17).
   d. Those around Him testified of Him being as such (Matt. 14:33, John 1:49).
   e. As the Bible says, a truth is established with two or three witnesses (Matt. 18:16).

2. Where do we come from according to the Bible?
   a. God said that He knew us before we were formed in the womb (Jer. 1:5).
   b. The scriptures say that God's Holy Spirit divides our joints and marrow (Heb. 4:12).
   c. The scriptures even suggest that we are still in the womb in this life (Isa. 46:3, 4).
   d. This is how intimately God knows and loves us.

3. How can we become, children of God, born of His Holy Spirit?
   a. Accept Jesus Christ of Nazareth as your Lord and Saviour. Accept His offering made for you, for the forgiveness of your sins. And confess your new found faith to Him and as God wills you to others.
   b. But ultimately, as the scriptures would suggest we are awaiting "new heavens", as the Bible speaks of "...new heavens and a new earth...", wherein dwells righteousness (2 Pet. 3:13, Rev. 21:1).
   c. That is, God's kingdom is not of this world, and His kingdom is a spiritual one first and foremost. Accepting His Holy Spirit, by cleansing you of your sins, through forgiveness of your sins in Jesus Christ of Nazareth, will no doubt give you that, "key of David", that we all need, to receive eternal life. Alleluia and Praise the LORD God, the Father, Almighty and His only begotten Son, Jesus Christ of Nazareth. Amen and Amen.

CHAPTER SEVEN
Summaries and Conclusion

Discussion: The Word of God

"…greater is he that is in you, than he that is in the world."
- 1 John 4:4

The reality is Jesus Christ of Nazareth has given us a gift of freedom in His Holy name. He did not come to give us a yoke or burden greater than what we already have, but He came to give us a light yoke (Matt. 11:29, 30). As He says of Himself, "Come unto me, all *ye* that labour and are heavy laden, and I will give you rest. Take my yoke upon you, and learn of me; for I am meek and lowly in heart: and ye shall find rest unto your souls. For my yoke *is* easy, and my burden is light." (Matt. 11:28-30). He did not come to condemn, judge or give us heavier burdens, but to lighten the load of sin we have accumulated from our natural birth into a sinful world (John 1:29). He has given us the Holy Spirit, a promissory note of sort, for eternal life in Jesus Christ of Nazareth's Holy name (Gal. 3:14). We have received God's Holy Spirit unto eternal life in the name of Jesus Christ of Nazareth, God's only begotten Son. Praise the LORD God, the Father, Almighty and His only begotten Son, Jesus Christ of Nazareth. Alleluia and praise the LORD. Amen and Amen. When reading through this chapters discussion question, consider what this "new life", means for you. How do you move forward with God, the Father, Almighty, His only begotten Son, Jesus Christ of Nazareth, and His Holy Spirit, and with others here on earth? Alleluia and praise the LORD. Amen and Amen.

Discussion Questions

1. How can you and I move forward in our relationship with God, the Father, Almighty through His only begotten Son, Jesus Christ of Nazareth, with His Holy Spirit and others here on earth?
   a. Starting or continuing a prayer life is a great start. Applying the blood offering of Jesus Christ of Nazareth to your life, in prayer.
   b. Reading the Holy Bible of God, with a new light, understanding that the scriptures do indeed speak about Jesus Christ of Nazareth's life, as He is the Living Word of God; not just part of the scriptures, but all of them speak of Jesus Christ of Nazareth and our relationship with Him. Alleluia and praise the LORD. Amen and Amen.

c. Fellowshipping with others whom are like minded, and sharing your testimony may also be a good way of sharing your "burdens" (Jam. 5:16). As the Holy Bible of God says, "If we confess *our* sins, he is faithful and just to forgive us our sins, and to cleanse us from all unrighteousness." (1 John 1:9).

d. Last, wait for Him, rest in Him, and enjoy this renewed or "new" life that God has given you in Jesus Christ of Nazareth. The only begotten Son of God. As there is no other name under heaven whereby we can be saved (Acts 4:12). Thanks be to God, the Father, in Jesus Christ of Nazareth, God's only begotten Son, our Lord and Saviour, with His Holy Spirit. Creator of this world, and Redeemer of all of mankind. Alleluia. Amen and Amen.

Printed in the United States
by Baker & Taylor Publisher Services